American
Public
Administration

American
Public
Administration:

Past, Present, Future

Edited by

Frederick C. Mosher

A Collaborative Project of the
Maxwell School of Citizenship and Public Affairs,
Syracuse University,
and the National Association of
Schools of Public Affairs and Administration

The University of Alabama Press
University, Alabama

Contents

Contributors

ROWLAND EGGER is Eugene McElvaney Professor of Political Science at Southern Methodist University. He was Edward M. Stettinius Professor of Government and Foreign Affairs and the first Director of the Institute of Government at the University of Virginia and later served as Professor of Politics and Public Affairs at Princeton. He has served as advisor to a variety of agencies in the United States and abroad and is author or coauthor of a number of books and other publications related to public administration.

JAMES W. FESLER is Alfred Cowles Professor of Government at Yale University. During the period of 1946 to 1960 that he treats in this book, he was a faculty member at the University of North Carolina and then Yale, served as associate editor of the *American Political Science Review* and editor-in-chief of the *Public Administration Review,* and was the author of *Area and Administration* and editor and coauthor of *Industrial Mobilization for War* (the official history of the War Production Board) and *The Forty-Eight States.* He was also consultant with the first Hoover Commission on Organization of the Executive Branch, the Michigan State University Advisory Group in Vietnam, the United Nations, and various federal agencies.

LUTHER GULICK is Chairman of the Board of the Institute of Public Administration. He came into public administration in 1915 through the Training School for Public Service and the New York Bureau of Municipal Research. He is past president of the American Political Science Association and of the American Society for Public Administration, of which he was a joint founder. He has been active in research, writing, lecturing, and consulting, designed to improve government operation and management at all levels, international, national, state, and local. He was New

York City's first City Administrator and served in administrative capacities in a variety of federal agencies.

DON K. PRICE is Dean of the John Fitzgerald Kennedy School of Government at Harvard University. He previously served in various federal agencies, especially the U.S. Bureau of the Budget and the Department of Defense, the first Hoover and various other study commissions, as well as with the Public Administration Clearing House and the Ford Foundation. He is the author of *Government and Science, The Scientific Estate,* and other works.

ALLEN SCHICK is Senior Specialist in American National Government in the Congressional Research Service. He previously served as a consultant to the U.S. Bureau of the Budget, as a research associate and senior fellow at the Brookings Institution, and as a faculty member of Tufts University. He is author of *Budget Innovation in the States* and coauthor of *Setting National Priorities: The 1971 Budget* and of a number of articles on public administration and government budgeting.

ALICE B. STONE has engaged in various teaching and public service activities, primarily as a volunteer. She has served on the boards in several cities of the United Nations Association, the League of Women Voters, the Young Women's Christian Association and the "Committee of 100 of Washington, D.C." She became acquainted with many of the developments discussed in this volume while collaborating with her husband, Donald C. Stone, in publications, speeches, conferences, and educational enterprises.

DONALD C. STONE is Adjunct Professor of Public Administration at Carnegie-Mellon University. He is also Dean Emeritus, and was a founder, of the Graduate School of Public and International Affairs at the University of Pittsburgh. Previously, he had been Executive Director of Public Administration Service, Assistant Director of the U.S. Bureau of the Budget, Director of Administration of the European Cooperation Administration, and President of Springfield College. He has served as consultant and in other capacities to a variety of governmental, research, and educational institutions here and abroad. A past President of the American Society for Public Administration and of the National Association of Schools of Public Affairs and Administration, he is now

Chairman of the International Association of Schools and Institutes of Administration. He is the author of a variety of publications in this field.

DWIGHT WALDO is Albert Schweitzer Professor in the Humanities in the Department of Public Administration, the Maxwell School, Syracuse University. Previously, he served as professor of political science and Director of the Institute of Governmental Studies at the University of California, Berkeley, and in the U.S. Bureau of the Budget and the Office of Price Administration. He is the author or editor of many professional works including *The Administrative State*, and much more recently, *Public Administration in a Time of Turbulence*. Since 1966 he has been editor-in-chief of the *Public Administration Review*.

Foreword

In May 1974, the National Association of Schools of Public Affairs and Administration (NASPAA), which comprises 145 universities with public-administration programs, held its annual conference at Syracuse, New York. The choice of Syracuse was significant since 1974 marked the fiftieth anniversary of the Maxwell School of Citizenship and Public Affairs at Syracuse University. Maxwell was the first full-fledged school of this kind in the United States on a university campus and one of its primary missions was to prepare people for public administration. Many months before the 1974 NASPAA meeting it had been agreed by the leadership of that association and the Maxwell School that it would provide a fitting occasion for a thoughtful review of the development of study and practice in public administration. Most of the essays in this volume were initially prepared for, and were presented and discussed at, that conference in May.

The original idea for these essays grew out of conversations in 1970 between the late Roscoe C. Martin and me concerning the upcoming Golden Anniversary of the Maxwell School in 1974. Among many other activities—symposia, conferences, and lectures —one along the lines of these essays was discussed. Professor Martin, who served as chairman of the Anniversary Committee until his untimely death in 1972, and I agreed that our first need was to find an appropriate person to act as intellectual leader and administrative coordinator of the undertaking. The logical choice was Professor Frederick C. Mosher, one of the most notable of the field's scholars and practitioners. Further, he is an alumnus of the school, served for eight years as a faculty member, and is a son of Maxwell's first dean.

Subsequently, after NASPAA had decided to hold its 1974 meetings in Syracuse, the president of that organization, Dr. Clyde J. Wingfield, president of Bernard Baruch College and also a Maxwell alumnus, joined with me in asking Professor Mosher to coordinate the development of essays for presentation at the NASPAA conference and for subsequent publication. He accepted and proceeded to hold a number of meetings and interviews with leaders in the field to develop a theme and plan for the essays. Following his consultations with colleagues, Professor Mosher decided on a series of papers, each of which would deal with the developments in public administration thought and education of given periods of time, mostly in the historical past but closing with the present and future. Each author would be chosen partly on the basis of his own personal experience—as student, professor, or administrator—during the period about which he wrote. (Of course, some exception to this qualification had to be taken for the author dealing with the future, but Dean Price, like any good administrator, is concerned more about the future than about either the past or present.) Each of the historical essays would deal with a period more or less distinctive and unique, though overlaps would be inevitable. Each would be a scholarly study in the sociology of knowledge and of education in public affairs, laying stress on: the nature of the environment, culture, and thinking during the period; the sources and nature of significant changes from earlier periods; and the legacies from that period that we inherit to this day. All would avoid a chronology of events.

The essays, following presentation by their authors at the NASPAA conference, were discussed and criticized by selected commentators and by others in attendance. Each author had a subsequent opportunity to modify and edit his paper, prior to its submission for this publication.

The essay by Dr. Luther Gulick was initially prepared not as part of this program but as one of a series of Maxwell Lectures, which were presented during the National Conference of the American Society for Public Administration, also held at Syracuse in connection with the School's Fiftieth Anniversary.* It constitutes a bridge from the beginnings, which considerably antedated the Maxwell School, to prognostications about the future. It seemed to Dr. Gulick, Dr. Mosher, and me a fitting epilogue for this volume.

For me to comment on the content of the essays in this volume would be superfluous. Professor Mosher's introduction provides the setting and summarizes the intellectual trends and countertrends that characterize the history of the field. The vigorous debate produced by the presentation of the essays at the conference highlights the field's current vigor—marked as it is by healthy controversy. Despite the controversy, it is worthy of note that the NASPAA conference at which these essays were presented saw the association adopt unanimously a report of its Standards Committee establishing guidelines for the content of programs leading to the Master's degree in Public Administration. Such agreement represents a growing intellectual consensus within the field, and these essays provide the background for understanding the nature and content of that consensus.

The staffs of both the Dean's Office of the Maxwell School and the Office of the National Association of Schools of Public Affairs and Administration contributed substantial time and effort to the necessary administrative details of the presentation of the essays, as well as to the preparation of this volume. They have my thanks.

August, 1974   ALAN K. CAMPBELL
*Dean, Maxwell School of Citizenship
and Public Affairs, Syracuse University
and
Vice President and President-Elect,
National Association of Schools of
Public Affairs and Administration*

---

*The Maxwell Lecture Series, which has been published by the Maxwell School, includes, in addition to Dr. Gulick's paper, others by Stephen K. Bailey, Jesse Burkhead, Harlan Cleveland, Abe Lavine, Al Marshall, William Morrill, James Sundquist, Dwight Waldo, and John Young.

Introduction:
The American Setting

FREDERICK C. MOSHER
Doherty Professor, University of Virginia

The readers of this volume should not expect, and will not find, a series of smooth-flowing, contiguous essays on the history of thought in the field of public administration. This is partly because of the way in which the papers were written. Each author was given a block of time in the past, present, or future and some suggestions as to what kinds of material seemed important and relevant during the period he was treating. But each also had virtually complete sovereignty on the subject matter he would treat, the emphasis to be assigned different topics, and the manner in which the material should be organized. Thus, to a major extent, each essay is an independent contribution that could stand by itself, associated with the others only loosely by the threads of time. Some subsequent editorial suggestions were offered to minimize obvious overlapping and inconsistencies, but these essays remain essentially independent contributions, written by scholars of eminence, each of whom had particular experience in and acquaintance with the period of which he wrote.

A second reason for differences in the style and content of the essays that follow is that the periods of which the various authors wrote were, in most cases, so different from each other. For example, much of what seemed and was important before the Great Depression became quite suddenly almost irrelevant during the New Deal and World War II. And the intellectual ferment in the social (behavioral) sciences, treated with such insight by Professor Fesler, was probably the most distinguishing feature of

1

the period following the war. Indeed, one of the conclusions almost inevitably drawn from this overview of the development and growth of public administration is the degree to which it has been dependent upon and responsive to its immediate social and intellectual environment. This is not to suggest that there were not connections between and among the periods, or that each period did not leave imprints that affected those that followed it. But the manner in which these essays were structured encouraged a focus on the period in time, leaving the major responsibility for interconnecting the themes to the reader.

A third source of disparity among the essays is of course the differing experience and perspectives of their authors. Although all of them have practiced, studied, taught, and written about public administration, they have done so at different places and different times. Their respective views are no doubt indicative of the wide differences of opinion in the field as a whole (although, as indicated later, public administration is in no way unique in this respect). Nonetheless, there are in these studies recurring themes, recurring problems, often differently viewed and defined. Some of the problems refuse to go away: the relations between management and public policy; the fact/value relationship; the linkage between public administration and the social sciences, particularly political science; and the linkage between public administration and other professional education, especially business administration and law. Like other fields of study and action, public administration has experienced a variety of new perspectives, slogans, and approaches, most of which have added new elements or emphases to the field, and have reinvigorated it. One thinks, for example, of economy and efficiency, administrative management, POSDCORB, performance budgeting, work measurement, human relations, cost-benefit analysis, PPBS; and today, of productivity, management by objectives, the new federalism, affirmative action, organization development, policy analysis, and the systems approach, to mention a few. However valid, important, or different these approaches may be, it seems desirable to examine them from time to time in relation to each other and in terms of the periods during which they emerged. Knowledge must be cumulative, if it is to contribute to understanding. New ideas and points of view are most valuable if they are seen, evaluated, and applied from the perspective of what has gone before as well as from the broader perspective of what was and is happening in related fields of study and action. It may therefore be useful to explore, very briefly, the differences, similarities, and interdependencies of public administration and other fields, particularly in the social sciences and professions.

PUBLIC ADMINISTRATION AND OTHER HIGHER EDUCATION

The first third of the present century was a period during which, among many other things, the professions and professional education were born, or in a very few cases, revivified. It was a period during which many of the occupations we now recognize as professions asserted that claim—accounting, business administration, city planning, forestry, engineering, foreign service, journalism, nursing, optometry, public health, social work, teaching, and many others. During that period, too, the older, recognized professions like medicine and law took major steps to strengthen pre-entry education for admission into their ranks. It is not accidental that this same period encompassed the professionalization of higher education in at least two senses: the professors organized themselves, developed standards of entry, and began their long battle for tenure; and, more important for our purposes, the object and the substance of a large part of higher education became preparation for career occupation—that is, in most cases, for professions. The nineteenth-century colleges, privately and community endowed, church supported and governed largely for the acculturation of upstanding Christian young men—though earlier challenged by the Morrill Acts and their gestures towards the applied arts and practices—began to give way to the socially and occupationally oriented institutions, both public and private. University interest in science in this country was scattered and sporadic until late in the nineteenth century and did not flower until World War II and, later, after Sputnik in 1958. The United States was certainly not a leading source of "pure" scientists until

World War II. But it became a leader in technology and applied science in the late nineteenth and early twentieth centuries, and subjects in these realms became dominant in our academic institutions.

The beginnings of a self-conscious public administration during this same period were therefore basically consistent with the directions of other occupational and educational developments. They were not scientific except in a very applied sense—roughly the sense of Frederick Taylor in his expression of "scientific management". They were not grounded in a profound theory of society or even of organization and management—any more than most of the other fields developing at the time were theoretically based. Like them, public administration was pragmatic, problem-oriented, sustained by faith in progress, efficiency, democratic government, and what we now call meritocracy. The early public administration, like some other societal developments, grew out of concern about public corruption and scandal. It was a reform movement, directed against clear and present evils that rational and well-intentioned people could correct. Like other movements associated with the Progressive era, it reflected a fundamental optimism that mankind could direct and control its environment and destiny for the better.

During the three-quarters of a century since its birth as a field of study, public administration has experienced, been challenged by, and to some extent responded to, many of the same kinds of environmental and internal forces as have other fields of thought, study, and practice. The impact of many of these is the subject of the essays that follow: the explosion of the Great Depression and the New Deal that endeavored to cope with it; World War II, which set off a near revolution in thought and concept as to the content and conceptual base of public administration; the incursion of paradigms and theoretical approaches from many other fields of study and the accompanying pressure toward scientism; the legislative explosions of the sixties; followed by the disappointments and the disillusionment of Vietnam, civil rights, and Watergate. The accompanying essays on the periods since World War II (by Doctors Fesler, Schick, and Waldo) indicate the absence of an agreed theoretic base for public administration, of a core and of firm boundaries for the field, and even of a definition of what it is. Public administration is undergoing, according to some, an "identity crisis" or, according to others, an "intellectual crisis."*

The extent to which these allegations are true is a matter for legitimate concern and discussion. And now is surely an appropriate time for those of us who are in this field to indulge in some thoughtful introspection about where we are, how we got here, and whither we are tending. Hopefully, this volume will contribute to such self-examination. But we should not assume that public administration is unique in its self-doubts and internal disagreements. All the social disciplines and professions (and many of the physical ones with which this writer has any familiarity) are undergoing the same kinds of trauma—as to purpose, content, paradigm, methodology, core, boundaries, and indeed the legitimacy of their existence. Economics, sociology, psychology, political science, law, city planning, education, business administration, and even medicine and engineering are entertaining the same kinds of doubts and internal ferment. We are not alone.

The disappointments, frustrations, failures, and disasters of the past decade have undoubtedly contributed to the current malaise in the educational and academic specialties. But probably a more enduring source of concern is the growing realization within each discipline and profession of its innate inability to handle real problems of the world within its own traditional confines. Those problems stubbornly refuse to respect academic, professional, and vocational boundaries. And as "relevance" to real social problems is increasingly demanded by society, the inadequacy of disciplinary and professional differentiations, at once traditional and artificial, will increasingly foment discontent.

Is crime a problem of ethics or poverty or housing or ballistics or education or drug control or immigration or police? Is it

---

*See particularly Vincent Ostrom, *The Intellectual Crisis in American Public Administration* (University, Ala.: The University of Alabama Press, 1973; rev. ed., 1974).

a problem for economics or political science or psychology or sociology or public administration or law or city planning or medicine or transportation engineering or criminology? Clearly, it is all of these and none could respond effectively by itself. There are few if any public problems about which the same generalization would not be equally applicable. Almost from its beginnings, public administration sought to transcend these difficulties by refusing to specialize, by insisting on cross-fertilization among specialties. This was, and perhaps is, at once its greatest strength and its most vulnerable feature.

In its origins and development public administration was part of a larger movement toward professionalization, and its experience in many ways resembled those of other fields. Yet it has always had certain distinctive features, many of which discouraged and still discourage its rapid and large-scale acceptance and growth. Among its handicaps, in comparison with most other professional fields, have been:

(1) the antagonism of much of society and of almost all of the emerging professions to politics and to government generally; (in a business oriented society, private endeavor has been more respectable and prestigious; most of the professions, in their drive for status, endeavored in every possible way to divorce themselves from politics, at least in the public eye);

(2) long-standing fear of concentrated governmental power in America, dating to colonial times; (from its beginnings, rightly or wrongly, public administration has embraced centralization of authority, responsibility, hierarchy—in short, bureaucracy);

(3) the widespread aversion among and within the professions to organized effort in contrast to their general preference for individual autonomy and responsibility, a feeling transferred from the image of the oldest and most respected professions, law and medicine; (public administration, like business administration, has of

course from the outset had to do with behavior in large organizations); and

(4) the emphasis in public-administration literature and education on generalism in a society which was increasingly impressed with and dependent upon specialized expertise in function, in occupation, and in knowledge; (most of American public administrators are products of specialized education and experience in a specialty deemed appropriate to the functions of the agencies they are administering; thus, in terms both of temporal sequence and of perceived importance, public administration is, for most of them, a second profession, if a profession at all).

To these were added other difficulties, a good many of which were shared with other emerging professions: lack of—or slow development of—career opportunities for graduates in the field; shortage of financial and other resource support except for a few scattered philanthropists at a few scattered institutions; and the reluctance of governments to provide public support for the development of administrative talent for themselves.

PUBLIC ADMINISTRATION IN THE UNITED STATES AND IN THE WORLD

Among the many occupational and professional fields with which it grew up in this country, public administration was thus unique in many respects, and handicapped in some. It also differed from many of them in that most of its character depended in only a minor way upon intellectual and vocational developments in other nations. Though it had distant roots in some of British constitutional history, in the largely abandoned German cameralism, in foreign military reforms (adapted to the American military establishment around the turn of the century), it was for the most part an American invention, indigenous, and *sui generis*. With only a few exceptions—some paragraphs by Hamilton in *The Federalist* papers, some interesting observations by de Toqueville, some rhetorical complaints by Lincoln and other political leaders

—the subject as one for science, study, or generalization was largely ignored in the century following the drafting of the Constitution. As a profession, it did not exist. In intellectual terms, it was picked up by a scattering of scholars in the late nineteenth and early twentieth centuries—Wilson, Goodnow, and others—and they drew on European literature and examples. But, as the article by the Stones in this volume makes clear, the real origins of public administration lay in the cities, especially the big ones, not in theories of sovereignty or the state or the separation of powers. The cities were where most government was, where most action was, where most problems were, where the services of public administrators could most demonstrably be made more effective, more honest, and less costly.

So in the United States, probably more than any other country in the world, public administration as practice, as field of study and as self-conscious profession, began in the cities. This was possibly the first time in modern history that concern about public administration focussed on the cities from the outset; virtually all European administrative thought, literature, and education began with the nation-state and worked downward. In the United States, the progression was reversed. We started with the cities; worked up to the states during the state-reorganization movement beginning around 1910 and subsiding in the thirties; focussed on national administration during the depression, New Deal, and World War II; went on after that war to international and comparative administration; and reverted partially to the states and cities during the trauma of the sixties—the decade of Vietnam, civil rights, ghettoes, and civic revolt. We are back to the cities now, though in a much different social, economic, and political context than in the early years of this century. In this history, public "administrationists" have learned, among many other things, that the governmental layers (cities, counties, states, nations, multinations) are hardly separable, any more than problems and functions (such as crime, welfare, economy, transportation, drugs, population, food) are separable.

One other significant difference of the United States from most of the rest of the world was that we have had no administrative class; and, at least after the Jacksonian era, we had no social class from which our public administrators could habitually be drawn and educated for public service. As de Toqueville remarked long ago, in the absence of a recognized aristocracy or, later, any consciously planned linkage between higher education and public administration, the principal posts in government fell to lawyers—totally in the judiciary and largely among legislators and administrators. But lawyers were typically neither trained nor experienced in public administration—as they were, for example, in continental Europe—and few of them planned careers in public service. As specialism in education and in governmental functions proliferated during the present century, top administrative posts were increasingly preempted by professionals in appropriate fields. In this respect, the problem of American public administration has been essentially opposite to that in countries whose administrations were based upon either the British or the continental administrative class traditions. Theirs, to this day, has been to develop and encourage specialists within, or in competition with, the administrative classes—whether predominantly Oxbridge scholar-amateurs or administrative lawyers. Ours has been, basically, to develop more generalized perspectives among administrators, whether or not their initial orientation was in a particular specialism.

The essays that follow, like this introduction, are based in American culture and, in anthropological terminology, are no doubt culture-bound. There is justification for this: American public administration is largely indigenous and peculiarly American. Of the many students and writers identified in the succeeding pages, only a very few were not Americans, and indeed these are principally footnote references: Weber, Fayol, Keynes, Urwick, Crozier and a few others. During and since World War II, the United States has been heavily involved in technical assistance in the public administration of a great many of the nations of the world, new and old. Many of our transient "experts"—and no doubt more of their foreign listeners—were dismayed and chagrined that many tried-and-true American ideas, techniques, and formulae were not particularly useful, or were completely irrelevant, away from home. (One may even speculate that the American experts learned more from the experience than did the governments they were endeavoring to assist.) This volume may be of some interest both to those interested in cross-cultural communication about public administration of whatever nationality, and to those students and practitioners of the field in the United States. For better or worse, it should help us—and them—understand how we got this way—or these many different ways.

*   *   *

As editor of this volume, I would like to express my appreciation to all the authors for their contributions and for their cooperative spirit in working with NASPAA, the Maxwell School, and me over many months. I am also gratified by the efforts of those who, upon request, prepared and delivered critiques of the various papers at the Syracuse meetings. They included:

> Brewster C. Denny, University of Washington
> Nathan D. Grundstein, Case Western Reserve University
> John Holmes ,University of Virginia
> Albert C. Hyde, State University of New York at Albany
> Robert J. Mowitz, Pennsylvania State University
> Laurence O'Toole, Syracuse University
> Clara Penniman, University of Wisconsin
> Dallas L. Salisbury, Syracuse University
> Orion White, University of North Carolina

Finally, I wish to thank, for their ideas, effort, and time, those who helped me in planning and organizing the series. They included:

> Stephen K. Bailey, American Council on Education
> Don M. Blandin, National Association of Schools of Public Affairs and Administration
> Alan K. Campbell, Maxwell School, Syracuse University
> James Carroll, Maxwell School, Syracuse University
> Morris W. H. Collins, Jr., College of Public Affairs, American University
> George A. Graham, National Academy of Public Administration
> Laurin L. Henry, Department of Government and Foreign Afairs, University of Virginia
> Mordecai Lee, Brookings Institution
> Frank Marini, San Diego State University
> Thomas P. Murphy, Institute of Urban Studies, University of Maryland

1. Early Development of Education in Public Administration

ALICE B. STONE AND DONALD C. STONE

In this study we describe the development of education in public administration in response to national and local dissatisfaction with the performance of government. Research and training programs of private agencies and universities stimulated administrative reform. At the same time, the need for administrative knowledge and competence to plan and implement such reform encouraged the establishment of research and training programs.

The struggle to develop multidisciplinary professional education in public administration is in many respects a dismal story. However, a few centers that originated before 1933 have survived to provide leadership in public service education today. Most of those that did not survive left important legacies of broader-based political-science departments and a cadre of service-committed graduates.

FEDERAL REFORM: A PRECONDITION OF PROFESSIONAL EDUCATION

To comprehend the seedbed in which public administration education first rooted and developed, one must be aware of the condition of government before the turn of the century. Not until well into the twentieth century was there any serious recognition of the function of administration and of the idea that professional training was feasible.

The corruption and patronage of the administration of President U. S. Grant is probably the base line from which reform movements struggled toward higher standards of governance. Post-Civil War history is replete with illustrations of guilt and malfeasance by high and low officials, by contractors, lawyers, and pensioners. Leonard D. White describes the offenses vividly: "During the 1870's there was both incompetence and dishonesty in the large custom houses: discipline and integrity among the navy-yard labor forces were at low ebb; the Indian service had been roundly condemned by Garfield; land agents connived at irregularities, and surveyors made fraudulent claims for work not performed."[1]

The smashing of the Whiskey Ring in 1870 by the indictment of 230 persons through the efforts of the secretary of the treasury only brought his forced resignation, while his predecessor, found guilty of gross negligence and incapacity, was rewarded by transfer to the judicial bench.

The Republican administrations after Grant brought gradual improvement in performance and reputation. The two Democratic administrations of Cleveland were no less progressive, but to illustrate that partisan politics has not changed much in seventy-five years we quote from the 1896 Republican platform, where to our knowledge the term *administrative management* was first used.[2]

> For the first time since the civil war the American people have witnessed the calamitous consequences of full and unrestricted Democratic control of the government. It has been a record of unparalleled incapacity, dishonor, and disaster. In administrative management it has ruthlessly sacrificed indispensable revenue, entailed an increasing deficit, eked out ordinary current expenses with borrowed money, piled up the public debt by $262 million in time of peace, forced an adverse balance of trade, kept a perpetual menace hanging over the redemption fund, pawned American credit to alien syndicates and reversed all the measures and results of successful Republican rule.

Struggles for power between legislative and executive branches preempted the post-Civil War battlegrounds. The reformers, looking for integrity, economy, and efficiency, gathered sufficient forces to create the Civil Service Reform League in 1881, a beginning in the change of the political climate. The assassination of

President Garfield triggered the passage of the Pendleton Act in 1883 and the creation of a bipartisan Civil Service Commission. Competitive examinations and protection from political pressures were introduced. This was a turning point in the federal administrative system that made public-service education relevant.

The issue of federal employee tenure was not settled until the Pension Act of 1920, which confirmed it as a principle. Meanwhile, there was much resistance to the setting up of "a college-trained aristocracy." The first examinations were geared to the common public-school product.

Preconditions. Establishment of personnel policies and practices that require knowledge and competences suitable to the administrative tasks of government was one precondition for the development of university education in public administration. Universities could not be expected to prepare students for public service in the absence of a definitive market. (This does not imply that a ready response would have resulted, inasmuch as universities have never paid much attention to public-service manpower needs.) Albeit, a good personnel system should have clarified the market.

This leads to the second precondition: governments must have definable and well-supported administrative policies and processes. This requires an understanding of administrative functions and systems and of managerial tasks and methods. No civil service system can prepare specifications for administrative or managerial positions unless such functions, tasks, and responsibilities have been identified and the requisite competences/education prescribed.

The story of the development of education and training for public service is thus irrevocably linked to administrative reform and improvement. Effective administrative leadership and systems are both the consequences and the stimulators of public-administration education. This linkage and interaction is apparent—at times dramatically so—in the struggle to overcome political patronage, malfeasance, disorder, special privilege, and waste in government.

The Early Situation. One of the many necessary reforms—and certainly the most urgent—pertained to the civil service at all levels. As we shall see, the need was most acute in the cities where government was both extensive and visible.

Until long after Grant, there was no recognition of the role of administrative management in the executive branch, and no recognition of the concept of the President as general manager, even though this concept seems implicit in the Constitution. Executive leadership and management are essentially twentieth-century innovations.

Departmental organization was casual, sometimes bordering on anarchy. Congress provided in 1789 for single-headed departments, but with no consistency in internal arrangements. For instance, the Treasury Department's administration was prescribed in detail, but the State and War departments were left to set up their own systems. Very little had been done to rationalize departmental administration or to develop methods of control and accountability. There was no budget system. Accounting was loose and unsystematized.

Until the Presidency of Theodore Roosevelt the initiative in administrative reform and economy remained in Congress. A joint committee under Dockery and Cockrell (1893–1895) brought about numerous departmental improvements in accounting, records, "business methods," and productivity of clerks. Presidents provided no executive leadership. Leonard D. White observed: "They seemed, as in a sense they were, more remote from the administrative system than Congress; they displayed no responsibility for systematic inquiry into the methods of its public business; they had no plans for its improvement; they watched aloof while Congress groped for better organization and procedures."[3]

Progress After 1900. Theodore Roosevelt began to assert the executive role of the Presidency. New kinds of administration were essential. Measures to cope with monopoly, trusts, relations between capital and labor, and conditions of employment involved regulation and use of boards of experts for investigation and non-political determination of facts. New concepts of regulatory administration crystallized.

President Taft's Commission on Economy and Efficiency, headed by Frederick A. Cleveland of the New York Bureau of Municipal Research, recommended an executive budget and other administrative reforms, but they were rejected by Congress. Although generally a weak President, Warren G. Harding contributed great strength to executive administration a decade later by implementing a number of the Taft Commission's proposals. President Wilson had vetoed what became the Budget and Accounting Act of 1921 on the ground that it unconstitutionally deprived the President of removal power over an officer he had appointed. If Wilson had been willing to suffer a little Congressional excess, his incumbency might have realized more joy. Harding approved a reenacted bill in 1921.

Wilson experienced the reality of trying to make an impact with a White House staff of only three, and no budget office. We recall a comment by Eleanor Wilson McAdoo years later, when she was informed of the role of the Budget Bureau in 1940. "My father would have liked that," she said. "He was always distressed because he had so few persons who could help him."

General Charles G. Dawes,[4] the first director of the Bureau of the Budget, with the support of President Harding, had a remarkable impact on administration and budgeting. Dawes appointed a chief coordinator and some twenty interdepartmental committees. For the first time the President brought together and addressed at least two thousand of the principal officials and employees. The reclassification of positions, improved pension legislation, and extension of personnel covered by civil service were other important advances made in the 1920s. Such initiatives brought about much improvement in departmental management throughout that decade. Heads of agencies were buttressed with budget and personnel offices. Chief clerks became miniature assistant secretaries for administration. Independent establishments were brought under presidential control.

Expert Assistance. These accomplishments could not have been achieved without the assistance of the expert staff of the New York Bureau of Municipal Research and the Institute of Govern-

ment Research. The latter was established in 1916 in Washington,
D.C., by Robert Brookings of St. Louis as a means of applying to
federal problems the systematic, analytical approaches that the
New York Bureau had so effectively used in cities and states.
W. F. Willoughby, Henry Seidemann, and others of its staff
worked intensively with General Dawes, the Civil Service Commission, and various departments in producing budget, personnel,
and other reforms. Frederick Cleveland, who served both the
bureau and the institute, helped to give continuity. The demand
for trained staff generated by these efforts increased the demand
for persons trained by the New York bureau's training school and
the Institute for Government Research.[5]

From Hoover to FDR. Herbert Hoover pushed these reforms
further but was shackled by a divided Congress and lack of
political/executive skill. By this time the Presidential staff included
three secretaries to the President, two executive officers, one chief
administrative officer and eleven assistants, plus five junior administrative officers. "Executive" and "administrative" were new
words in the White House lexicon.

Hoover was a strong advocate of reorganization. In 1924, while
secretary of commerce, he proposed the reorganization procedure
finally enacted in 1939. His Commission on Recent Social Trends
helped to pave the way for some of President Franklin D. Roosevelt's social and economic reforms. If Hoover had not been over-
whelmed by economic collapse, his Presidency might well have
been noted for advances in organization and management and in
better-trained manpower. But the adoption of Secretary of the
Treasury Mellon's strategy of liquidation and retrenchment made
this a period of curtailment, of jetisoning employees, and not one
of educating them.

The developments during the first third of the century both
stimulated and discouraged response by the universities. Opportunities for university professional graduates were increasing.
Public management had been greatly enhanced, but the routes to
the post of chief clerk were still crowded with messengers on the
make. There were no classification and recruitment arrangements

that provided direct entry at beginning or higher levels either for public administration graduates or for experienced practitioners.

CITIES AND STATES: IMPACT ON PROFESSIONAL EDUCATION

Important as national and state developments were in generating new concepts of administration and in revealing the need for trained personel, it was in the cities that the most significant changes occurred. Education for the public service was initiated principally to fulfill an early demand for persons capable of evaluating and improving municipal government. Administrative reform first flourished in the cities.

The Impact of City Government. For most people what happened in city hall had more effect on their lives than what happened in the statehouse or in Washington. It was in the cities, primarily, that life had to be serviced and regulated. It became incumbent upon city government to control lawlessness, to pave the streets, to supply pure water, to remove waste, to protect health, to provide mass education.

The planning and implementation of such services and facilities obviously required trained manpower and, even more, elected officials who had both a concern for effective and impartial performance of services and some awareness of their technical, fiscal, and administrative requisites. Unless officials shared such concerns there could be no recognition of the personnel competences and the training required.

By the turn of the century, 40 percent of the population of the United States lived in cities, as compared with 6 percent a century earlier. The total urban population in 1900 was thirty million plus a few thousand. The sheer necessity of extinguishing fires, suppressing crime, and providing transportation and running water forced a modicum of public service.

Patronage and Corruption. Unhappily, many cities were under control of political cliques and bosses who used their power more for their own advantage than for providing livable communities for their constituents. The spirit of Andrew Jackson was still pervasive. Few had challenged his observation that "the duties of all public offices are, or at least admit of being made, so plain and simple that men of intelligence may readily qualify themselves for their performance;..." Except for the relatively few engineers, doctors, accountants, and similar specialists, most positions were filled on the basis of political patronage.

The bosses maintained their power by obligating their supporters and their extended families through the largesse of the public payroll. This enabled them also to levy regular tribute to finance the party and, frequently, to line their own pockets. However, the major sources of graft were selling of franchises, construction of public facilities in areas where the political bosses had purchased land, and kickbacks in the award of contracts. "Dirty tricks" did not begin in 1972. The chronicle of municipal bossism is filled with examples of injury and threats to noncooperators, fleecing of innocent persons, and bribery for cover-ups. In this respect, corruption and malfeasance at the local level were reflected in state and national governments. City governments were in some ways a laboratory for sordid and despotic practices not illuminated by the searchlight of national publicity and congressional surveillance. Many state and national politicians learned their lessons in their home towns.

Some political chicanery and corrupt practices grew out of the nature of state constitutions. Our Constitutional fathers thought of America in terms of an agrarian society. Thomas Jefferson believed that cities were a prime source of evil. The federal Constitution did not mention or recognize the existence of cities. State constitution drafters and legislators alike organized state governments to represent and serve territory (i.e., rural interests) and thus discriminated against cities.

Little wonder that cities, for the most part, were dreary and dangerous places in which to live. Often the larger cities were centers of crime and vice, poverty, disease, and congestion. They suffered from poor transportation, miserable housing, inadequate sanitation, limited or no recreation facilities. Libraries were nonexistent. Schools deteriorated with untrained teachers. James

Bryce had already declared American city government to be the most conspicuous failure in the commonwealth.[6]

Prelude to Reform. Since these conditions affected the privileged and educated as well as the poor, efforts at reform started early. By 1894 there were eighty-four citizen associations and clubs in different cities attacking general deterioration or specific abuses. These groups organized the first national conference for good city government in 1894. From this meeting emerged the National Municipal League—the strategy center for many municipal reforms in the subsequent decades.

Reform campaigns were organized, and some won, at the polls. Electing honest officials, in itself, produced few results other than to curtail privilege and kickbacks temporarily. Lacking knowledge of the essentials of public administration and good practice, the new regimes were not equipped to make much real improvement in governance. They, too, had to rely on ill-prepared employees.

Disenchantment with the reformers opened the way for the political machines to take over again. Boss Tweed was thrown out in 1871 but Tammany Hall was back in the saddle in New York City in three years.[7]

Newspaper stories and articles in national journals had begun to make people generally aware of the deficiencies in the public trusts. Lincoln Steffens, in particular, aroused the country to an awareness of the extent of municipal mismanagement through his book *The Shame of the Cities*, published in 1904. He found a fundamental relationship between political corruption and industrial privilege.

Greater access to information and use of communications made it easier for citizen groups to ferret out local scandals and to press for reform than to affect the national government. This largely explains why administrative reform took root and brought about greater change in city government prior to substantial improvement in state and federal administration.

The 1906 Turning Point. The foregoing conditions and forces in New York City provided a fertile setting for change that ulti-

mately brought into flower the profession of public administration
and the creation of variously titled educational programs in public
affairs and administration. The old intuitive approach of simply
"throwing the rascals out" and electing new officials failed for a
number of reasons. The new officials had no training, no understanding of "management," no supporting staffs. They obviously
needed more than honesty. No one had gathered enough facts
about governmental operations and conditions to determine where
the major problems lay, so that solutions could be developed. R.
Fulton Cutting, a wealthy civic leader, joined with Frederick A.
Cleveland, William H. Allen, and Frank Tucker to establish the
New York Bureau of Municipal Research. After a period of planning, Cutting enlisted Andrew Carnegie and John D. Rockefeller
to join in financing the bureau for a term of years. It was incorporated in 1906, with Henry Bruère as its director.

While the bureau had a common-law and a charter right of
access to public records, Tammany Hall refused entrance to the
doors of City Hall. Rather than appeal to the courts, the bureau
decided to make its first study out of doors, specifically an ap-
praisal of the condition of the streets of Manhattan. The investi-
gators were able to compile information about appropriations for
construction and maintenance and relate these to the quality of the
streets that would have resulted if funds had been expended
effectively. In the ensuing furor, the chairman of the bureau was
sued for $100,000 libel by the Manhattan borough president. The
city's committee of accounts made a report denying the validity
of the bureau's findings. Mayor George B. McClellan, who was
feuding with Borough President Ahearn, appointed a young
lawyer, John Purroy Mitchel, to make an investigation. Mitchel
verified the facts in the bureau's report, and Ahearn agreed,
although protesting the conclusions. The mayor then referred the
reports to Governor Charles Evans Hughes, who in turn held
hearings and in due course removed Ahearn for incompetence.
This action, in 1909, was the first formal removal of a local official
for malfeasance in the United States, according to record.[8]

Reform Momentum. Tammany Hall provided free advertising

by labeling the bureau as "The Bureau of Municipal Besmirch." Subsequent mayors, notably Mitchel, who was elected on a reform ticket in 1914, enlisted the help of the bureau in effecting many improvements in budgeting, accounting, public works, public health, purchasing, and other fields.

Other cities, hearing about the Manhattan street survey and subsequent studies, called on the bureau for aid. Common use of the term "survey" originated at this time. This new approach to the solution of public-service problems became infectious, and resulted in numerous reorganization surveys in a number of states. By 1925 some 235 studies had been made.

Invariably, the bureau recommended that research bureaus be established in both cities and states as citizen-sponsored, voluntary organizations. When public officials became convinced of their value, they established units within the governmental structures themselves. Los Angeles City and County and the City of Toledo were pioneers. The administrative-management work of the U.S. Bureau of the Budget and comparable units in federal departments and state governments were likewise products of this movement.

The survey reports constituted a new kind of literature about public administration. They developed facts about the functioning of governments, the advantages and disadvantages of alternative policies, administrative arrangements, and procedures. Principles, doctrine, and requisites of good organization were delineated. Consequently, the New York Bureau of Municipal Research became the advocate of the short ballot (originally initiated by Richard Childs), executive leadership with legislative oversight, the executive budget, position classification and personnel administration, consolidation of duplicating and overlapping agencies into unifunctional departments, elimination of administrative boards—all to the end of making governments more effective and responsible. Above all, the bureau demonstrated the value of the analytical approach in solving policy and administrative problems. The establishment of public administration as a field of study and professional practice could not have taken place without this empirical experience.

These same concepts were applied by the bureau in its state

government surveys. For example, the executive leadership role of governors had become well established by the early 1930s. California had made the first bold moves in 1911. The 1915 Constitutional Convention in New York, staffed by New York Bureau leaders, prepared a remarkable document, which was, however, defeated at the polls. Its proposals, including the concept of the governor as general manager, influenced action in other states and were subsequently implemented in New York by Governor Alfred E. Smith. The states that had made the most progress by 1931, in addition to New York and California, were Illinois, Massachusetts, Maine, Pennsylvania, Virginia, Michigan, Maryland, Wisconsin, Ohio, South Dakota, and Tennessee.[9] As at the federal level, these steps were essential to establish the value of trained administrators and to provide cooperative links between universities and states in fulfilling their administrative needs.

Comparative Study and Professionalism. Exchange of experience and knowledge about the new field of public administration was fostered in several ways. Comparative study of administration first began when bureau personnel moved from city to city and state to state conducting surveys. Comparison and exchange of information became a major purpose of the Governmental Research Association, founded in 1915. It brought together annually the heads and staffs of research bureaus. Committee reports and annual proceedings were gold mines for the young student, researcher, and official alike.

A similar development of significance was the organization of public officials and public bodies into professional and public interest associations. The American Society for Municipal Development (founded in 1894) became the American Society for Municipal Engineers, which merged in 1935 with the International Association of Public Works Officials to form the American Public Works Association.

The awakened interest in improved administration extended the city-manager form of government widely. To share experience and develop professional standards, the managers organized the International City Managers' Association in 1913. Police chiefs, fire chiefs, municipal finance officers, and civil service officials also organized. State leagues of municipalities multiplied and coordinated their efforts through the American Municipal Association, which later became the National League of Cities. All these associations circulated information about this new field of public administration by means of newsletters, reports, meetings, and advisory services. Both state and local governments afforded a ready-made laboratory for comparative study. This stimulated the application of new concepts and practices under varying conditions.

Facilitating Efforts. The work of professional and public-interest associations was greatly strengthened with the financial assistance of the Laura Spelman Memorial of New York. In the late 1920s a plan was developed to bring a number of the principal associations together under one roof. The instrument created to do this was the Public Administration Clearing House, headed by Louis Brownlow, a former journalist, commissioner of the District of Columbia, and city manager. This concentration in Chicago, at 1313 East 60th Street, later became known as the "1313" public-administration center.

The International City Managers' Association (ICMA) arrived in Chicago first (1929) from Kansas. Then came the Civil Service Assembly,[10] followed by the Municipal Finance Officers Association, the American Municipal Association (AMA), the American Legislators Association (ALA), the American Public Welfare Association, the American Public Works Association and others. The ALA soon created the Council of State Governments, which in turn gave birth to the Governor's Conference. In 1933 the Public Administration Service, a joint consulting, research, and publications agency, was established.

From the start, the "1313" family stressed the need for in-service training of public officials and better pre-service education by universities. Some of the organizations offered short courses, and all encouraged governments and universities to do so. The AMA provided a clearing house on training materials and methods, and assisted its constituent municipal leagues conducting courses. The staff of the several associations lectured in these training efforts and developed close ties with university centers.

Another stimulus to governmental interest in administrative reform was the Social Science Research Council's appointment in 1928 of a Committee on Public Administration. In addition to conducting and stimulating studies, the committee had the special mission of bringing public officials in closer contact with scholars. The aim was to encourage official interest in applying the results of research and in acquainting the producers of research with practical problems. The Rockefeller Foundation made this work possible.

Scientific Management. In 1880, Frederick W. Taylor initiated an approach to management in industry that brought substantial changes in industrial management and had a spin-off into government. The principles of scientific management as developed by Taylor and others associated in the movement—the Gilbreths, Gant, Dodge, Hathaway, Cook, Person, and others—were ultimately comingled with the concepts initiated by the New York Bureau of Municipal Research and other contributors to the governmental research movement. Both contributed to administrative improvement in government and provided primary root sources for instructional programs.

Taylor stressed the use of factual, analytical approaches in place of rule-of-thumb or intuitive methods; careful selection, training, and assignment of personnel; and friendly cooperation between management and employees in planning and carrying out the work of the organization. He applied behavioral/human relations principles as then understood.

Taylor's philosophy and methods attracted wide public attention in hearings before the Interstate Commerce Commission in 1910–1911. Their application in government agencies was retarded at first by a lack of management-conscious officials, but their eventual successful utilization in military arsenals paved the way for extensive application in new agencies in the 1930s. A few universities that emphasized the functions of management incorporated Taylor's principles into their curricula.

Complementary Forces. In summary, we see four parallel and interacting efforts to improve government over several decades:

a. the growth of citizen reform organizations,
b. the analytical and problem-solving approaches of the governmental research or bureau movement, extending from municipal to state and federal governments,
c. scientific management as a propagated method of solving public as well as private-enterprise problems,
d. the advent of professional and public-interest associations, dramatized by the "1313" cluster.

Individually and collectively these stimulated university interests in government and made possible professional (action-oriented) education in public administration. If World War I and the subsequent economic depression had not intervened, these forces might have enjoyed more favorable circumstances and financial support.

DEVELOPMENT OF PROFESSIONAL PROGRAMS

Universities responded slowly to the need of the public service for professionally prepared personnel. Around 1900, Harvard University is reported to have considered the establishment of a graduate school for civil servants and diplomats. The idea was finally abandoned because of lack of career opportunities in either the civil or diplomatic services. Instead, the university founded the Harvard Business School.

In the 1920s, home-rule and council-manager movements created a much wider market for professionally trained administrators. State reorganization, with its enhancement of the executive role, increased the demand from that source. Not until the creation of the emergency agencies in the 1930s did the federal government begin an earnest search for administrative talent. Civil-service examinations did not focus on the recruitment of persons competent in public administration until that time.

Categories of Education. Four kinds of education related to public administration should be distinguished.

FIRST is the study of history, government, and public affairs as a part of liberal arts or citizenship education. The purpose is to provide an awareness or appreciation of the role of public administration in society and to encourage students to become interested in government.

SECOND is the study in depth of one or more disciplines, such as political science, sociology, or economics, with special reference to their analytical and policy contributions to public affairs. Teaching and research are principal career objectives of this kind of education.

THIRD is professional study with a clinical component to develop competence as an administrative practitioner, either as a generalist manager, staff officer, researcher, consultant, or educator.

FOURTH is the acquisition by a specialized practitioner (engineer, lawyer, public health or medical doctor, social welfare worker, agronomist) of administrative knowledge and competence as a functional or program manager.

We are dealing here with the third and fourth categories, both of which should be the focus of any school or program of public affairs/administration. Since the first two categories are often viewed as education in public administration, it is important to be aware of these distinctions.

Professional education in public administration is concerned with application, operations, and performance, not primarily with theory, abstractions, and research methodology. It draws on all relevant disciplines and professions in developing the insights and skills needed to plan, determine policy, organize, manage, and implement programs and operations. It is concerned with the interfaces of policy, administrative processes, managerial leadership, program technology, use of analytical tools, environmental factors, human and ethical values, and social and political forces. It is problem-oriented with a major clinical component. It is concerned with the functions, operations, and substance of what is being planned and executed.

A medical school, for example, requires substantial inputs from biology, anatomy, physiology, neurology, and other sciences. But a collection of courses in these disciplines does not produce a medical practitioner. Similarly in public administration, inputs from political science, economics, law, sociology etc., are necessary, but they do not in themselves constitute professional education for public administration.

In the following pages these distinctions are maintained. Professional education in public administration would be severely crippled without the development of a substantial descriptive and theoretical body of knowledge. As we shall see, only a handful of university programs organized before 1933 became genuinely professional and multidisciplinary and achieved an enduring institutional status.

Early Contributions. History, political philosophy and economy, law, and journalism have yielded much understanding about government and its administration. *The Federalist* papers, de Tocqueville's *Democracy in America*, Bryce's *The American Commonwealth*, and Adam Smith's *Inquiry Into the Nature and Causes of the Wealth of Nations* are patently illustrative. These early writings were mostly descriptive. In contrast, Woodrow Wilson's 1887 essay on *The Study of Administration* was epochal in delineating the conduct of government as a field for analytical study and generalization.

There were as yet few administrative concepts, doctrines, or recognized principles and practices; there was no system of administrative analysis; there were no textbooks. But we had an indefatigable scholar at Columbia University, sometimes referred to as "Father of Public Administration" because of his prolific writings and ardent teaching. Frank J. Goodnow's book on *Comparative Administrative Law*, published in two volumes in 1893, was the first American treatise on public administration. This was followed in 1900 by *Politics and Administration*. He turned next to the study of municipal home rule, finding in local government the principal locus of administrative activity.[11] These were oriented to the first two categories of education listed above, not to the professional education of practitioners.

Other scholars were also laboring in the vineyard. Students of government are familiar with the early contributions of Theodore Woolsey, J. W. Burgess, Beatrice and Sidney Webb, Henry George, W. F. Willoughby, J. A. Fairlie, E. L. Godkin, H. D. Lloyd, Charles Merriam, and other "greats." Their treatises contributed philosophy, background, and insights but very little in the way of professional knowledge on *how* to plan, organize, and manage programs and operations. In the decades from Woolsey to Merriam the newer disciplines of administrative law, politics, economics, and other social sciences were replacing the older philosophy, theology, and classical studies in the curricula. In the first decades of the twentieth century, higher education became increasingly professional with the flowering of education for medicine, engineering, business administration, architecture, library science, social work, etc. Agriculture and the mechanical sciences in the land-grant colleges had already established the service orientation of those state institutions. Though largely privately oriented, the professions provided a more hospitable venue for public administration than the previously prevailing arts and classics.

The Training School for Public Service. The first genuine professional school of public administration began outside of academia in response to a very specific market. The Training School for Public Service was founded in 1911 by the New York Bureau of Municipal Research to meet both its own and the urgent staffing needs of bureaus in other cities. Springing up wherever their progenitor made surveys, these new bureaus drained off the New York staff by attractive offers. Professional and civic associations and a few municipal governments were by this time also looking for administratively trained personnel. Mrs. E. H. Harriman contributed substantially to the founding and maintenance of this school.

Though technically separate, the training school functioned almost as a part of the New York bureau. The latter's staff became its instructors and directed its operations. The school occupied bureau quarters, and used its library. Students were assigned to work on bureau projects. The aim was to provide persons who had already mastered some profession with a background in government, the functions and processes of administration, and with research techniques.

In 1912, Charles A. Beard of Columbia University reported to the American Political Science Association's Committee on Practical Training for the Public Service (of which he was a member): "The Training School fulfills every requirement of a university. . . . In my opinion one year at the Training School is equal in discipline and academic training to a year spent in any university with whose graduates I am acquainted."[12]

When Beard became director of the Training School for Public Service in 1915, he broadened and strengthened the curriculum. The school's distinctive contribution became the development of generalizations and clinical methods regarding organization, management, and administrative practice. Here we see the disciplinary fragments assembled and put into an operational framework. The school, which was incorporated into the Institute of Public Administration in 1922, developed cooperating relationships with a number of universities and became a pilot in professional education programs at the graduate level.

Response by Universities .The December, 1913 final report of the political science committee cited above endorsed training for government careers and advocated direct contact between universities and government. Unfortunately, the committee found no group of public employees concerned about their training and no interested public authority. World War I also diverted attention. In any event, White says: "The universities failed to respond in any impressive manner to the challenge put forth in 1913 by the American Political Science Association."[13] In the 1920s the situation began to change. Resourceful professors at various universities labored long and diligently to develop courses and to stimulate students to enter public service. University curricula gave increasing attention to government, public issues, and public administration. Such changes were usually in favor of the first and second categories of education listed above, not the education of professional practitioners. It has been asserted that in the years before the New Deal (i.e., 1933) between thirty and forty university programs in public administration were inaugurated. However, relatively few of these were truly professional or multidisciplinary in character. Many were so subordinated to political science departments that their survival was in doubt. Many efforts atrophied or died when their mentors retired. Only a few with academic autonomy could compete for funds and achieve prestige within the university as well as in the external world.

The professionally focussed programs drew heavily on the educational format of the Training School for Public Service and utilized concepts, survey reports, and comparative studies emanating from the bureau movement. Stimulated in considerable part by the broadening concerns of associations of public officials, the amount of useful professional literature and text materials grew rapidly. University efforts generally stressed municipal administration, although some also dealt with state and federal administration.

Each major effort to create a school or substantial program in public administration is an interesting case of institution building. Comparatively, such cases provide a means of assessing the causes of success and failure. The Appendix to this volume contains brief case histories of the Training School for Public Service and of the ten university-related endeavors that we believe to be most significant. Arranged roughly in chronological order of their founding, they include:

> **The University of Michigan,** which in 1914 established a one-year master's program in municipal administration, including a joint program with engineering in public works administration. Many decades later, the program evolved into the Institute of Public Administration and, more recently, the Institute of Public Policy Analysis.

> **The University of California, Berkeley,** which, partly through its Bureau of Public Administration, in 1920 began offering courses and seminars in various aspects of public administration, providing a growing number of graduates

for public service. It was not until the 1960s, however, that a formal degree program was established in public administration, followed by the founding of what is now known as the Graduate School of Public Policy.

Stanford University, which in 1921 began a program in public administration within its political science department. After its founder passed from the scene, the program disintegrated.

Syracuse University, whose Maxwell School of Citizenship and Public Affairs was established in 1924 and to which was transferred a large part of the program of the Training School for Public Service. It encompassed graduate work in all the social sciences as well as a public administration program and was the first semi-independent school with its own dean (originally director), and it continues to thrive after more than a half-century of continuous operation.

The University of Cincinnati, which in 1927 began a program somewhat like Stanford's but including joint degree arrangements with other units of the University and which inaugurated the "co-op" or work-study principle in the study of public administration.

The University of Southern California, which in 1928/29 established the first totally professional school in this field in the nation and which became, and remains, one of the most innovative and influential enterprises of its kind.

The University of Minnesota, which established a public administration center with a well-rounded program for both generalists and specialists. The center was not formally established until the mid-1930s, but its activities had been developing for many years before then. It has recently become a School of Public Affairs.

Columbia University, which as early as 1915 was encouraging students to study and perform field work at the New York Bureau of Municipal Research and its associated training school, and which incorporated the Institute of Public Administration in 1931. Neither the program nor the marriage were enduring; the Institute disengaged itself in 1942.

The University of Chicago, which made enormous contributions to the study of public administration in the 1920s and 1930s through its faculty and graduates, but it did not establish any formal degree program in the field.

The Brookings Institution, which was given that name in 1927 following the merger of predecessor organizations in Washington. It granted degrees in economics and government as well as conducting a variety of research activities.

Other Institutions. Several other universities made important public-administration contributions during this period. The University of Pennsylvania is reported to have offered courses as early as 1888, the same year as Columbia University. Its political science department gave much attention to public administration, but no formally organized professional program developed until the Fels Institute of State and Local Government was established.

The University of Wisconsin, like Minnesota, initiated courses in public administration in the 1920s and enlisted increasing student interest during the 1930s, feeding a substantial number of graduates into state and municipal civil services. Contributing to this lively interest were: (1) the tradition of reform and high purpose in state and local government; (2) the stimulating impact on students of the LaFollette leadership; (3) the constructive state civil-service system, which stressed recruiting good persons and promoting them; (4) the cooperation of the Wisconsin Municipal League whose own training program was coordinated closely with the university; and (5) the large number of professors of political science, economics, and law who had first-hand government experience.

Despite these favorable conditions, Wisconsin did not achieve more than a loose collection of courses, research activities, and cooperative relations. There was no integrated program, no systematized student/faculty interaction, no professional headquarters.

George Graham aptly comments with respect to Chicago, Columbia, and Wisconsin: "To give this sort of training, something more than an academic cafeteria is desirable. A training table is probably not necessary, but a coach and dietition would be useful; the counter crew and cashier are not quite enough."[14]

The University of Illinois was another institution that offered courses in public administration in the early years. It began to do so in 1909, when John A. Fairlie, a committed scholar in municipal and state government, came to Ilinois from the University of Michigan and initiated a cluster of courses in public, national, and municipal administration. Courses in county, state, judicial, and international administration were soon added. The result was an unusual harvest of master's and doctoral degrees. The faculty was prolific in its writings and generous in serving on state and local advisory groups. Like Wisconsin, Chicago, and Columbia, no permanent professional organ was established, and Illinois became another story of what might have been had there been effective internal institution building.

Harvard offered a number of courses in government and administration during the first two decades of this century. A research bureau, established in 1913, emphasized "practical work" in government. The official Harvard Register for 1929/30 lists graduate government courses taught by administratively sophisticated persons like Arthur Holcomb, Carl Friedrich, Rupert Emerson, and Christian Herter. A cluster of courses reflected the university's traditional interest in municipal affairs. These included State and Local Administration by John Sly, Municipal Government by Ernest Griffith and Hugh Elsbree, Municipal Administration and Administrative Process, both by Tom Reed of Michigan, and City Management by Miller McClintock. Don Price and Arthur Maass now teach under the same title the course on National Government listed for Holcomb in the 1920s, all of which contributes to the enigma of what was political science and what was public administration at Harvard.

The *Municipal Yearbook* of 1937 reported about twenty-five other colleges and universities to have announced programs in public administration prior to 1933.[15] Most of these consisted of a few courses offered in political science departments, many at the undergraduate level. Fewer than ten subsequently developed into multidisciplinary professional degree programs.

University Research Bureaus. A parallel development to university instruction in public administration was the establishment of university-sponsored municipal, legislative-reference, and research bureaus. They collected and published information about state and local governments, provided reference services, and made studies on their own initiative or at the request of government officials and legislators. They were the university counterpart of the citizen-sponsored governmental research bureaus. As indicated in the case histories, these units sometimes served as springboards for launching academic programs.

The Wisconsin Municipal Information Bureau, founded in 1909, was the first such bureau, followed by Kansas in the same year. Both were administered by their university extension divisions. In its 1913 report, the Committee on Practical Training of the American Political Science Association noted the existence of university research bureaus with "some emphasis upon practical work in eight institutions: Oregon, Texas, Washington, California, Wisconsin, Cincinnati, Harvard, and Iowa." By 1931 fourteen university governmental-research agencies were flourishing: Wisconsin, Cincinnati, Minnesota, Oklahoma, Michigan, Colorado, Harvard, MIT, North Carolina, Florida, Kansas, California, West Virginia, Columbia.[16]

Some of these bureaus were later combined with schools or institutes of public administration. In this way, the four-fold role of comprehensive schools emerged: (1) to provide pre-service and in-service professional education of graduate quality, (2) to upgrade public employees through short courses, (3) to engage in research to produce theory and applied knowledge for both teaching purposes and operational guidance, and (4) to provide advisory assistance and information to governments.

Education of Specialized Administrators. Concurrently, universities began to educate students in their various professional schools for specialized public-service fields. Some of these efforts were linked with public-administration programs.

We would go far afield to try to consider all such specialized training efforts. We therefore note only a few. Obvious are Annapolis and West Point, both founded in the nineteenth century and committed to training officers for the armed services. Before the turn of the century there was a growing number of teacher training institutions, and by 1928 there were 339. Some of the larger ones, such as Teachers College of Columbia, offered a curriculum in education administration and engaged in research and survey work.

University programs in civil engineering were among the first forms of public-service education. Railroad engineering was oriented to private enterprise, but highway and sanitary engineering brought graduates into government. Courses in municipal engineering were introduced in the first decades of this century, with options in that field developing in a few universities. Harvard established the Erskine Bureau of Street Traffic Research in 1925 and in the same year Texas A. and M. offered a program in the department of municipal and sanitary engineering to prepare students for municipal and other administrative positions.

Several of the early public-administration programs included course work in municipal engineering or public-works administration. Collaborative programs also came early in this field. The first was a 1914 joint master's degree program in public-works administration offered at Michigan in cooperation with the school of engineering. USC and Cincinnati followed suit in the 1920s.

Social-work education began in independent schools with principal emphasis on private charity. By 1929 twenty-four social-work schools had affiliated with, or had been established in, universities in which some attention was given to preparation for public service.

Training for public-health work began at MIT as early as 1886. Harvard awarded its first doctorate in public health in 1911. The School of Public Health at Yale, founded by Dr. C. E. A. Winslow, became a national center. By 1930 there were eighty-nine universities granting advanced degrees in this field.

Police-service training blossomed around 1930, when the New York City Police Acadamy was reorganized to become the leading center for police training. The FBI Police Academy soon followed. Several state leagues of municipalities established police-training courses. Universities entered the field: Willamette University in 1929, Redlands (California) Junior College in 1928, and Northwestern University in 1932.[17]

Some early programs in public administration included courses in city planning. Schools of architecture and engineering also introduced courses, most of which focussed on design. Some of these grew into city-planning programs. By 1933 eighteen universities were offering courses, but Harvard had the only independent School of City Planning at that time. It required a bachelor's degree and three and a half years of graduate work to attain the degree of "Master of City Planning".[18]

ASSESSMENT OF SUCCESS AND FAILURE: LESSONS FOR THE FUTURE

We believe that the foregoing account, amplified by the case histories in the Appendix, points to a number of requisites for professional education in public administration. The final outcomes at the universities were largely preordained by the manner in which the program were structured and institutionalized. Few programs had built-in survival qualities.

The Comparative Picture. The annual survey of institutions conducted by the National Association of Schools of Public Affairs and Administration (NASPAA) provides a current profile on each public-administration program. The association's 1974 report, *Graduate School Programs in Public Affairs and Public Administration*, lists 104 graduate programs of some kind in the United States, compared to some 39 reported training programs in 1933. Of these 104, approximately 50 have enough identity and standing to be designated a school, department, center, or institute. Among the 50, fewer than 20 have the structure, authority, and scale of a comprehensive professional school of public affairs/administration. This contrasts with 2 or 3 in 1933.

One of the problems in assessment is the failure to classify programs according to the four categories of public-service education described at the beginning of the preceding section of this essay: (1) liberal arts/citizenship, (2) social-science discipline, (3) general professional practitioner, and (4) specialized practitioner.[19] Consequently, a university can publicize a category (1) or (2) program as though it were a professional one when it may consist only of existing political-science courses including two or three labeled public administration. Not until 1974 were recognized standards available for professional master's degree programs.[20]

In assessing the adequacy of professional educational resources, account must be taken of the varied training centers and programs provided by government agencies, professional organizations and other auspices. These have always provided a substantial part of in-service training.

An Overview. The university effort and its yield reflect the casualness with which the nation has viewed and understood the importance of effective and honest conduct of public affairs. The lack of foresight, scarcity of funds, unresponsiveness of faculties, unresourcefulness of governments have been very discouraging. There were always participants who thought the universities were doing great things. With a few exceptions, we believe the aggregate of efforts were fragmentary, haphazard, and meager.

A tabulation of the early years shows that the Institute of Public Administration (Training School for Public Service), Michigan, Syracuse, Cincinnati, and Stanford together produced 375 graduates of masters' programs (or equivalent) before 1931. Of these, 162 held public positions divided almost equally among federal, state, county, and city governments. Another 96 were employed by quasi-governmental agencies such as leagues of municipalities, governmental research and consulting units, and professional organizations. Fifty-three were engaged in teaching, 46 in business, 5 in other work, and 13 unknown.[21] *The Fifty Year History of Brookings* reports that by the 1930s 65 former students or staff members were serving government.[22] These professional graduates were augmented by programs at colleges and universities in categories (1) or (2) as described above.

While few in number, the *professional* graduates injected much leaven and innovation into many governmental units. In their various capacities, they introduced new concepts and systems and demonstrated the requisites of effective administration. If a national network of influential schools such as USC and Syracuse had been established in that same period—each enrolling 200 to 300 students—would not the conduct and integrity of professional public service throughout the land be of far higher quality today? The cost would have been infinitesimal in relation to the result.

Education for Program Fields. Few public administration programs made any significant contribution to the education of functional or program administrators. They failed to recognize that most of the managerial and related administrative posts in government at all levels are found in such operational fields as public works, health, law enforcement, welfare, and public enterprise. USC was the principal exception (see the Appendix). We have offered above a few illustrations of special programs conducted by other kinds of professional schools, but most of them lacked an adequate managerial component. There were not many effective collaborative programs.

We discern several reasons for this oversight. Most administration programs were too limited and insufficiently oriented to practice either to enroll students with specialized functional or sectoral backgrounds or to develop collaborative relationships with other schools. Other faculties were largely oriented to the private sector and saw little relevance or need for a public-administration input. These included schools of education, which historically viewed their field as a separate branch of government (if a part of government at all). Government agencies were mostly interested in recruiting professional specialists and technicians at the junior levels and so overlooked the need for managerial competence and the possibility that training would help provide it. The Michigan, Cincinnati, and USC programs in public-works engineering and administration were exceptional in this respect.

Assessment of Capability. As a means of evaluating the institutional capability or potential of the early programs—and today's programs—we propose an adaptation of a system that we designed for an international organization. The purpose was to stimulate underdeveloped countries to make self-assessments of the administrative capability of their governments and agencies as a first step in organizing administrative-reform and improvement programs. The application seems apt because most university programs in this field were and are underdeveloped, and their organization and management are also immature.

Our analysis indicates that the capability or performance of a school or program in public affairs and administration reflects the ratio between two rough aggregates.

First, an effective mix of

IL —Institutional Legitimization

PM —Political Mandate, i.e., support of purposes and programs by university authorities

EL —Executive Leadership by dean or director and program heads

FIA—Facilitative Internal Administration: organization, systems, and processes

R   —Resources: human, physical, informational, monetary

Second, a limited number of obstacles

S   —Saboteurs from political science, business administration, or other units which historically have opposed establishment of strong programs in this field

LS —Lack of support by local, state, and federal agencies for the educational and research product of the school

CO —Extent of reliance of university on Collegial Organs for administrative and budgetary decisions

ED —External Disasters such as economic depression, wars, and changes in government, which erode responsibility for supporting education and research (e.g., Title IX, HUD fellowships, EPA training grants)

ID —Internal Disasters such as scandal in the library, heart failure of a successful dean, domination by a disciplinary or analytically preoccupied faculty

The capability—even the survival potential of any institution—can be calculated by use of an algebraic formula.[23]

$$\text{Capability} = \frac{(\text{IL} + \text{PM}) \times (\text{EL} + \text{FIA}) \times \text{R}}{(\text{S} + \text{LS}) \times \text{CO} \times (\text{ED} + \text{ID})}$$

By applying a scale (e.g., 1 to 10) to each element, a rating for a school can be made. Too many years have elapsed to make informed appraisals of programs covered by our case histories. Nevertheless, some of their comparative strengths and weaknesses are made readily discernible by this assessment process. Obviously, it is the process, not the numerical result, that has value.

Requisites for Success. Our chronicle of the birth, successes, maladies, and death of programs should help in the development of survival strategies. Unfortunately, there was no association of schools nor an academy until the 1960s to formulate strategy and to develop criteria and standards.

Six principal requisites of an effective professional school can be derived from the case assessments to guide a university that seeks a major role in public affairs/administration.

First, the university must accord the same kind of recognition and priority to a school of public affairs/administration that it does to business administration, law, and other professional schools.

Second, the school must have effective managerial leadership, that is, a dean and program heads knowledgeable about and convinced of the importance of professionally oriented education and capable of carrying out the necessary managerial tasks.

Third, it must have an organic (institutional) status that assures continuity and support in the university system. The unit must be able to appoint faculty with many disciplinary and professional backgrounds without being controlled by any one discipline, and able to compete for funds and attention. A school with lesser status is at an enormous disadvantage in external negotiation, in serving as the university portal for contacts with government, and in achieving cooperative and joint programs with other professional schools and with the disciplines. Since the employment market is largely in functional or sectoral fields, the ability of universities to respond with administratively trained persons depends upon how well they can develop interprofessional resources and cooperation.

Fourth, the school must have sufficient resources to cover important curricular areas and to engage in research and services. Emaciated programs never attracted the best students, earned respect within the university, or created confidence from without. Assignment to an old World War I barracks or to a building abandoned by some other school hardly reflected distinction on the field. Of the schools described earlier, not one had a building designed for it before the mid-thirties.

Fifth, the school must have fellowship funds. Alternatively, research funds that can be used for research assistants can partially offset lack of fellowships. (Leonard D. White enriched the field with enormous production of material in the early crucial days because of ample research funds and excellent assistants.)

Sixth, the school must have support services: recruitment, placement, counseling, attendance at meetings, field work, project development, publicity, publications, etc.

Constraints. A number of common road blocks or deficiencies may be identified that prevented the above requisites from being fulfilled at most of the universities.

First is the amorphous character and diversity of the public sector. Administration is a generalist occupation, one that calls for what Harlan Cleveland graphically refers to as being concerned with the "situation as a whole." Education in public administration could not become a discrete field of practice such as engineering or law because it was not as easily defined and recognized. Moreover the demarcation between teaching public administration from an historical, cultural, or social-science perspective and from that of a profession concerned with operations and the management of change is too little understood. Leaders who carried the professional torch and endeavored to clarify these ambiguities in their respective universities—Anderson, Beard, Bromage, Cottrell, Egger, Fairlie, Gaus, Gulick, Lambie, Lowrie, Macmahon, May, Mosher, Olson, Reeves, Short, White, and other heroes—should be enshrined in the public-administration hall of fame.

A correlative obstacle was the lack of recognition of the administrative or managerial function involved in rendering public service. The early civil-service systems gave little recognition to this factor in classification or recruitment. The council-manager movement, the National Municipal League, the Civil Service Reform League, bureaus of governmental research, and a few professional societies were only beginning to have real impact by 1933. The American Society for Public Administration was not yet born.

A third constraint restricting collaboration within and outside of the universities was the assumption by specialists that their knowledge of technology automatically qualified them for managerial responsibilities. A good policy or plan was often assumed to be self-implementing. Lack of recognition of the elements of administration and the policy and implementation role of program managers insulated lawyers, social workers, engineers, scientists, medical doctors, and other specialists from cooperative efforts.

Finally, there were the restraints that most political science faculties placed upon public-administration professors within their ranks. Even where support was given, the portion of the budget that could be assigned to public administration was small. A multidisciplinary and professional faculty was incompatible with the concept of a disciplinary department whose primary aspiration was to educate Ph.D.s for teaching and research in the discipline.

Contrast With Business Schools. Education for public administration and business administration had parallel beginnings. The need for professional education for the public sector was much greater, in as much as the functions are far more complex. Business schools that generally met the requisites for success outlined above spawned rapidly during the first third of the century. Today there are more than ninety graduate schools of business, which have many times the resources and recognition accorded to public administration.

Business programs were first initiated by departments of economics. How could business administration be emancipated from economics departments while public administration remained the captive of political science? One suggested reason is that political scientists are more sophisticated in the politics of hegemony and thus more skillful in maintaining dominance over a subordinate group. The principal reason probably lies in the American ethos regarding the capitalistic system and the noxious effect of government, or the propagated fiction that the less government the better.

Large companies recognized early the value of training in economics and business. Most university trustees were businessmen and as such they understood business schools, as did the corporate givers. Affluent graduates were a potent source of support. Their allies outside the university gave the deans of business schools leverage inside.

University Support. This contrast in the origin of schools of business and public administration suggests some generalizations as to the conditions under which universities are able to start programs in new fields. One or more of the following conditions appear to be essential:

a—Availability of a strong group of faculty members who are convinced of the merit of a new program and will lobby for it. Since it has been found to be exceedingly difficult under university decision processes to restructure academic units and change priorities, this criterion standing alone is seldom successful.

b—Resourceful leadership by the university president or chancellor. Even if sympathetic, he can be outmaneuvered by faculty power blocs. He needs some face cards in his hand to win this trick.

c—Strong conviction by influential trustees who understand the field, take up the cause, and elicit external support.

d—Substantial external financial inducement. Private philanthropy and foundation funds brought into being the Training School for Public Service, Maxwell, and Brookings. Grants for training and research have produced great thrusts in science, engineering, agriculture, health, and medicine.

An adequate combination of these supporting forces is seldom available. The inability of programs at such prestigious universities as Wisconsin, Illinois, Ohio State, Chicago, and Columbia to muster enough internal support and funds to make them operationally effective is very sobering.

What About Curricula? Was the quality of the curricula as good as failing memories think, or as bad as some of today's quantitative analysts and behaviorists suggest? Were they doctrinaire, lacking in empirical validity, deficient in scientific analytical methods, overly preoccupied with structure, devoid of human content, and beset with folklore and gadgetry?

In some programs the course work was little more than an extant political-science curriculum with public-administration additives. The New York Training School, Brookings, and USC curricula represented development from a zero base and thus were designed as integrated packages. This is obviously the best way, but few programs had the requisite freedom and resources. Initially, they were bound by traditional political science requirements that left little room for executive management, program administration, and other professional subject matter.

By the 1930s, the three movements or streams of professional input described earlier had considerably matured: (1) the governmental-research movement, with its emphasis on improvement in organization, processes, and management of governments; (2) the scientific-management movement, with its focus on planning of work operations, systems, personnel selection and development, and the function of management; and (3) a rapidly growing recognition (reflected partially in the first two streams) of the effect of employee attitudes and behavior on performance, and of the human relations and motivational responsibilities of managers. The works of Mary Parker Follett and Oliver Sheldon, the Hawthorne experiments and their subsequent flow of literature, and other writings contributed greatly to professional curricula and to the developing emphasis in government at all levels of the role of executive leadership and consultative management.

The scarcity of resources and the lack of sufficient contact with the three streams of inputs prevented the majority of programs from attaining adequate breadth, particularly in relation to policy and program fields. Most of the early programs, however, opened up the new and crucial aspect of administration, namely *management*.

Management was found to be a visceral process, utilizing as much knowledge and analysis as conditions warranted or permitted. Ferreting out and analyzing the facts was the cornerstone of early instruction. Until the invention of the computer there was little temptation to assume that good decisions could be assured by an engorgement of information, identification of variables, and delineation of alternatives. The aim was to help the student to develop background knowledge, competences, and motivations necessary to build effective organizations and processes capable of getting something done.

In the absence of textbooks, much of the course work was inductive. Students worked on problems, examined surveys and reports, and sought ways to improve administration and performance. There may have been too much emphasis on "pat" solutions and techniques, and on personnel and fiscal procedures. Perhaps what the curricula lacked in administrative theory, organization behavior, decision models, and analytical methods was partly compensated by their emphasis upon pragmatic skill in improving the conduct of public services.

In brief, the best curricula in the 1920s and early 1930s provided the graduate with a lot of operative mileage, both immediately and for a lifetime. They generated a sense of mission, ethical standards, and confidence that public service could be advantaged by better management. Concerned with managing change, they had to understand the political and social environment. They were oriented to becoming managers or participants in solving problems of concern to managers.

Concluding Note. Since the obstacles to establishing strong university programs in public administration were insuperable in many places and persist to this day, our assessment may discourage interest in this field. The contrary is our hope.

Against great odds, schools and programs have provided good instruction and research. They have stimulated wide interest in public affairs. They have produced high-quality graduates. They have provided the architects and the builders for countless advances—virtual miracles in the performance of governments.

With increasing enlightenment in respect to the administrative needs of the public service, many new and strengthened professional schools, training institutes, and research centers should be realized in future years, whether comprehensive schools in large universities, or more limited efforts in smaller ones. It is important, however, that the architects of new programs know whether they are developing a category (1), (2), (3), or (4) enterprise, and important that prospective students and the market for their talents are not misled as to the nature of the product. All categories are desirable. Whatever is offered should have excellence. No more than fifty or sixty universities should try to create a comprehensive school of public administration to embark on category (3) and (4) programs. An institution should have pride in category (1) and (2) efforts, but such programs should not be misrepresented as fulfilling the objectives of (3) and (4).

NOTES

1. Leonard D. White, *The Republican Era: 1869–1901* (New York: The Macmillan Company, 1958), p. 367. (Hereafter cited as *Republican Era*.)
2. The Republican Platform of 1896, St. Louis, Mo., June 16, 1896. From Henry Steele Commager (ed.), *Documents of American History* (New York: Appleton-Century-Crofts, seventh edition, 1963), Document no. 341, p. 623.
3. White, *Republican Era*, p. 91.
4. Who later became Vice President, 1925–1929.
5. Case descriptions of the Training School for Public Service and of the Brookings Institution are contained in the Appendix to this essay. The contributions of the New York Bureau are discussed in the next section.
6. Quoted in White, *Republican Era*, p. 383.
7. Denis T. Lynch, *Boss Tweed* (New York: Boni and Liverwright, 1927), p. 16.
8. Luther Gulick, The National Institute of Public Administration, NIPA, 1928.
9. Leonard D. White, *Trends in Public Administration* (New York and London: McGraw-Hill Book Company, Inc., 1933), pp. 176–200. (Hereafter cited as *Trends*.)
10. Later changed to the Public Personnel Association and subsequently to the International Personnel Management Association.
11. John D. Millet, *History of the Faculty of Political Science* (New York: Columbia University Press, 1955), Chapter XII.
12. Bureau of Municipal Research, No. 670, "Efficient Citizenship," March 18, 1914, pp. 5–7.
13. White, *Trends*, p. 261.
14. George A. Graham, *Education for Public Administration* (Chicago: Published for the Committee on Public Administration of the Social Science Research Council by the Public Administration Service, 1941), p. 310.
15. The *Municipal Yearbook* is published annually by the International City Managers' (now Management) Association (ICMA). The source of this listing is the 1937 *Yearbook*, Table III, pp. 223–27.
16. White, *Trends*, p. 327.
17. Ibid., p. 264.
18. Howard K. Manhinick, "Training for the City Planning Profession," in *Public Administrator's News Letter* (January 1933).
19. Preliminary guidelines, notably for establishing a comprehensive school of public affairs/administration, were included in *The Response of Higher Education to the Administrative Needs of the Public Service*, Donald C. Stone, NASPAA, 1971.

20. *Guidelines and Standards for Professional Masters Degree Programs in Public Affairs/Public Administration*, NASPAA, 1974.

21. Schedule compiled by editors of the *Public Administrator's News Letter*, Public Administration Clearing House, Chicago.

22. Charles B. Saunders, Jr., *The Brookings Institution: A Fifty-Year History* (Washington D.C.: The Brookings Institution, 1966), p. 65.

23. Credit is due Warren Ilchman who first suggested this kind of presentation, although he was not consulted in preparing this document.

2. The Period of Crisis: 1933 to 1945

ROWLAND EGGER

INTRODUCTION

The period that the architects of these essays on university education and public administration have characterized as the period of crisis corresponds with deceptive neatness both to Franklin Delano Roosevelt's tenure as President of the United States and Adolph Hitler's dictatorship of the Third Reich. Only the former of these coincidences is important to our purpose. The twelve years spanned by the dates 1933 and 1945 undoubtedly constituted a period of crisis, during which the people of the United States came to grips with the national purpose in terms that had not been confronted since the Civil War, and with their international obligations in terms that had never before been encountered.

The Roosevelt Revolution was the fourth of the five authentic social revolutions we have experienced in our national history. The first was, of course, the War of the Revolution and the aftermath culminating in the Philadelphia Convention, which established firmly and irrevocably our nationhood. The second was the era of Andrew Jackson, which changed fundamentally and irrevocably the homology of the American Presidency and the nature of the party system. The third was the incumbency of Abraham Lincoln, which changed fundamentally and irrevocably the nature of the Union. The fourth was the age of Franklin D. Roosevelt, which changed fundamentally and irrevocably the national purpose of the Republic. The fifth, which began with the Warren Court and is still in progress, is changing—slowly and painfully, to be sure, but also fundamentally and irrevocably—the structure and functioning of the national society, and belatedly bringing to reality the egalitarianism of which Thomas Jefferson dreamed, but which he probably never fully comprehended.

The period of the two New Deals and World War II did a great many things to, for, and about a great many people and a great many aspects of our national life. Public administration, far from remaining modestly in its customary rear pew in the cathedral of the great transformation, became an element of prime importance in the entire undertaking. At no time in the history of the country did the professoriate receive more deference or command more attention as its members roamed freely the corridors of power. At no time did graduates specialized in the newly emergent art and science of public administration encounter more interesting job opportunities on the basis of their still-damp diplomas.

In a more precise sense, however, public administration's revolution was both more and less than Roosevelt's revolution. It was more than Roosevelt's because it began to incorporate and make operative what may be called secular trends in the value-free philosophy of management science quite alien to the essentially moral thrust of the Roosevelt revolution or, for that matter, the essentially theological approach of the President's Committee on Administrative Management. It was less than Roosevelt's because it never developed any clear criteria of the role of public administration in social change, and left the discipline without very many clear and viable standards of conduct for weathering the social and political conflicts through which a democratic polity charts its course.

THE UNITED STATES IN 1933

In 1933 the United States was a shambles. An economy that had promised two chickens in every pot and two cars in every garage had, in a three-and-a-half year tailspin, reduced itself to virtual immobility. Private savings had long since been exhausted in the events of mere physical survival. State governments were probably not financially, and certainly not morally, competent to deal with massive unemployment and distress. Local governments were going bankrupt hand over fist. The government in Washington remained hopelessly entangled in the cocoon of its outworn doctrines of political and economic laissez faire. The only redeeming feature of the whole sorry panorama was the infinite patience and quiet desperation of the American people, and in places that too was beginning to wear thin.

The Economy. This is not the time to recite the litany of the economic debacle following Black Friday in 1929. It is important to the purposes of this symposium primarily as it illuminates the social-economic problems with which the country was confronted when Roosevelt came to power in 1933, the dimensions of the crisis, the political decisions that the size and urgency of the crisis forced upon the government in Washington, and the administrative implications of these political decisions which, *pari passu*, changed radically the terms of reference of the entire enterprise of education for the public service.

The numbers do not require—indeed, they do not permit—elaborate comment. They are the statistics of disaster.

	1929	1933	% Change 1929–1933	1937	1941
Gross national product	181.8	126.6	−30.4	183.5	238.1
Personal consumption	128.1	103.5	−19.2	132.1	154.3
Private domestic investment	35.0	4.0	−82.8	27.0	36.7
Federal expenditures	2.9	5.3	+89.3	9.6	30.7
State and local expenditures	15.6	14.6	−6.4	16.4	16.9
Employment					
Number unemployed	1.6	12.8	+825.0	7.7	5.6
Unemployed as percentage of labor force	3.2	24.9	+678.1	14.3	9.9
Federal employment	0.6	0.6		0.9	1.4
Trade union membership	NA	2.7		7.0	10.2
Federal surplus or deficit	0.7 S	2.6D		2.8D	6.2D
Economic indices					
Manufacturing production	58	36	−37.9	60	88
Farm prices	148	70	−25.7	122	124
Wholesale prices	62	43	−30.6	56	57
Per capita GNP	1492	1007	−32.5	1423	1784
Family income distribution					
Top 5 per cent	30.0				24.0
Top 20 per cent	54.4				48.8
Second 20 per cent	19.3				22.3
Third 20 per cent	13.8				15.3
Fourth 20 per cent }	12.5				9.5
Bottom 20 per cent }					4.1

Source: U.S. Bureau of the Census, *Historical Statistics of the United States, Colonial Times to 1957* (Washington, D.C.: Government Printing Office, 1960).

Translated into human terms, they are the apotheosis of degradation and despair. American literature is replete with novels, plays,
poetry, and solemn social analyses documenting the bad things
that happened to good people in the economic prostration of the
Depression. John Steinbeck's *The Grapes of Wrath* is one of these,
but it is only one of many. Even the measured language of official-
dom sometimes achieved the level of literate and moving prose.

> This study of the human cost of unemployment reveals that a
> new class of poor and dependents is rapidly rising among the
> ranks of young, sturdy, ambitious laborers, artisans, mechanics
> and profesionals, who until recently maintained a relatively high
> standard of living and were the stable, self-respecting citizens and
> taxpayers of this State. Unemployment and loss of income have
> ravaged numerous homes. It has broken the spirit of their mem-
> bers, undermined their health, robbed them of self-respect, de-
> stroyed their efficiency and employability. Many households have
> been dissolved; little children parcelled out to friends, relatives or
> charitable homes; husbands and wives, parents and children sepa-
> rated, temporarily or permanently.... Men, young and old, have
> taken to the road. They sleep each night in a new flophouse. Day
> after day, the country over, they stand in the breadlines for food
> which carries with it the suggestion "move on," "we don't want
> you." [1]

Rural America was no whit better off. By 1933 the level of
farm prices was down more than one-half from 1929. Eggs could
be bought for a penny each, and a pound of butter for fifteen
cents. Mortgage foreclosures on farms were rife until armed
resistance in the Midwest and elsewhere brought them to a stop
and a moratorium was declared, a procedure legitimized by the
Supreme Court in 1934.[2] Of the agricultural strike in Sioux City
it was written that:

> ...Roads were blockaded, fist fights broke out, arrests were
> made, and gun toting, exhortation, vituperation, picketing, storm-
> ing of jails and capitol buildings, and stopping of trains and auto-
> mobiles were among the other events that took place. In some
> places the old Populist cry of 'raise less corn and more hell' was

heard; in others Hoover was likened to Louis XIV, and the actions of strikers were compared to those of the Boston Tea Party and William L. Garrison. . . .[3]

The State of the Government. Historians disagree on President Herbert Hoover's convictions with respect to the use of governmental power, especially the power of the national government, in coping with economic and social catastrophe. Walter Lippmann[4] and Broadus Mitchell[5] give him high marks on his intentions and some of his actions. It is true that he did send Jesse Jones and the Reconstruction Finance Corporation into the fray with money to bail out the holders of state and municipal bonds in default. A distinguished Catholic divine of the period is reported to have remarked of this interesting foray in dribble-down economics that he doubted whether the Good Lord, whose omniscience comprehended even the fall of the sparrow, would consider his obligation to these, the least of His creatures, satisfied by tossing a horse a bale of hay. In any case, it is not recorded that there was a notable accretion of sparrows to the standards of the President's party in the 1932 elections.

In his autobiography,[6] published twenty years after he left office, Mr. Hoover comes through as the sort of humanitarian and interventionist that nobody suspected him of being at the time. Andrew Mellon, it appears, was the real Social Darwinist, who espoused liquidation of labor, stocks, farmers, real estate, and apparently everything else that could be liquefied. He even thought, according to Hoover, that a panic could purge the rottenness of the people, make them work harder, live a more moral life, adjust their values, and give enterprising people the opportunity to pick up the pieces from the less competent. On the other hand, Mr. Hoover tells us, he, Mills, Young, Lamont, and Hyde all felt that the powers of the government should be used to "cushion" the situation.

Whatever President Hoover's recollections of the state of affairs may have been, what he said and did at the time made the difference. When Congress, under the control of the opposition party, passed bills for national intervention in the crisis, he told it that rigid economy was the real road to the relief of farmers, workers, home owners, and every element of the population; that their proposals embodying increases of federal expenditures of over forty billions during the next five years represented a spirit of spending in the country that must be abandoned; and that the country could not squander its way into prosperity.[7] So it was that Mr. Mellon's Social Darwinism—if it was his—continued to dominate national policy for the thirteen months that remained of Mr. Hoover's term.

In short, when Franklin Roosevelt succeeded President Hoover in March, 1933, he confronted a country with one-fourth of its labor force out of work, underemployment rife, farm prices far below the cost of production, mortgage indebtedness defaulted in increasing volume, bank failures rampant, commerce stagnant, domestic investment all but disappeared, and a population whose morale, caught between dumb misery and utter outrage at the way in which the traditional virtues had played them false, which had probably never in American history been at a lower ebb. If, as Roosevelt told us in his inaugural, we had "nothing to fear but fear itself," it is equally true that the people of the United States in 1933 had plenty in their past and their immediate prospects about which to be fearful.

The State of the Art. Public administration, as an art and as a science, was in 1933 in what Dwight Waldo has correctly identified as its "period of orthodoxy."[8] It was in a period of intense activity, especially at the levels of state and municipal government, it was pragmatic, it was experimental, it was reformist, and there was little time for theoretical abstraction concerning either its ends or its means. But Waldo is using the term in a much more precise and much less ambiguous sense. He is telling us that public administration had not yet challenged its major premise, which is the separability—and separateness—of the discipline and its amenability to analysis and elaboration on the basis of criteria and principles different from those involved in the mere application of legal rules on the one hand, and equally different from those that had dominated political science in its attempts to identify and define the phenomena of governmental action. In short, it continued to embrace, without basic skepticism, the Wilsonian dichotomy.

If in 1933 public administration had not challenged its major premise, some of its minor premises were in a state of turmoil and even downright disorder. Fayolism and Taylorism had already begun to clarify and confuse both the organizational and operational aspects of administrative orthodoxy.[9] The fact that the Maxwell School is a "School of Citizenship and Public Affairs," and was so named as early as 1924, tells us something about William E. Mosher's lifelong commitment to the notion of "efficient citizenship" as a basic ingredient of good public administration.[10] The intellectual incompatibilities of F.J. Goodnow[11] and W.F. Willoughby,[12] on the one hand, and L.D. White,[13] on the other, regarding distinctions between "executive" and "administrative" functions challenged several minor premises and even made a dent in the more basic notion of the separability of administration and politics. And the city-manager movement was an outright denial of the even more sacred principle—the separation of powers.

In short, the orthodoxy that permeated thinking about the content and method of the discipline at the opening of the crisis period should be recognized, but not overrated. The orthodoxy was grounded not in the impermeability of a set of monolithic doctrines or beliefs, but rather in the harassments of a discipline so concerned with meeting its immediate problems that it had little time or energy for theorizing.

The Institutions of Administrative Development. In 1933 the institutions of administrative development were already firmly grounded, especially those for the improvement of state and local government. Reform organizations, such as the National Municipal League and the National Civil Service Reform League, had been in effective operation for many years. Professional organizations of state and local officials and associations of state and local governments, perhaps best exemplified in the "1313" complex—then the "850" complex—in Chicago, were, thanks to the stimulus of the Spelman fund, providing extensive services to their constituencies in the improvement of administration. State leagues of munici- palities, with their satellite organizations of public-works officials, finance officers, city managers, etc., were all but universal.

Nor were the colleges and universities lacking in interest in the development of public administration. By 1933 about thirty-five educational institutions had established training programs which purported to prepare students for employment in public admin- istration. Some of these were important foundations which con- tinue to this day to exercise major influences in the development of public management. Some have fallen by the wayside. Some have so changed their interests and emphases that they no longer bear a discernable relationship to administration. Some were inconsequential from the beginning.

Of these thirty-five training programs twenty were in public— state or municipal—institutions and fifteen were private. They were scattered from coast to coast, and from the Canadian bound- ary to the Gulf of Mexico. While there were certain concentra- tions—six in California and six in Ohio, for example—it was not a parochial movement. The distribution pattern seems to have been related less to any notable environmental exigency than to the interest, energy, and enthusiasm of many of the familiar figures of academic political science who labored mightily in the vineyards of state and local government in the earlier decades of the twen- tieth century.

On a less formal—or in any case less pretentious—basis forty-one colleges and universities had introduced instruction in public administration into their curricula by 1933. Most of these were courses in municipal administration, since there was not even a textbook in general public administration prior to Leonard D. White's contribution, which was first published in 1926. Some of these institutions subsequently developed integral training pro- grams for the public service. In some cases the introduction of public administration into the academic curriculum was an out- growth of efforts in extension programs. Some appear to have been designed to prepare students for work in graduate institutions offering public-service training. Some were introduced simply to enrich the undergraduate political-science offering. As in the case of the formal training programs, the distribution was widespread and appealed to public and private institutions alike.

A third institutional manifestation of university involvement weighing heavily in the climate of 1933 was what has been called the "bureau movement." Deriving from such nonacademic origins as the New York Bureau of Municipal Research, founded in 1906, it spread quickly to other metropolitan areas and thence to the universities—mainly state institutions, which had an important stake in servicing the research needs of state and local governments. While in 1933 the bureaus were almost entirely involved in state and local administration, they served an important purpose in bridging the gap between the academy and the cutting edge of public administration in the governments they served.[14]

THE FIRST NEW DEAL

Like public administration itself, the First New Deal was in the main pragmatic, experimental, and opportunistic. As Frances Perkins wrote:[15]

When Franklin Roosevelt and his administration began their work in Washington in March 1933, the New Deal was not a plan with form and content. It was a happy phrase which he had coined during the campaign, and its value was psychological. It made people feel better, and in that terrible period of depression they needed to feel better.

But the long, hard road to recovery involved a great deal more than merely making people feel better. The New Deal had its own difficulties finding the road.

The Government in Action. Roosevelt was inaugurated on March 4, and immediately called the Congress into special session on March 9. Meanwhile, confronted with an unprecedented spurt in bank closures he declared, under the authority of the Trading with the Enemy Act of 1917, a bank holiday. When Congress met it was presented with an Administration proposal, the Emergency Banking Bill, which enabled the Federal Reserve Bank to issue notes on the security of the assets of sound banks and permit them immediately to reopen under Treasury license. This stopped the bank panic with ultimate losses of something more than a billion dollars by banks that Treasury had refused to license. Very few licensed banks failed. The bill was passed within four hours of its introduction on March 9, and was signed that evening. Roosevelt also moved to maintain the festive atmosphere by immediately legalizing 3.2 beer and initiating steps to repeal the Eighteenth Amendment, which occurred within a year.

On March 18 a draft of the Agricultural Adjustment Act was sent to Congress that, after extended debate, emerged on May 12. It gave the farmers much of what they had been fighting for during almost a half-century, in the form of protected prices for their surpluses, inflated money with which to pay their debts, and cheap credit. This time the rural sparrows, at least, didn't have to depend on dribble-down.

On March 21 Roosevelt sent to Congress a message asking for authorization of a Civilian Conservation Corps for the immediate employment of 250,000 young men for conservation work in the national forests, for authorization of the Public Works Administration, and for cooperation between labor and management, under government supervision, in expanding industrial employment. The CCC was authorized and funded quickly, and the PWA and NIRA authorizations were included in the National Industrial Recovery Act, signed on June 16.

On May 12 the President signed the Federal Emergency Relief Act, which was in the main a program for assisting state and local governments in direct relief payments. A portion of the funds appropriated under the legislation was available to the states on the basis of one dollar of federal funds for every three dollars of state and local funds expended for relief of the unemployed. On May 15 he signed the Tennessee Valley Authority Act, and on May 27 the Federal Securities Act establishing the registration of stocks traded on the exchanges with the Federal Trade Commission. On June 5 he completed the job, initiated under the Emergency Banking Relief Act, of taking the country off the gold standard by signing the gold clause repeal resolution, which made all debts and contractual agreements payable in legal tender. On June 16 he signed the Glass-Steagall Act creating the Federal Deposit Insurance Corporation and expanding federal control of the banking system and the NIRA, as noted above; he then left for Campobello. The Hundred Days was over.

Most of this initial First New Deal legislation, it should be noted, was of the sort Herbert Hoover could have signed if he had not been bemused by the dollar marks. With the exception of federal assistance to the state and local governments, much of it had, indeed, been urged by Hoover. Roosevelt's Economy Act, moreover, which cut veterans' pensions and reduced federal salaries by 15 percent, delighted the conservatives. Despite the reputation he subsequently enjoyed for his free hand with the tax-payers' money, the Hundred Days exhibited little to frighten either the money changers in the temple or the malefactors of great wealth.

These measures, and especially the prospects of more to come, produced a false boom. Between March and July, 1933, the pro-duction index rose about 80 percent, farm prices almost 50 percent, and stock prices in the neighborhood of 70 percent. But it was a purely speculative advance founded on cheap credit, anticipated inflation and future profits, inventory expansions as hedges against price increases, and the attempts by manufacturers to increase stockpiles in anticipation of NIRA-induced cost in-creases, production limitation, and more comprehensive price con-trols. In July the market crashed, and the country was back to square one.

Meanwhile, the machinery of relief and rehabilitation was grinding with all deliberate speed. The CCC was proceeding with its specific and limited mission with some dispatch. The Public Works Administration created by Title II of NIRA was designed to stimulate the construction industry by providing funds for a massive public works program. "Honest Harold" Ickes, secretary of the interior, administered the title, and his quite proper concern with scrupulous honesty in the awarding and supervision of con-struction contracts made for a very sedate rate of unemployment relief. NRA's Blue Eagle was flying on one wing in its efforts to stimulate and spread industrial employment. Winter was coming on.

Harry Hopkins had never liked the dole, which was the essence of FERA. He wanted to provide work relief for employables that would reincorporate their skills and their spirits in the work force, rather than merely keep their souls and bodies together with subsistence payments. This involved a degree of centralized control and a level of funding that Roosevelt found uncongenial, but Hopkins' persuasiveness, the statistics of resurgent unemployment, and the fact that hard weather was on its way led him on November 8 to establish the Civil Works Administration, which was a short-run experimental program in direct federal work relief. It terminated April 1, 1934, but in its short life it pumped almost $1 billion into the purchasing power of American employables who had worked for their money, even if sometimes the work was no more permanent than raking the leaves. It got Roosevelt through the winter of 1933/34.

By 1935 Roosevelt was ready to accept on a continuing basis Hopkins' formula for handling employables through direct federal work programs. On May 6 the Works Progress Administration, subsequently renamed the Work Projects Administration, was launched, funded at $4 billion. Some estimate of the scope and variety of WPA projects may be gained from Rauch's recital of a random selection from a small fraction of its accomplishments during its first two years: [16]

> . . . 1634 new school buildings, 105 airport landing fields, 3000 tennis courts, 3300 storage dams, 103 golf courses, 5800 traveling libraries established, 1654 medical and dental clinics established, 36,000 miles of new rural roads, 128,000,000 school lunches served, 2,000,000 home visits by nurses, 1,500 theatrical productions, 134 fish hatcheries, 1,100,000 Braille pages transcribed, and 17,000 literacy classes conducted per month.

During the remainder of the First New Deal additional important legislation was enacted. The Resettlement Administration was established in May to deal with the seamier aspects of farm tenancy and sharecropping. On May 11 the Rural Electrification Administration was set up. The National Youth Administration came into operation on June 26. The Wagner-Connery Act, establishing a new National Labor Relations Board to supervise bargaining agency elections, was signed on July 5. The Social Security Act was signed on August 14; some of its titles were of immediate application, such as Aid to Dependent Children, Aid to the Blind, and the medical titles, but the economic impact of Unemployment Compensation and of Old Age and Survivors Insurance would be delayed until covered employment requisites could be complied with and until reserves could be built.

Meanwhile, the Supreme Court had girded its loins to do battle with the President of the United States. On May 6, 1935, it declared the Railroad Retirement Act of 1934 unconstitutional.[17] On May 27 it declared the National Industrial Recovery Act of 1933 unconstitutional, although the Blue Eagle had been a sick bird almost from the outset.[18] On January 6, 1936, the court struck down the Agricultural Adjustment Act.[19] On May 18 the court invalidated the Bituminous Coal Conservation Act,[20] and on May 25 the Municipal Bankruptcy Act of 1934.[21] In a wholesale reversion to nineteenth-century doctrine the court even struck down a New York minimum wage act.[22] While Congress was able to salvage some of this legislation by enactments meeting the court's objections, the series of 1935–36 decisions effectively ended the First New Deal.

The Government. The years 1933 through 1936 were times of extraordinary development and experimentation in public administration, especially in the national government. The multipurpose authority, marked by the establishment of the TVA, was a very significant administrative innovation. And while the government corporation was not wholly new to the American scene at the time of the First New Deal, the use of the corporate device was enormously expanded and its applications multiplied during this period. But experimentation and innovation have their price, and the First New Deal was not exempt.

Roosevelt had very little confidence in the ability of the "old line" departments or the civil service of 1933 to carry out the programs that in time came to make up what is called the First

New Deal. Many legislative leaders whose names were associated with New Deal enactments were reluctant to see their administrations absorbed into ongoing programs, where their performance could not be readily observed and monitored. So it was that practically every new program involved the creation of a new agency.

The First New Deal was not notable for the symmetry of its administrative architecture or for the orderliness of its administrative processes. Indeed, the tasks to which it had set itself fitted poorly into the established administrative structures, and the thrust of the New Deal itself was alien to the experience and outlook of the government clerks of the 1933 bureaucracy. And Roosevelt himself—no Social Darwinist—was not averse to the survival of the fittest in the administrative milieu. So it was that a large number of new agencies with novel mandates, unorthodox procedures, and occasionally indefinite boundaries came into being. It was the heyday of the alphabetical organizations.

Quantitatively, staffing in the First New Deal was not a problem. The supply of educated and experienced personnel for the intermediate and lower echelons was far in excess of demand. At the upper levels relevant experience was hard to come by, since no American government or organization had performed the kinds of functions on the scale the government then set for itself. Harry Hopkins' experience as a social worker at Christadora Settlement House in New York City, or even as Governor Roosevelt's chairman of the New York State Temporary Relief Administration, provided very little background for running the Civil Works Administration or the Works Progress Administration. And in those days even Tommy the Cork (Thomas Corcoran) was a neophyte in the labyrinthine ways of Washington. Top management was experimental, innovative, ad hoc, and frequently impromptu; it had to be. There was, nonetheless, a considerable influx of people, many of whom turned out to be excellent administrators, from the academic departments and faculties, from the settlement houses and state and local welfare agencies, and from myriad other sources. The contribution of Harvard was beyond the call of duty, and sometimes even of decency. The TVA, under David Lilienthal's tutelage, sometimes looked like a University of Wisconsin Extension Division project. Even Dean William E. Mosher left the Maxwell School for a while to direct a rate study for the Federal Power Commission. As Edmund Wilson has testified, Washington was a very entertaining place in those days.[23]

Serious students of administration, meanwhile, were concerned with the ability of public personnel systems to respond to the challenges of the new state. A privately financed investigation by an ad hoc Commission of Inquiry on Public Service Personnel conducted extensive research and held an extended series of public hearings in 1933/34. Its report, issued in 1935, is comparable in many significant aspects to the Macauley report of 1854, which established the foundations of the British civil service.[24] Although warning against a closed career service, the commission did come out emphatically for the development of a transferable, high-level administrative class in the United States Civil Service for staffing managerial posts in the departments, bureaus, and agencies. Forty years later we have still failed to deal adequately with this problem. During this period Roosevelt also established the National Personnel Council, to the head of which he appointed Frederick M. Davenport. One of Davenport's earliest ventures in this assignment was to launch the National Institute of Public Affairs, which was achieved with the aid of the Rockefeller Foundation. The institute, for a fourteen-year period until its functions were taken over by the Civil Service Commission, brought into Washington each year from thirty to fifty of the "brightest and the best" of current college graduates for internships in the federal departments and agencies. Some pretty good men went through this experience, including several who later turned up as ambassadors, assistant secretaries, and even one chairman of the Civil Service Commission.

In 1934 Roosevelt set up the National Resources Committee, subsequently renamed the National Resources Planning Board. This board was charged with the development of plans for the use and conservation of natural and human resources for the guidance of federal policy, and with promoting and improving the planning capacities of federal, state, and local agencies. In addition to many seminal documents on national resources, it has had an enduring influence in its highly successful efforts to develop and strengthen resource planning in the states and their political subdivisions. Much of the state planning machinery now in existence is in one way or another a heritage of the NRPB programs in the prewar period.

The Academy. The period from 1933 to 1937 was one of great quantitative progress in the expansion of training for public administration, in university research and service to state and local governments, in elevating and broadening the intellectual interests of those in the academy concerned with public administration, and in liberating the academic machinery of research and training from its preoccupation with state and local administration. During the period, fourteen institutions of the alleged higher learning established training programs in public administration; three of these in the District of Columbia continue with no small prosperity to the present day. In addition, twenty-nine institutions introduced instruction in public administration into their regular curricula. Perhaps more significant was the shift in emphasis of older training programs in the direction of a concern both with the federal government and functionally to the programs in which the federal government played an important role in policy and finance. This tendency was important in some public-administration training programs, but it also affected professional education in schools of social work and even in schools of law, which began to rediscover administrative law.

Relationships of cause and effect are as difficult to discover in public administration as in quantum mechanics, but of the enrichment of the intellectual resources of the academy during this period there can be little doubt. Throughout the earlier periods, and well into the 1930s, public administration training had been conceived primarily in terms of the traditional staff functions—planning, personnel, organization, budgeting, procurement, accounting, etc.—and even those within fairly mechanical criteria of economy and efficiency. Early in the period, Mayo's *Human Problems of an Industrial Civilization* was published, and the findings of the Hawthorne experiments began to make their way into the literature of management, public and private.[25] Although a full translation of Max Weber's *Wirtschaft und Gesellschaft* would not come until the middle 1950s, Carl Friedrich and Taylor Cole published in 1932 their *Responsible Bureaucracy*, which set the stage for a debate on the bureaucratic obligation that has turned out to be as relevant in 1975 as it was in 1933.[26] This was not, of course, the first assertion of the "generalist" primacy in administrative ideology, but it did open the issue and define the terms of a major debate in the academy that has survived even the hegemony of the high-temperature physicists and the latter-day logical positivists. In 1934 Louis Brownlow told us that the primordial concern of the administrator is with "human relations, with human values, with those deeper economic, social, and spiritual needs of the human beings whose government, in its administrative branch, he represents."[27] Pendleton Herring likewise called for a revised conception of the bureaucratic function that would permit a meaningful synthesis of interest-group pressures and the requirements of equality and freedom in the formulation of alternatives and the decisions of broad policy in implementing the program choices of the legislature.[28] Lucius Wilmerding distinguished succinctly the "administrative" class from those who carry out the orders, and of the former said: "Although he must be learned in the law, experienced in the consequences of administrative action, skilled in public finance, and able to understand the purely technical considerations involved in a problem, he is neither a lawyer, a politician, a financier, nor a technician. . . . His specialty is method rather than subject matter."[29] And William E. Mosher took the logical next step in pointing out that public administration is itself a discipline and a method that is learnable and teachable.[30] Indeed, during much of this and the succeeding period one of the major problems of training in public administration was the superimposition of broad administrative and managerial skills on civil servants with specialized education and experience—making city managers, for example, out of civil engineers, and making welfare administrators out of social case workers.

Two other events in the academy that influenced profoundly the teaching of public administration should be noted. In 1936 John Gaus, Leonard White, and Marshall Dimock published a series of lectures designed to illuminate pathways of development in public administration.[31] These essays not only emphasized the necessity of long-term planning in public affairs; but also assisted greatly in breaking the art and science of administration out of the rigidities that its own orthodoxy had imposed upon it, and also foreshadowed many important later developments and made explicit the inadequacies of the then current approaches to research and training. The same year John Maynard Keynes published his classic commentary on employment, interest, and money.[32] It may be, as Paul Appleby always insisted, that Keynes had no influence on Roosevelt, who apparently accepted Churchill's dictum that "wheresoever there are two economists there will be three opinions, two of which are Keynes'." But Keynes' ideas had a profound effect in the Treasury and at many levels of government below the White House, as well as amongst members of the academy occupied with problems of public finance and fiscal policy.

In 1934, meanwhile, the Social Science Research Council had established a Committee on Public Administration, with the aim of upgrading academic research in the field and bringing it into closer and more operational contact with innovations in administrative methods and procedures. Until its activities were brought to a halt by American involvement in World War II, the Committee poured a steady stream of significant new research into important developing areas of national, state, and local administration. While most of the publications of Committee-sponsored research appeared during the Second New Deal, their origins were in most cases earlier. Notable studies of city-manager government,[33] of grant systems in the United States and Canada,[34] of social security administration,[35] of Federal work relief,[36] of agriculture and public administration,[37] and of education and public administration[38] were planned and funded by the Committee. A highly provocative series of monographs on the scope and methods of research in public-personnel administration,[39] administrative law,[40] the administration of public tort liability,[41] and NRA code administration[42] had great influence on research subjects and methods in the academy in both the Second New Deal and in the postwar periods.

THE SECOND NEW DEAL

The First New Deal, as has been noted, was terminated with a series of adverse Supreme Court decisions in 1935 and 1936. Although legislative revision salvaged some of what the court had struck down, a considerable momentum had been lost. In a very real sense the 1936 election was a referendum on Roosevelt and the New Deal. He was returned to the White House with the electoral votes of every state except Maine and Vermont. The Democratic Party was returned to power with 85 of the then 96 seats in the Senate and 333 of the 435 seats in the House. But Roosevelt had earlier indicated to Roy W. Howard, head of the Scripps-Howard newspaper chain, that the substantial completion of the experimental stage of the New Deal would lead to a "breathing spell." And under pressure from Morgenthau, the secretary of the treasury,[43] he again began to veer heavily toward budget balancing and the reduction of federal expenditures. Late in 1936 the economic recovery that had been mainly sparked by WPA expenditures began to frighten the timid souls in the administration, of whom there were a good many, and the spectre of a runaway boom of the 1928/29 variety was resurrected.[44]

> ...It was therefore determined that...by drastically reducing the number of workers on WPA rolls, the administration planned to balance the budget within a year. WPA rolls had been considerably reduced late in 1936, and early in 1937 the policy was announced of discharging about half of those remaining. By August only one and one-half million persons were still employed by WPA.

On Black Tuesday, October 19, 1937, the stock market again disintegrated. Seventeen million shares were traded in a market more reminiscent of the 1929 debacle than anything that had happened in between. Morgenthau's assertion and Roosevelt's hope that a balanced upturn in private employment would solve the disequilibrium between prices and spending power were again in ashes. With sporadic oscillations the economy continued to degenerate. The indices of industrial production fell from 117 in August, 1937, to 76 in May, 1938. Wholesale prices declined from 87.9 to 78.1 in the same period, and farm prices dropped from 123 to 92. Employment in manufacturing industries was 112.7 in August, 1937, and 84.7 in July, 1938. Payrolls declined from 108.7 in August, 1937, to 71.1 by July, 1938. There was a midterm election in November.

On March 25, 1938 the market took another sickening lurch. This time Roosevelt did move. He instructed Henry Wallace and Jessie Jones—an unlikely combination—to work out a program for housing, flood control, rural rehabilitation, and loans to industry. He asked Congress for $1.25 billion for relief for the period July 1, 1938, to March 1, 1939, for $50 million to keep the CCC in operation, and for $300 to $400 million in increased borrowing authority for the RFC.

The late start in 1938 was insufficient to check the sharp downturn quickly, and despite some improvements the year-end figures were unfavorable. The gross national product declined $8.4 billion —the first loss since Roosevelt had assumed office. Unemployment had increased by 2,600,000, and constituted nineteen percent of the labor force. Personal-consumption expenditures, gross private domestic investment, manufacturing production, farm prices, and wholesale prices were all sharply down for the year. The only element that prospered was trade union membership, which increased by about one million during the year.

The Government and the Economy. Some time during the latter part of 1938 Roosevelt apparently reached the conclusion that he had been calling on private industry for tasks to which it was intellectually and morally unequal. In February the Congress had passed the Agricultural Adjustment Act, which salvaged what was salvageable from the AAA, but was particularly directed to the problem of unmanageable agricultural surpluses such as those produced by the "good" year of 1937. It involved fundamental changes in persuasive techniques from benefit payments for not

farming to production allotments and the purchase by the government of surplus production at parity prices, thus effectively steril-
izing the surplus production, stabilizing prices, and, it was hoped,
improving agricultural practices and land use. The Federal Crop
Insurance Corporation was another administrative innovation of
this period, created mainly to deal with problems of crop failure
such as those created by the Dust Bowl. The new agricultural
legislation continued the soil-conservation practices of the old
AAA, but Congress never funded the Farm Security Administration adequately. It would take World War II to pull the poorer
farmers out of their difficulties and give them a transient prosperity without solving their fundamental problem, which is what
happens to the price of agricultural products between the farm
and the supermarket.

The Fair Labor Standards Act of 1938 attempted to extend
minimum wages and maximum hours to the work force in general,
affording protection especially to those elements in the labor force
not able at that time to protect their interests through collective
bargaining. It became a battleground for the AFL and CIO (then
living apart), it was emasculated by the Southerners to preserve
their "favorable" wage differential, and it was delayed several
years in coming into full operation by a coalition of conservative
Republicans and anti-Roosevelt Democrats. What Roosevelt got
out of Congress was indeed a poor thing in comparison with what
he had requested. But it did provide the occasion three years later
for a new court to make a clean break with its antique jurispru-
dence and definitively to legitimatize national control over labor
relations.

Early in the First New Deal, Roosevelt had embraced economic
nationalism when he torpedoed the London Conference on the
very pragmatic grounds that until the United States was able to
revitalize its own economy it was not in a position to undertake
international commitments with respect to currency valuations
and other efforts to ease trade restrictions. This policy was
drastically abated in the Second New Deal. The process was
gradual, of course, and had begun with the passage of the
Reciprocal Trade Agreements Act in 1934, through which the

United States attempted to clamber down with as much dignity as possible from the excesses of the Smoot-Hawley tariff of 1930. And the Good Neighbor Policy had been proclaimed very early in the First New Deal. As a practical matter, however, tangible results in terms of substantial increases in trade volume were slow in developing. During the period 1937-1941, however, there was a significant increase in the number of agreements negotiated under the Reciprocal Trade Agreements Act, and in the volume and value of exports and imports.

By 1939 pump-priming and the effects of the new legislation and increased activity under old legislation were beginning to become apparent. The gross national product jumped by almost $14 billion to $189.3 billion, unemployment dropped by almost one million, manufacturing and farm price indices rose slowly but steadily, and the wholesale price index held firm. There was a substantial improvement in real wages. But what put the United States clearly on the road to economic recovery was the outbreak of the war in Europe.

The Government in the Second New Deal. There were four major events in the Second New Deal that profoundly conditioned the orientation of education for public administration. The first of these was the Reorganization Act of 1939, which permitted the implementation of the Report of the President's Committee on Administrative Management. As early as 1935, Roosevelt had been acutely aware of the administrative deficiencies of the federal establishment, which were multiplied and exacerbated at state and local levels as the number of federal agencies providing "categorical" grants and administrative supervision for relief and economic rehabilitation multiplied. Indeed, he was not insensible of the fact that his own reservations, and those of his principal colleagues in the legislative branch, concerning the bureaucratic establishment had contributed to the administrative chaos and confusion. In 1935 he appointed his Committee on Administrative Management, consisting of Louis Brownlow as chairman, Luther Gulick, and Charles Merriam. Many members of the academy were involved in the preparation of the committee's report. I was not one of these, and may therefore observe with propriety that it was the first comprehensive reconsideration of the Presidency and the President's control of the executive branch since 1787, and is probably the most important constitutional document of our time. The findings and recommendations of the committee, frequently criticized on doctrinal grounds by exponents of the "new public administration," continue to occupy a central position in the perennial debate about how to manage the government's business.

Probably the best summary of the thrust and purpose of the report is in Brownlow's memorandum for the committee:[45]

The report should recommend:

That the staff of institutional agencies should be made directly responsible to the President; that the President establish a White House secretariat which will include not only such functions as have been exercised in the past, but which under an executive secretary will establish the direct lines of communication with all of the staff agencies except the Budget (which should report directly to the President);

That through the development of such a White House secretariat the President coordinate the work of the line and operating agencies with respect to information and recommendations;

That to facilitate coordinated over-all management and to improve internal agency administration a single responsible administrator be placed at the head of all administrative agencies, staff and line, which are now headed by boards and commissions;

That while no recommendation may be made at this time for the segregation of administrative duties from the quasi-judicial duties of the regulatory agencies now in existence, the danger of the development of an irresponsible Fourth Branch of the government be recognized and that consideration be given in all future regulatory legislation to the devolution of such work upon the regular departments of government as already has often been done;

That the President be given continuing power, subject to a Congressional veto of the type provided in the Economy Act of 1933 to regroup, rearrange, consolidate and reorganize the departments, agencies and bureaus; and that to facilitate his work in this respect there be developed in the Bureau of the Budget the research function already provided by law;

That in the presence of an emergency the temporary creation of emergency agencies to handle new types of activities is not only justified but necessary; that as the emergency situation lessens the new activities be fitted into the permanent establishment by order of the President (subject to the same type of Congressional veto suggested above);

That to effectuate these recommendations which are to be elaborated in detail, it is necessary to establish direct lines of relationship which will enable the President to control effectively the fiscal machinery of the government, to extend the merit system to all branches of the Executive, excluding only policy-making positions, to command the research and intellectual resources of an adequately equipped planning agency, to require the coordination of statistical and reporting services and to establish a coordinated scheme for the clearance of legislative recommendations or reports proper to the sphere of the Executive as well as provide clearance and control for the issue of Executive Orders and administrative rules and regulations which require presidential authority or approval;

That effective Congressional control of the Executive cannot be exercised by detailed and uncoordinated legislative action whether by general law or limitations attached to particular budgetary items or appropriation bills or by the type of control exercised by the Comptroller General who is the agent of Congress but who in fact is irresponsible to either the Executive or Legislative branch; but that Congressional control of the Executive will be advantaged by a concentration of administrative responsibility upon the President in accordance with the Constitution, and will be made fully effective only by the creation by Congress of its own agent to review and audit the conduct of the Executive Branch and to report to Congress through committees especially set up by the two houses of Congress to receive and digest the results of such review and audit.

The report of the committee, which was submitted in 1937, was inundated in the melee attendant upon the President's Supreme Court Reorganization Plan, which he sent to Congress on February 5, 1937. By 1939, however, Congress was prepared to deal with reorganization. Despite criticism and opposition, Congress not only passed reorganization legislation, but improved substantially on the traditional formula requiring positive Congressional approval of organization plans. The Reorganization Act of 1939 provided that reorganization plans submitted by the President would have the force of law if, within sixty days after submission, they had not been vetoed by both houses. With this legislation in hand, Roosevelt moved swiftly toward administrative reorganization.

The authorities of the Reorganization Act of 1939 fell somewhat short, it is true, of the committee's and of Roosevelt's goals. The separation of pre- and postaudit was not achieved. In deference to the lobbies, Congress exempted a number of agencies, as it always does, from the reorganization power. But a substantial part of the committee's program could be accomplished under the act. The White House Office was expanded, the Executive Office was established and the Bureau of the Budget and the National Resources Planning Board transferred to it, the Federal Security Agency (in lieu of the Welfare Department the President wanted) was put together, and a considerable list of agency transfers and reorientations was put under way. The net effect was substantially to enhance the role of the President as chief administrator.

A second development of importance to the universities was the establishment, beginning in 1938, of departmental personnel offices to handle departmental personnel programs and to deal with the Civil Service Commission. In this period, the commission, largely as a result of the efforts of Leonard D. White and Arthur Flemming, developed and introduced a type of general examination designed to provide an entrée into the Civil Service of able college and university graduates seeking nontechnical administrative positions. While the examination system conferred no special benefits upon graduates of public-administration training programs, it did open up an important avenue into the federal service for interested and able young men and women, including those from training programs.

A third event of great importance to the improvement of communication between the academy and the public service was the organization in December, 1939, of the American Society for Public Administration.[46] This development, which had been in the making for some time, sought, on the one hand, to provide for public administrators a vehicle for the consideration of vital cur-

rent issues of public management and, on the other, to forge closer
links between the academy and the public authorities who were
the primary consumers of the academy's research and training
activities. It was also designed to bring together the various administrative specialties—finance, personnel, planning, public works,
public welfare, etc.—in a forum where common interests and in
some cases mutual conflicts might be examined and more adequately defined. Shortly after the society was constituted, it began
the publication of *Public Administration Review*, under the
editorship of Leonard White and Don Price. William E. Mosher,
dean of the Maxwell School, was the society's first president.

In its 1937 report, the Committee on Administrative Management had stated forcefully the need for a continuing research and
advisory capacity in the Bureau of the Budget to work on problems of organization and procedures. Executive Order 8248,
which Brownlow wrote for Roosevelt immediately following the
passage of the Reorganization Act of 1939, instructed the bureau
quite specifically "to conduct research in the development of
improved plans of administrative management, and to advise the
executive departments and agencies of the Government with
respect to improved administrative organization and practices."
To this end, Harold Smith, whom Roosevelt appointed as director
of the budget when the bureau was transferred from the Treasury
Department to the Executive Office, established a Division of
Administrative Management as one of the four coordinate divisions
of the bureau and named Donald C. Stone assistant director in
charge of the division.

The pressures created by the implementation of reorganization
plans, abetted no doubt by a certain tenacity on the part of the
assistant director, produced in relatively short order a remarkable
flowering of "O and M" machinery throughout the executive
branch. In due course the movement spread to the states and to
many larger municipal governments. The idea of in-house organization and management research was certainly one of the most
significant and productive achievements of the Second New Deal,
and was an important influence in shifting the preoccupation of

training programs from their exclusive concern with state and local affairs to a larger perspective.

Training for Public Administration in the Second New Deal. From 1937 through 1941 fifteen universities established training programs in public administration. They stretched from Harvard to Hawaii and from New Hampshire to Florida. Twenty-six institutions reported the initiation of courses in public administration, and these also extended from Yale to Alaska and from Connecticut College to Nevada. More significant, however, than the number of new programs or their geographical distribution is the shift that may be noted, during this period, not only in the newly established training institutions but among many of the older ones as well, to concern with opportunities in federal agencies for their products. Harvard and Yale had, of course, been mainly interested in the federal market, and Princeton, after an initial emphasis in the early 1930s with New Jersey state and local government likewise became involved with national government. It is difficult to assess the impact of such programs as that of the National Institute of Public Affairs internships, the change in the nature of Civil Service examinations, and the opportunities offered by the burgeoning O and M movement, but it seems clear that there was a general recognition of the close relationship between the kinds of public service training that had developed in the universities and the usefulness of this training to relatively rapid advancement in the federal service. The training programs at state and local institutions, on the other hand, adapted much less rapidly to changes in the market, probably because of the intimacy which many had built up in training, research and service relationships with the state and local governments they had been organized to serve. But a little later, when the impact of the war in Europe, and the eventual American involvement, became clear these too responded to the brighter opportunities in Washington.

If it was not a period of great quantitative expansion, it was one of profound reconsideration, analysis, and self-analysis. In 1938/39 George Graham made field studies of sixteen university programs of various types as the foundation for his notable report published in 1941. Thirty-three years later his pages are still pregnant with meaning and sound advice, albeit within a vastly changed context, for those involved in the preparation of students for public service and for the retooling of specialists for broader administrative responsibilities. He sums up his findings in these words:[47]

> The record of universities in training men for public adminis-
> tration is on the whole a creditable one. So far as this survey has
> been able to appraise the evidence, students entering a formal
> training program have not been misled about their opportunities
> or the difficulties ahead of them. The training given has proved
> useful. Most faculty members interested in public administration
> have been on the lookout for evidence of what is needed to make
> training effective yet have been cautious in modifying existing
> types of postgraduate training. If the universities have erred, it
> has been in the direction of conservatism rather than experimen-
> tation. A safety factor has been the policy of limiting the number
> of students in training for public administration to a relatively
> small group. The policy has been general, and exceptions have
> been few.
>
> It probably should be continued, not only because the market
> has not yet been determined, but also because quality is more
> important than quantity; even the strongest institutions have not
> the resources to handle more than a few people at a time and to
> do a good job. Probably no general increase in the number of
> graduate students concentrating in the social sciences should be
> anticipated or attempted. Rather, students preparing for the pub-
> lic service are more apt to come from among those who, a few
> years ago, would have thought only of teaching. To many, ad-
> ministration now offers the most attractive career available.
>
> So far so good, but what of the future. Educational institutions
> have done the best they could, and the best was good enough for
> the times. But what was once good enough is no longer adequate.
> Administrative knowledge and administrative practice have im-
> proved so much—for this improvement universities are partly (if
> indirectly) responsible—that yesterday's theory has become to-
> day's routine . . .
>
> Practice in the best-managed governmental organizations has
> pretty well caught up with the theory. Furthermore, the change
> in the character and scope of governmental functions has pro-
> duced a new and more difficult set of administrative problems.
> Today faculties are teaching all they know about public adminis-
> tration and maybe a little bit more. We cannot perpetrate the

past upon the future without committing the fraud that we have to the present avoided.

Research is perhaps the only escape—research that involves the mutual assistance of a broader body of scholars, that is enriched by close collaboration with public officials, and that is related to fundamental problems of government and administration. Without this sort of activity the universities will not be able to meet the needs of the present and the future. Graduate training for public administration worthy of the university tradition must be based upon and closely related to research.

The Academy in the Second New Deal. If the Second New Deal did not immediately usher the art and science of administration into the new and sometimes beautiful dimensions of behavioralism, multilinear regression, and chi square, it was nonetheless a period of remarkable creativeness. Some of the new literature originated in the government itself. Studies undertaken or commissioned by the National Resources Planning Board, for example, developed new and original approaches to vital social and economic problems. Its program for a federal "Public Works Reserve," which involved the creation of a shelf of preplanned and engineered state and local public works projects for execution in slack economic times, led not only to the development of new concepts for long-term planning but also to the integration of Keynesian notions about compensatory spending into works programming. A study of urban life in the 1930s forecast with remarkable prescience what actually happened in the cities in the 1960s and 1970s. Its studies of resource availabilities and requirements, and resource management, laid the groundwork not only for wartime priorities and allocations but likewise provided the foundations for postwar ecological analyses that we had not the wit to understand and use.

Centralization and decentralization simmers constantly on the cookstove of public administration and rarely stays on a back burner very long. The period of the Second New Deal was rich in the literature of this controversy. The report of the Committee on Administrative Management is generally supposed to have been the authentic official statement of the case for centralization, although Luther Gulick, a member of the committee, and James

Hart, a staff consultant, had argued the case for centralization some years before. Pendleton Herring had likewise made a strong argument for centralization based upon the necessity for achieving unity in the purposes of the state, rather than mediating and arriving at an algebraic sum of the purposes of conflicting interest groups. The committee, looking to some sort of coincidence between the President's political power and his legislative responsibilities, sought two objectives: (1) to assure the President of the dominant and timely voice in policy formulation; and (2) to make certain the President had the resources for an independent judgment of policy issues, and would not be at the mercy of representatives of contending interests. Indeed, the essence of "administrative management" was to enable the President to maintain continuous access to the mainstream of policy formulation and administrative action throughout the executive branch, to be able to call up the issues that he deems of political or administrative importance, and to decide them on the basis of information and criteria independent of the claims of conflicting pressures.

Gulick's views on centralization, which found congenial company among his colleagues on the committee, had been argued in some detail as early as 1933.[48] At that time he had made a case for centralization on the grounds of: (1) its advantages in planning processes; (2) its utility in management in achieving economies of scale, conflict reduction, and elimination of overlapping; (3) its contribution to increased specialization, higher levels of expertise, and larger career opportunities; and (4) its effectiveness in providing foci of citizen attention and control and in reducing the citizen's task to manageable proportions. This period was also enriched in its intellectual history by the revival of the "holding company" theory of administrative organization, although this time in a somewhat different context. The notion that Congress and the President should preside with a light hand over a series of relatively independent enterprises had been cogently argued by Willoughby,[49] Coker,[50] Edwards,[51] Walker[52] and others over a considerable period. In 1938/39, however, it reappeared as an element in the controversy over the fundamentals of departmentalization. Schuyler Wallace, who had been a member of the staff of the Committee on Administrative Management, published in 1941 a study of the problems of departmental structure and departmentalization in the federal government that made a very persuasive case, in some quarters at least, for the building of departments on the holding-company principle.[53] Although the consequences arrived after the period that this essay is supposed to review, the Department of Defense and the Department of Health, Education and Welfare are clearly the monuments to the principles so cogently argued by Professor Wallace.

Wallace's argument was based in the main on: (1) the alleged efficacy of decentralization, through the holding-company device, in pushing decision making out to the scene of operations and relieving the center of problems with which, by reason of its remoteness, it could not deal realistically; (2) the superior claims of autonomy versus coordination in enhancing the legislative role in its oversight of executive agencies; (3) the unsatisfactory nature of prevailing principles of departmentalization, i.e., function, process, clientele, territory, for determining the overall departmental structure; (4) the differentiation between the regulatory agencies with quasi-legislative and quasi-judicial responsibilities and the "regular" administrative work of the government; and (5) the limited utility of the staff agencies, such as the Bureau of the Budget, the Civil Service Commission, and others in achieving interdepartmental integration. David Lilienthal, arguing from the experience of the Tennessee Valley Authority, took the same general line as Wallace, but emphasized in addition the necessity of involving the public in operations of the government—cooperation, rather than mere compliance—and of coordinating the work of state and local governments involved in realizing common objectives.[54] Ordway Tead carried Lilienthal's first principle further by insisting that democracy in administration, which of course implies decentralization, is the touchstone of administrative efficiency; the representation of interests on the one hand, and informed agreement among the groups involved, he said, are the criteria of good administration and good government.[55]

During the period of the Second New Deal, public administration began also to question the transmitted wisdom that had permeated much of the thought and writings of the academy in past times. It dared to ask itself what it meant by "principles" of public administration, to question whether there was or could be a theory of organization, and to reconsider its accepted value system centered on "economy and efficiency."

Willoughby, for example, had long proclaimed the cause of rationalism in public administration.[56] In 1937 he affirmed unequivocally the existence of principles of administration comparable to the "laws" of even the exact sciences, and insisted that these principles could be discovered and their significance analyzed by the application of rigorous scientific methodology to the phenomena of management. A. B. Hall, on the other hand, argued that the problems of public administration derived from and were determined by the scope and content of the policies it attempted to administer.[57] White also expounded the case for pragmatism in suggesting that the term "principle" should be restricted to a hypothesis that had been verified at least to the extent that it had a prima facie verification, and that conformed to reality within the possibilities of currently available evidentiary processes.[58] Finer thought that public administration ought to sort out its notions of principles—those that expressed a presumably objective statement of cause and effect on the one hand, and those normative principles that are essentially ethical statements.[59] E. O. Stene carried the notion of principles to the point of developing quite precise definitions, formulating equally precise propositions, and emerging with categorical axioms.[60] All these exercises were healthy and constructive, not in the sense that they provided especially significant answers for a discipline searching for organizing ideas but rather as demonstrating the deficiencies of accepted doctrinal attitudes and as maintaining the vulnerability of the discipline to new ideas and new criteria.

The theory of organization also came in for some hard looks during this period. Stene's proposition building and axiom derivation, which had at least the virtue of methodological clarity and consistency, went a considerable distance in breaking loose organization theory from pristine empiricism. But it also led to organizational principles that were neither self-evident nor scientifically demonstrable within the terms of the then available evidence. Gulick took another approach; he told us that "Theory of organization . . . has to do with the structure of coordination imposed upon the work division units of an enterprise. . . . Work division is the foundation of organization; indeed, the reason for organization."[61] Some years later, by then oblivious to the source of the idea, I found myself writing for the prime minister of Pakistan that "The essential purpose of administrative organization is to liberate human energies—to set men free, within an agreed jurisdiction, to get on with their jobs without interference. From a structural point of view, its objective is to create, in a pyramidal scale of descending responsibility, units as nearly self-contained— as nearly able to 'settle' matters assigned to them—as possible. From a political and managerial point of view, its objective is to establish the formal framework of communication and command by which responsibilities are fixed and coordination assured. From an operational point of view, its objective is to provide a basis for the maximum degree of decentralization consistent with the nature of the work being done, which is a *sine qua non* of efficient and economical administration." George Graham expressed the central idea with great cogency in observing that organization is a means to an end, and cannot be appraised apart from its use and purpose. He also reminded us that government organization is not only concerned with its members but also involves forces in the entire governmental system and sometimes in the entire society.[62] None of these observations settled finally the question whether there could be a distinct and integral science of organization, applicable to all purposes and to all situations in all occasions, but it is equally true that the New Deal experience made clear again and again the dominant influence of purpose and method in determining structure.

Economy and efficiency had long been the touchstones of administrative change and reform even before Franklin Roosevelt ever got to the White House, and they have persevered since, though with appreciably modified connotations. For a considerable period in modern administrative history, economy and efficiency were equivalent to the minimization of expenditures. After

Roosevelt's Economy Act had spent its force and the New Deal had recovered from its original trauma, the need for redefining both terms became a matter of some urgency. While there was no quarrel with the basic notion of economy as the achievement of predetermined objectives with the minimum expenditure of resources,[63] efficiency was another matter. Dimock had, early in the period, essayed a redefinition of efficiency in essentially utilitarian terms that implied optimum satisfactions for the persons engaged in the work.[64] He was followed shortly by Ridley and Simon, who were interested in establishing benchmarks and measurements, and who made the important distinction between adequacy of service, which is an absolute, and efficiency of service, which involves accomplishment relative to available resources. There were other penetrating contributions to the debate on this subject during the period, but it seems clear the conflict was less over technical definitions of efficiency than over social and administrative values.

Efficiency inevitably involves a prior question—efficiency for what? And "what" is a word imputing value. The answer, more often than not, is a matter of perspective. In 1943 the Bolivian Development Corporation was engaged in building a highway from Cochabamba to Santa Cruz, to connect the mining and industrial highlands with the rich agricultural lowlands. The corporation was the primary owner of tractors, bulldozers, draglines, and other earth-moving equipment. The problem arose of the servicing and maintenance of this equipment. The engineering staff produced analyses indicating that the most economical method would call for the establishment of a major repair center in Santa Cruz and a series of strategic substations along the route, which would be able to handle corporation equipment. But there were many tractors and trucks in the hands of agricultural producers in the region that were out of use because repair and servicing facilities were not available. Query: should the corporation mind its own business, or should it use its requirements to build a machinery service system capable of meeting the needs of both the corporation and the private agricultural sector? It depends on the answer to the value question: is one building a road or developing an economy? As Dwight Waldo has quite accurately pointed out, efficiency is a function of the hierarchy of purposes. The ends that are important only in terms of other ends tend to be relatively constant in all organizations, but the ultimate and less mechanical purposes are less likely to be constant in their efficiency.[65]

THE WAR

Pearl Harbor carries the date of December 7, 1941. Actually, the transformation of both politics and economy to a war footing had begun some time before. Some political historians—among them the late Charles A. Beard, who is not without credentials as one of the founders of the American Society for Public Administration—think our involvement was a Roosevelt plot from the beginning. That Roosevelt saw and recognized at its true value the possibility of American participation, and did everything he could to prepare the country for involvement, is beyond question. That he in fact attacked the Japanese at Pearl Harbor is less clear.

Statistics mean little in the highly artificial context of a war in which the United States met not only its own economic requirements for a virtually completely mobilized nation but was also the Arsenal of Democracy, as well as the principal supplier of both civilian and military requirements of many nations associated with us in the shooting war, of whose democratic intentions inquiry would have been, and still is, both tactless and footless. As a matter of record, even with price and wage controls, rationing, and all manner of devices designed to avoid inflation (and to contain such inflation as could not be avoided), the GNP increased by 74 percent between 1941 and 1945. Unemployment for all practical purposes disappeared altogether; a substantial part of the civilian labor force, indeed, was frozen in strategic occupations and to some degree in specific jobs. From 1941 to 1945 average hourly earnings in industry increased a little more than 40 percent, wholesale prices about 20 percent, and agricultural prices about 55 percent.

The story—even the highlights—of the country's military, economic, social, and moral mobilization for war hardly needs recounting at this time. Many of us were there and have been talking about it ever since. The superb collection of war histories, moreover, faithfully preserves the record, in a way never previously achieved in American history, for those who were not there, or were not there all the time. We all know how Roosevelt shelved the War Resources Board's proposals for an industry-dominated industrial mobilization, how he went back to 1916 legislation and established a National Defense Council, and how he used the Reorganization Act of 1939 to put the entire mobilization process under civilian control in the Executive Office. We remember how he bullied a foot-dragging Congress into the enactment of wage-and-price-control legislation with one of the most drastic threats in the history of presidential/congressional relations. We remember how our "groups of friends and neighbors" functioned under the aegis of the Selective Service Act, and how the Office of War Information operated. We remember about transportation priorities, and getting bumped by Elliot's dog and lesser breeds without the law.

The Government in Wartime. The Second World War added several dimensions to the operations of the United States government that were to change fundamentally ideas concerning the metes and bounds of public responsibility, the nature of international relations, and the substance of the administrative process. All these were to be reflected, some quite immediately, in the role of the universities as institutions and the role of members of the academy as individuals in the prosecution of the war effort.

The United States had, of course, had previous experience with military mobilization. The draft—such as it was—dated from the Civil War, and during World War I most of the essentials of what was to be known as "Selective Service" had been fairly well worked out. But civilian mobilization—of industry, transportation, distribution, agriculture, finance—on the scale and to the degree of prevision achieved in World War II was a new experience for Americans. It involved cooperative efforts in the allocation of scarce resources, in the construction of facilities, in the conversion of programs to war purposes, in the programming of operations, and in the entire management of logistics in a totally coordinated way that was utterly alien to an economy built on the notion of occasionally perfect competition. It involved rationing, price control, and distribution—in effect, a commercial system that for the time at least had abandoned the dictates of the market in its decisions. It called for, and secured, in short, an entire complex of decisional criteria and techniques and an operational milieu in which persuasiveness and egalitarianism in the pursuit of a common purpose were the effective sanctions. To be sure, the "honor system" implicit in the self-assessment basis of income taxation had much in common with the ways in which civilian mobilization was managed, but it was far short of the intimacy and comprehensiveness that characterized relationships between governmental agencies and the civil population during the war. And it evoked profound changes in attitudes and behavior on the part of both those who for the moment were the regulators and those who were the regulated. As Herbert Emmerich was fond of pointing out, the extraordinary achievement of the United States in civilian mobilization was in a major degree the function of the success with which the mobilizers coped with the human problems of an industrial civilization.

In the second place, the position of the United States as the supplier of the sinews of war not only to its own armed forces but to the entire United Nations brought many American administrators—including a substantial number from the academy—into contact with the inner workings of foreign governments and foreign bureaucracies in a way that would have been impossible in other circumstances. For all manner of reasons—from control of basic economic supplies to dominance of foreign-exchange holdings—American civil servants found themselves functioning virtually as cabinet members in the decisional processes of foreign governments. This involvement, it should be pointed out, cut both ways. Jean Monnet, who headed the French procurement mission in Washington in the early days of the war, frequently knew more about what was going on at different places in the United States government, especially on the economic and procurement fronts, than either the White House or the Executive Office, and it is reported that his superior information was not without potent influence in our own decisional processes. In any case, as a consequence of these experiences, the study of comparative government and administration, which had hitherto been primarily institutional description and by definition noncomparative, was never the same again. While there is little evidence that these involvements laid any special foundations for the transmogrification of comparative studies into the pure behavioralism of the Comparative Administration Group, for example, many of the old restraints were eliminated and the way was paved for a vastly more perceptive and realistic approach to the understanding of cross-national and cross-cultural political and administrative phenomena.

In a closely related vein, the war involved many Americans in international and what Charles Ascher refers to as "supranational" administration. The work of UNRRA, to take a single example, exposed a fair number of American civil servants to experience in cross-national and cross-cultural environments that had previously been available to no more than a handful in the League of Nations and the International Labor Organization. In another vein of equal, and perhaps greater importance, the experience involved members of Congress and political leaders generally in relationships that made fully comprehensible the nature and extent of the obligation of the United States in the postwar world. In a very real sense, the depth and intimacy of our wartime involvements with foreign political leaders and foreign bureaucrats made UNRRA, the Greek-Turkish Aid Program, the Marshall Plan, the IBRD, and the AID Program logical, understandable, and inevitable.

The Universities in Wartime. The war period had a very salutary effect on university training for the public service for quite unusual reasons. In the first place, it ended "business as usual" and compelled drastic changes in program and purpose to meet the needs of the emergency. Unlike medical schools and certain other professional training organizations, public administration had no special treatment in the Selective Service System. In the normal course of events, therefore, they were confronted with making do so far as students were concerned with 4-F's and women, since these were the only two groups within the SSS age brackets that it was not eager to embrace. Moreover, the market for the kinds of people who tended to populate public service program faculties was most favorable, both in Washington in civilian employment and in training positions in the armed forces. A good many programs, in consequence, either folded altogether or maintained a low profile during the war.

Two groups of institutions that had developed viable training programs, however, waxed strong during the war period. Many, especially those which were strategically located in relation to military establishments and to war-related industry, were able to accomodate their programs to a new market, and they spent a busy and constructive period training personnel with supervisory and managerial responsibilities in military and industrial installations. Another group, among the leaders of which was the Maxwell School, developed training programs for the considerable number of foreigners who came to the United States for training during the war years. These were mainly, though not exclusively, Latin Americans, and many were sponsored by the Coordinator of Inter-American Affairs. The Division of Administrative Management of the Bureau of the Budget was likewise involved in this undertaking. Even today, thirty years later, it is difficult to visit a Latin American capital without encountering a senior official who served time in the States during the war. Many of these relations persisted and formed the foundation for lucrative AID contracts for the training programs in their subsequent reincarnations. Whether the fact that the assistant director for administrative management of the Bureau of the Budget had moved over to handle AID administration had any connection with this interesting coincidence must continue to be speculative.

On balance, however, the significant impact of the war period on training for the public service did not take place on the campuses or affect the people who stayed at home to mind the store. Never in the history of higher education have so many faculty members been provided with so expensive postdoctoral training in public administration at so high levels of both political and administrative responsibility as occurred during World War II. There had, of course, been a considerable amount of "in and outing" during Roosevelt's previous terms, especially in the

Second New Deal, but the quantity of the flow was miniscule in comparison with the events of 1941 to 1945.

The exodus of faculty who went to administrative positions, as distinguished from research posts, was important for the subsequent development of training for two major reasons. First, public-administration training in the universities had hitherto been concerned almost entirely with staff operations—organization, budgeting, planning, personnel management, procurement, etc. But the war-period inflow was involved in line administration to a degree of which it had previously had little experience. The tasks in the war agencies were directed to devising and constructing machinery and procedures that had immediate impact on the behavior of people and resources—that got something done or didn't. Cause/effect relationships were drastically foreshortened. Heavy emergency pressures were prevalent in almost every aspect of the daily business. This environment differed enormously from the atmosphere of deliberation and suspended judgment that tends to characterize much staff work.

Second, war-time administrators were heavily involved in policy processes at many levels, but the involvement was especially acute at the levels at which the refugees from university faculties found themselves. Because of the large number and complex configurations of the interests involved, the engineering of consent for policies and policy changes was more difficult and more time-consuming at the very moment when there was less time in which to achieve it. The searing experiences of professors turned administrators and policy makers are responsible for no few of the very basic changes in the discipline's approach to administrative processes which have characterized postwar training for the public service.

The Academy in Wartime. The effect of the war on the literary production of the academy was curiously mixed. Since a considerable part of the membership was involved in administration or in military service, neither of which leave much time or energy during major crises for contemplation or composition, there was some abatement of the rich flow of prose that characterized the Second

New Deal. On the other hand, the series of administrative histories produced by the confluence of imagination in the Bureau of the Budget, the war agencies, and the academy have documented and enriched the literature of public administration and our understanding of crisis management in ways that have not been equalled in any previous conflagration anywhere in the world. These histories, which provide orderly and critical accounts of the experiences of the United States government's civilian agencies in accomodating their organization and procedures to the necessities of mobilization and support of the war effort, and which recount in considerable detail the establishment and program development of the ad hoc machinery of industrial mobilization, price and wage control, etc., afford access to important lessons of large scale management that are of continuing and major significance in the literature of the profession.

What did the academy learn from its experiences during the war? A number of books, based upon happenings in the war agencies, have been written, and they have provided useful and penetrating insights into various specialized aspects of crisis government. But the most sophisticated overview of how we performed and what we learned is an assessment prepared for the edification of the Southern Regional Training Program. In this volume Gulick enunciated the following conclusions:[66]

> 1. The American governmental system was found to be fully adequate for the management of the war....
> 2. A clear statement of purpose universally understood is the outstanding guarantee of effective administration....
> 3. Translation from purpose to program is the crucial step in administration....
> 4. Co-ordination is the indispensable dynamic principle of effective action....
> 5. Administrative operations may be subjected to control by various techniques other than the limitation of expenditures....
> 6. Planning is an essential and continuous aspect of management, and is greatly enhanced by specialized information, though it is difficult to establish stable and effective working relations among planning, programming and operations....
> 7. When geographic dispersal of operations calls for decentralization of an organization, high technical standards and policy

uniformity can be maintained by integrated dual supervision....

8. Broad functional organization is more effective in activities requiring coordination than is organization based on commodities or on specific operating programs....

9. The danger of overloading the chief administrative officers is greatly increased in time of national emergency....

10. Competent personnel is, of course, indispensable, and the creative administrative genius is priceless. Nothing is so important except perhaps clear and sound policy direction....

11. The War gave us a new recognition of the importance of time in the administrative process....

12. International administration at the consultative level presents no new problems or principles with which we have not already had experience in the United States in our domestic affairs....

13. The support of public opinion is essential for good administration under American conditions....

14. Official representatives of organized interest groups are apparently more useful as advisers and as salesmen for government programs than as routine members of the administration....

15. Truly effective action in administration arises from singleness of purpose and clarity of policy, ardently believed in both by the leaders and by the public in all parts of the country and in all strata of society....

THE LEGACY

The administrative legacy of the years from 1933 to 1945 is not easy to determine. Like the period itself, the development of public administration was part of a continuum that began early in the century and has continued without serious interruption ever since. It would be exceedingly difficult, and probably not very profitable, to segregate those events of importance to the development of the discipline and to instruction in public administration that were peculiarly the product of the period of crisis. It is unquestionable that the events of the period gave history a push, and that many of the things that happened would not have happened the way they did in the absence of the kind of political leadership that was provided.

Without claiming more for the period than the facts warrant, however, we may derive some profit from looking at the important changes that, from whatever cause (including accident), came to pass during the twelve years under review. Obviously, the major change, and the one most portentious for the development of public administration, was the drastic expansion in the public conception of the obligations and responsibilities of government in social and economic affairs. While there were in some cases undoubtedly doctrinal factors present, the transition was on the whole markedly free of ideological content. In a very real sense, it was a reaffirmation of the traditional system of checks and balances applied to the larger societal sphere. There was little socialism in it. The assumption seemed to be that the allocation of benefits from the productivity of the economic system would continue to be settled essentially by the adversary process, which implied big business and big labor refereed by big government. There were, of course, conceptions of national minima that had to be preserved, but there was no notion that the government owed anyone a living—or a dividend. Indeed, what was actually achieved at the time was much less important than the forces that were organized and set in motion. The Fair Labor Standards Act of 1938 is by present-day criteria an absurdity. What is not absurd is the constitutional and political principle that the act established, under the aegis of which Congress thirty-six years later continues to enact minimum-wage legislation—in effect, continuing to referee the processes activated more than three decades ago. From the standpoint of public administration, this has opened an enormous spectrum of educational relevance and research opportunity, reaching from the Council of Economic Advisers to the local Employment Office, and from the FAA to the Dallas-Fort Worth Regional Airport.

A second important change that occurred during the Roosevelt years was the enduring emphasis upon presidential leadership, and especially upon the development of institutional facilities through which this leadership might be effectively exercised. The consequence has been to accord much greater importance to the civil service, and especially to the upper reaches of the executive bureaucracy, which has at the same time strengthened the career aspects of the civil service and exacerbated the problem of management at the bureau level—and sometimes above and below, as well. On balance, however, the federal service has been steadily upgraded in public esteem and confidence; it has steadily become more professional and better equipped with managerial and policy skills, and more able to run the government whatever the vicissitudes of politics.

A third important legacy of the years of crisis is the change in the nature of the federal system. The emergence of a truly national economy, and the emergency created by the time-lag in developing a truly national society, has of necessity shifted to the national scene the responsibility for most of the important policy decisions. This process was under way long before 1933, but the events of the depression and the war, and the measures undertaken under the pressures of both, defined in large measure the way in which government would be accomodated to these basic changes in the economy and the society. In our concern for liberty we have, in the United States, always assumed, in Leslie Lipson's words, that "Leviathan's grip is weaker when the skeleton is loose-jointed." Because the shibboleths of states' rights and local autonomy have for so long been a part of the political confessional, the New Deal left us with an unbalanced legacy in the relations between the states and the national government. And because economic dislocation is so much more readily observable than social failure, the imbalance has persisted for a longer time than normal tolerance dictates. But it did teach us what to do and how to do it, once we acquire the moral sensibility and political sophistication to proceed.

Perhaps the most important legacy of all, albeit one that is under considerable strain at the moment, was the lesson that we live in a limited and prescribed universe, inhabited by many other peoples, and that we cannot secede or alienate ourselves from the rest of humanity. The fact that our arrogance, and a certain ineptitude in *realpolitik*, have led us to interventional excesses cannot dim the luster of a series of actions in the war period and for some years thereafter that have not been equalled in history for their responsibility, generosity, and statesmanship.

NOTES

1. *Report and Recommendations of the California Unemployment Commission* (Sacramento, 1932), pp. 145–46.
2. *Home Building and Loan Association* v. *Blaisdell*, 290 *U.S.* 398 (1934).
3. Theodore Saloutis and John D. Hicks, *Agricultural Discontent in the Middle West 1900–1939* (Madison, Wis.: University of Wisconsin Press, 1951), pp. 443–44.
4. *The Method of Freedom* (New York: The Macmillan Company, 1934), pp. 32–33.
5. Brodaus Mitchell, *Depression Decade* (New York: Rinehart, 1947), p. 405.
6. *The Memoirs of Herbert Hoover: The Great Depression 1929–41* (New York: The Macmillan Company, 1953), p. 30.
7. Ibid., pp. 133–34.
8. *International Encyclopedia of the Social Sciences*, vol. 8 (New York: The Macmillan Company, 1968), pp. 148–49.
9. Henri Fayol, *Industrial and General Administration* (London: Pitman, 1930); Frederick W. Taylor, *The Principles of Scientific Management* (New York: Harper & Bros., 1911).
10. See, for example, W. E. Mosher, "The Party is the Crux," *National Municipal Review*, vol. 28, no. 5 (May, 1939), pp. 335–40, 354.
11. F. J. Goodnow, *Politics and Administration* (New York: The Macmillan Company, 1900).
12. *The Government of Modern States* (New York: D. Appleton-Century Company, Inc., 1919).
13. Leonard D. White, "The Public Service of the Future," in L. D. White (ed.), *The Future of Government in the United States* (Chicago: Public Administration Service, 1942).
14. See Dwight Waldo (ed.), *Government Related Research of University Bureaus* (Berkeley: University of California Press, 1960).
15. *The Roosevelt I Knew* (New York: The Viking Press, 1947), p. 135.
16. Basil Rauch, *History of the New Deal* (New York: Creative Age Press, Inc., 1944), p. 164.
17. *Railroad Retirement Board* v. *Alton Railroad Co.*, 295 *U.S.* 330.
18. *Schecter Poultry Co. and others* v. *United States*, 295 *U.S.* 495; the "hot oil" provisions of the act had previously been invalidated in *Panama Refining Co.* v. *Ryan*, 293 *U.S.* 398.
19. *United States* v. *Butler*, 297 *U.S.* 262.
20. *Carter* v. *Carter Coal Co.*, 298 *U.S.* 238.
21. *Ashton* v. *Cameron County Improvement District*, 298 *U.S.* 513.
22. *Morehead, Warden* v. *New York ex. rel. Tipaldom*, 298 *U.S.* 587.

23. *The American Earthquake* (New York: Doubleday, 1958), p. 536.

24. Commission of Inquiry on Public Service Personnel, *Better Government Personnel* (New York: McGraw-Hill Book Company, Inc., 1935).

25. Elton Mayo, *The Human Problems of an Industrial Civilization* (New York: Viking, 1931).

26. C. J. Friedrich and Taylor Cole, *Responsible Bureaucracy* (Cambridge, Mass.: Harvard University Press, 1932).

27. *National Municipal Review*, vol. 23 (May, 1934), p. 248.

28. E. P. Herring, *Public Administration and the Public Interest* (New York: McGraw-Hill Book Company, Inc., 1936).

29. Lucius Wilmerding, *Government by Merit* (New York: McGraw-Hill Book Company, Inc., 1935).

30. W. E. Mosher, "The Making of a Public Servant," *National Municipal Review*, 28 (June, 1939), p. 416.

31. John M. Gaus, Leonard D. White, and Marshall E. Dimock, *The Frontiers of Public Administration* (Chicago: The University of Chicago Press, 1936).

32. *The General Theory of Employment, Interest and Money* (London: The Macmillan Company, 1936).

33. H. A. Stone, D. K. Price, and K. H. Stone, *City Manager Government in the United States* (Chicago: Public Administration Service, 1940); H. A. Stone, D. K. Price, and K. H. Stone, *City Manager Government in Nine Cities* (Chicago: Public Administration Service, 1940); Frederick C. Mosher *et altera*, *City Manager Government in Seven Cities* (Chicago: Public Administration Service, 1940).

34. V. O. Key, Jr., *The Administration of Federal Grants to States* (Chicago: Public Administration Service, 1937); Luella Gettys, *The Administration of Canadian Conditional Grants* (Chicago: Public Administration Service, 1938).

35. Raymond C. Atkinson, Ben Deming and Louise C. Odencrantz, *Public Employment Service in the United States* (Chicago: Public Administration Service, 1941); Robert T. Lansdale, Elizabeth Long, Agnes Leisy, and Byron T. Hipple, *The Administration of Old Age Assistance* (Chicago: Public Administration Service, 1939); Walter Matschek, *Unemployment Compensation Administration in Wisconsin and New Hampshire* (Chicago: Public Administration Service, 1936); Robert T. Lansdale *et altera*, *The Administration of Old Age Assistance in Three States* (Chicago: Public Administration Service, 1936); Walter Matscheck and R. C. Atkinson, *The Administration of Unemployment Compensation Benefits in Wisconsin July 1, 1936 to June 30, 1937* (Chicago: Public Administration Service, 1937).

36. Arthur W. Macmahon, John D. Millett and Gladys Ogden, *The Administration of Federal Work Relief* (Chicago: Public Administra-

tion Service, 1941); John D. Millett, *The Works Progress Administration in New York City* (Chicago: Public Administration Service, 1941).

37. John M. Gaus and Leon Wolcott, *Public Administration and the United States Department of Agriculture* (Chicago: Public Administration Service, 1940).

38. George A. Graham, *Education for Public Administration* (Chicago: Public Administration Service, 1941).

39. Leonard D. White, *Research in Public Personnel Administration —Scope and Method* (Chicago, 1939).

40. Oliver P. Field, *Research in Administrative Law—Scope and Method* (Chicago: Public Administration Service, 1939).

41. Leon T. David and John F. Feldmeier, *The Administration of Public Tort Liability in Los Angeles 1934–1938* (Chicago: Public Administration Service, 1939).

42. Robert H. Connery, *The Administration of an N.R.A. Code* (Chicago: Public Administration Service, 1941).

43. John M. Blum, *From the Morgenthau Diaries* (Boston: Houghton Mifflin, 1959), p. 280.

44. Rauch, *History of the New Deal*, pp. 294–95.

45. Louis Brownlow, *A Passion for Anonymity* (Chicago: University of Chicago Press, 1958), pp. 376–77.

46. Donald C. Stone and Alice B. Stone, "The Birth of A.S.P.A.," *Public Administration Review* (January/February, 1975).

47. Graham, *Education for Public Administration*, n. 38, pp. 131–32.

48. Luther Gulick, "Politics, Administration and the New Deal," *Annals of the American Academy of Political and Social Science*, vol. 169 (September, 1933), p. 55.

49. W. F. Willoughby, "The National Government as a Holding Company," *Political Science Quarterly*, vol. 32 (September, 1917), p. 505.

50. F. W. Coker, "Dogmas of Administrative Reform," *American Political Science Review*, vol. 16, (August, 1922), p. 399.

51. W. H. Edwards, "The State Reorganization Movement," *Dakota Law Review*, vols. 1 and 2 (1927 and 1928).

52. Harvey Walker, *Public Administration in the United States* (New York: Farrar & Rinehart, Inc., 1937); See also David Truman, *Administrative Decentralization* (Chicago: The University of Chicago Press, 1940); John M. Pfiffner, *Public Administration* (New York: The Ronald Press Co., 1935), and G. C. S. Benson, *The New Centralization* (New York: Farrar & Rinehart, Inc., 1941).

53. Schuyler Wallace, *Federal Departmentalization* (New York: Columbia University Press, 1941).

54. David Lilienthal, *The T.V.A.: An Experiment in the 'Grass Roots' Administration of Federal Functions* (Knoxville, 1939).

55. Ordway Tead, *New Adventures in Democracy* (New York: McGraw-Hill Book Company, Inc., 1939).

56. In the introduction to G. A. Weber, *Organized Efforts for the Improvement of Methods of Administration in the United States* (New York: D. Appleton and Company, 1919); see also Willoughby's essay, "The Science of Public Administration," in J. M. Mathews and James Hart (eds.), *Essays in Political Science* (Baltimore: The Johns Hopkins Press, 1939).

57. In the preface to A. C. Millspaugh, *Public Welfare Organization* (Washington, D.C.: The Brookings Institution, 1935).

58. *The Frontiers of Public Administration, op. cit.*

59. Herman Finer, "Principles as a Guide to Management," *Public Management*, vol. 17 (1935), p. 287.

60. Edwin O. Stene, "An Approach to a Science of Administration," *American Political Science Review*, vol. 32, (December, 1940), pp. 1124–25.

61. Luther Gulick, "Notes on the Theory of Organization," in L. Gulick and L. Urwick (eds.), *Papers on the Science of Administration* (New York: Institute of Public Administration, 1937), p. 3.

62. George A. Graham, "Reorganization—A Question of Executive Institutions," *American Political Science Review*, vol. 32, (August, 1938), p. 708.

63. Luther Gulick, "Politics, Administration and the New Deal," n. 61, p. 191.

64. Marshall Dimock, *op. cit.*, n. 58, p. 116.

65. Dwight Waldo, *The Administrative State* (New York: The Ronald Press Co., 1948), p. 204.

66. Luther Gulick, *Administrative Reflections from World War II* (University, Alabama: University of Alabama Press, 1948), pp. 74–121.

3. Public Administration and the Social Sciences: 1946 to 1960

JAMES W. FESLER

If the years between the ages of thirty-five and fifty are among the most active of a man's professional life, his opportunity to review those years as they were played out in his chosen profession tempts him to nostalgic recollection. I shall try to place that period in perspective, rather than to relive it. Nevertheless, to quote Virgil's *Aeneid*, "I myself saw these said things; I took large part in them."[1] Aeneas, a commentator notes, "is not boasting; he sees himself as a part of the misery of Troy, not as a hero doing heroic deeds."[2] And so it is with me.

Ambivalence has always troubled the study of public administration. We have been importuned to choose between basic research and applied research, between theory building and data collection and analysis, between prescription and description, between *in vivo* clinical studies of "real administration" and *in vitro* studies of nonadministrators in sociopsychological laboratories.

The equivocal nature of our calling became deeply embedded, rather than exorcised, between 1946 and 1960. The real world pressed in on us, affecting our university setting, providing new models of scientific scholarship, suggesting new agendas for our research, and providing many of us with sensitizing experiences in the public service. Of even greater importance, public-administration scholars were challenged to absorb the theories, findings, and methods of the behavioral sciences. The appropriate response to this challenge was not self-evident, for the most sympathetic

97

response demanded abandonment of the field's identity in favor of a generic "administration" that had no species labeled "public."

FOREIGN AFFAIRS AND OVERSEAS OPERATIONS

The fifteen-year period of 1946 to 1960 was both a postwar period and a prewar period. America rapidly shifted its concern from the Fascist Axis to the Communist nexus. After the USSR's 1949 explosion of an atomic bomb, the world power structure became bipolar and the United Nations' potential as an independent political force became severely constricted.[3] The United States, in the meantime, had established the National Security Council, the Central Intelligence Agency, and the Department of Defense. The NSC was to illustrate the difficulties in devising structural and procedural arrangements for supradepartmental coordination of policy formation and implementation. The Defense Department demonstrated the hyperbolic quality of the phrase, "unification of the armed services."[4] And the CIA, with its budget, staffing, and activities hidden from view, was eventually to sharpen public concern over the contradictory claims of secrecy and accountability.[5] For most of the 1950s the secretary of state conducted foreign affairs as an itinerant negotiator and, not for the first time, neglected the institutional resources and needs of the Department of State.

The bilateral American foreign-aid programs, particularly the Marshall Plan and Point-Four Program, dramatically committed American resources (over $55 billion between 1945 and 1963) to nonmilitary assistance of allies, former enemies, and underdeveloped nations. The technical-assistance programs of the foreign-aid agency have particular relevance for the concerns of this paper. First, they enlisted the services of many of us, expanding our horizons (literally), enriching the experiential base for our teaching and scholarship, and laying the foundations of an "invisible college" that was to attain visibility as the Comparative Administration Group. Second, because the foreign-aid agency often enlisted universities as its agents in provision of technical assistance, "contracting out" came into our consciousness as a new form of delegated administration. We were slow to perceive its potential significance or, in the particular case of universities, to reckon the risks entailed as well as the benefits immediately enjoyed.[6]

Relative to the inherent importance and the vastness of America's undertakings in foreign affairs and national security, and those of the United Nations as well, their administrative complexities have been meagerly attended to by our community of public-administration scholars. To be sure, in absolute rather than relative terms, a number of our leading men wrote about these complexities.[7] And others contributed by invitation to governmentally initiated studies.[8] As teachers and scholars, we valued the informative hearings and trenchant reports on national-security organization and processes emerging from Senator Henry Jackson's Subcommittee.[9] Yet our enthusiastic reception of these and other public documents emphasizes the scantiness of private initiatives by students of public administration. The United Nations, like foreign affairs and national security, we left mostly to colleagues in the field of international relations. Walter R. Sharp, among others, argued that "only the more formalistic aspects of organizational machinery and internal 'housekeeping' services" were likely to be illuminated by those who thought that international administration was basically like other kinds of administration.[10]

SCIENCE AND ADMINISTRATION

Nature's orderly world (and, indeed, solar system) began to yield a series of dramatic disclosures that were to transform the disorderly world of human affairs. In 1946 the electronic computer was invented and soon the words "automation," "feedback," and "cybernetics" entered social scientists' vocabulary and altered modes of thinking.[11] Eventually the computer itself was to expand administrative agencies' capacities for storing, retrieving, and analyzing data, to impose new training requirements on social scientists whether in government or the universities, and to pose fresh dilemmas about centralization and protection of personal privacy.

Nuclear power altered the strategies of defense and foreign policy, the weapons arsenal, and the striving among the armed services for resource allocations. It also had important domestic consequences. The National Science Foundation and the Atomic Energy Commission were born, special care being taken to assure their responsibility to the President and Congress.[12] The National Aeronautics and Space Administration in 1958 began the remarkable success story whose climax was a civil servant's taking man's first step on the moon. Nuclear fission and space-satellite launchings enhanced the public estimation of the sciences.

All these developments affected political science (and its subfield of public administration), for in its new drive to be rigorously scientific, the model chosen was from the physical, not the biological, sciences. And so the machine model, rational and efficient, a neutral instrument teleologically designed to achieve predetermined ends, reentered public administration by the front door.

The biological and medical sciences also made striking advances, often with administrative side effects. When the tuberculosis death rate fell by 75 percent in the 1950s, new uses had to be found for TB hospitals, though their placement in nonpopulous locations made them poor prospects as general hospitals. When infantile paralysis cases fell by 90 percent, the National Foundation for Infantile Paralysis had to find new purposes to be served by its army of volunteer solicitors. As with TB hospitals, an organization's *means* sought *ends*, thus bringing in question a central premise of organization theory.[13] But the "succession of goals" concept was invoked, enabling organization theorists to proceed undismayed. Meantime, research aimed at other diseases was to attract large funds to the National Institutes of Health, a phenomenon facilitated by the supportive attitudes and official roles of Senator Lester Hill and Representative John Fogarty. Modern organization theory does not take much account of accidents that put the right men in the right places at the right time, but NIH appropriations quadrupled between 1954 and 1960.

Science and technology had never held so central a position in national policy and administration, nor had they demanded such pure acts of faith in experts or such bold choices when experts differed. Yet students of public administration wrote few studies of relevance. The notable exception was Don K. Price, whose *Government and Science*[14] eloquently set forth an agenda of concerns that should have attracted us. Many may have been attracted, but few performed.[15]

DOMESTIC AFFAIRS

Foreign affairs and atomic weapons deeply affected domestic affairs. An anti-Communist foreign policy was matched by persistence in tracking down the *bête rouge* within our gates. Public servants and university faculty members were compelled, in medieval fashion, to take "loyalty oaths" disclaiming Communist beliefs and associations. The mushroom cloud of the atomic bomb cast a pall whose message was, "There may not be a tomorrow." Though nothing has changed, we now can scarcely imagine the doom-saying mood of the new atomic age. McCarthyism and the bomb together put a chill on universities that goes far to explain why the undergraduates of the 1950s earned the tag, "the silent generation"—students weakly responsive to their courses in public affairs and more ambitious to do well than to do good.

For most of the 1950s the federal government service lacked the drawing power of the exciting New Deal and wartime years. The focus of action was on decremental and modestly incremental changes, "responsible" budgeting, and efficient management. Divided party control of the legislative and executive branches reduced the opportunities for dramatic actions even if the Republican administration had been inclined to propose them. What most mattered was that the national consensus came to embrace the legacy of the New Deal. The strange calm was reflected among political scientists, some of whom raised the plaintive cry, "Whatever happened to the Great Issues?"

For everybody it was a period of learning. The first Hoover Commission, reporting in 1949 to general applause, subscribed to the Brownlow Committee's model of a President-centered Executive Branch, though in 1937 Roosevelt's Brownlow-based measure had been shrilly attacked as the "dictatorship bill." The Presidency itself became a preoccupation of political scientists. But only in 1960 did a distinguished, fresh treatment emerge, Richard Neustadt's *Presidential Power.*[16]

The Commission on Intergovernmental Relations, established in 1953, seemed to be heading for a restoration of the Articles of Confederation. After its first chairman resigned at the President's request, the new chairman, Meyer Kestnbaum, brought the commission into the twentieth century and it produced a distinguished report.[17] Obsequies for state and local governments were in any event premature. In the 1950s their per capita general expenditures rose 92 percent, while the federal government lagged at 70 percent. As over half of the federal government's expenses were defense-related, its domestic-activity expenditures in 1960 were only half those of state and local governments.[18] Staffing of state and local governments with generalists and administrative specialists continued to be a major objective of state universities' public-administration training programs.[19] Yet the attractiveness of municipal and state employment was not high. Municipal (and, by extension, state) personnel practices were judged "unequal to the tasks of getting and keeping the number and caliber of . . . personnel required."[20] For the training programs the changing role of the city manager[21] and governments' increased reliance on specialized professionals for the conduct of operating programs posed difficult problems of adjustment.

In both 1949 and 1950, Congress rejected President Truman's proposed establishment of a department consolidating health, education, and welfare. In 1953, Congress speedily approved President Eisenhower's similar proposal. HEW, along with the Defense Department, seemed to our scholars a new phenomenon misleadingly dubbed the "holding company" type of department. In fact, it was to replay an old theme, the stubborn resistance of bureaus to departmental direction and coordination.

The period was also one of beginnings, whose potential lay mostly in the 1960s and beyond. As early as 1945 President Truman had boldly put compulsory national health insurance on the nation's agenda. In 1952 Candidate Eisenhower attacked it as "socialized medicine." Two years later President Eisenhower made a modest proposal (government reinsurance of insurance companies' health policies) that the American Medical Association viewed as "the opening wedge toward socialized medicine." A more important illustration of the point is the 1954 Supreme Court holding that racial segregation in the public schools is unconstitutional. Portentous, to be sure. But by 1960 only 6 percent of Negro students in the South were in schools with whites (a figure that was to reach 84 percent in 1970). This and other antidiscrimination decisions started the change that was, among other things, to mandate equal employment opportunities in the public service. Another noble beginning was the 1949 Housing Act's stated "goal of a decent home and suitable living environment for every American family." The act authorized one hundred and thirty-five thousand public-housing units a year for six years, as precisely quantified an "operational" goal as a new-day policy analyst could wish. But later measures limited each year's new contracts to, usually, thirty-five thousand units. Someplace here is a lessson for goal-demanders, but not an easy one.

If Congress demonstrated in the housing field its capacity to contradict itself sequentially, its Employment Act of 1946 proved its capacity to do so simultaneously. Congress declared it the policy of the federal government to afford "useful employment for those able, willing, and seeking to work, and to promote maximum employment, production, and purchasing power." On the other hand, all this was to be done "in a manner calculated to foster and promote free competitive enterprise."[22]

The act and the President's Council of Economic Advisers were striking innovations both in policy and in staff assistance for the President. The status of the discipline of economics rose with its strategic representation through the council, its capacity to smooth the business cycle so as to avoid depressions (though not recessions), and eventually its self-congratulatory assurance that it could "fine tune" the economy. Rarely did political scientists seriously address themselves to the policy roles and administrative peculiarities of the council, the Federal Reserve System, the Treasury, and other agents of powerful, albeit indirect, leverage on the economy.[23]

POLICY AND ADMINISTRATION

Students of public administration do not live in a vacuum. They are informed by their own administrative experience and by the communicated experience of others. They react to the winds of change sweeping through their disciplinary home of political science. Their approaches to public administration are affected by their other teaching and scholarly commitments—in the 1946–1960 period, mostly American government, state and local government (or intergovernmental relations), and government regulation. Especially in periods when disenchantment with old dogmas threatens to persist as self-indulgent negativism, some students of public administration are likely to search in neighboring and distant disciplines for ordering models, taxonomies, and methodologies. Others, also turning outward, may seek in other disciplines and philosophies a vision of man freed of bureaucratic shackles.

The early clues to the 1946–1960 period are found in two sets of people: those political scientists who served in Washington during World War II and those political scientists who published their dissertations between 1946 and 1950. The first group account for the collapse of the policy/administration dichotomy, for a new realism about administrative life (extending to sharpened sensitivity to human behavior in organizations), and for a renewed conviction that administration matters. The second group initiated the troubled search for ways of separating or blending normative and empirical, qualitative and quantitative, deductive and inductive approaches to the analysis of administrative phenomena.

Among the well-known contributors to the public-administration literature who served in Washington during World War II, I can readily name thirty,[24] so the total number must have been substantially greater. The academics among them who arrived clutching Leonard D. White's and John M. Pfiffner's textbooks found little occasion to consult them. Returning to the campuses they brought a zest for teaching and writing in a wholly new vein.

Their "new public administration" (though they wisely did not call it that) involved four changes in emphasis: (1) a shift from administrative specialties (e.g., personnel, purchasing, and workflow planning) to the line operations concerned with achieving public purposes; (2) a shift from the chief executive and major auxiliary-and-control agencies to administrative problems of the departmental and bureau levels; (3) a shift from general, abstract principles to appreciation of the varying contexts of individual departments and programs; and (4) a shift from the rather arid concern for efficiency and economy to a concern for how American public administration is (or should be) affected by the political values and processes of its democratic setting.

Realism was the prevailing mood and the classic policy/administration dichotomy became its victim. That the dichotomy is dead has been the cliché ever since. But two errors appear to be involved. One is the logical fallacy of assuming that if a boundary cannot be precisely drawn, no distinction can be asserted. We constantly deal in categories that shade into one another at the edges and yet are distinct at their cores. We surely know that there is more than a modest difference in degree between formulation of a foreign policy and a janitor's choice of which room to sweep first, even though both qualify as "decision making" and the janitor's discretion is sufficient to save him from the routine of "programmed decision making." The second error is overinterpretation of what the postwar academics were undertaking. At the levels at which they operated in the war agencies, they found policy and administration inextricably intertwined, and of absorbing fascination.[25] Both lower-level administration and the specialized administrative auxiliary services they found dull. Back on the campus they proposed to focus their teaching and research on the interesting, with the result that they seemed to exclude "mere" administration from the very definition of "public administration." They did not know that their excluded term would get smuggled back under the euphemism "delivery of services."

The intermixture of policy and administration was probably most influentially set forth in a jointly authored textbook and in a series of books by a distinguished administrator. The 1946 textbook *Elements of Public Administration*[26] was written by fourteen political scientists with World War II governmental experience and edited with remarkable skill by Fritz Morstein Marx. Paul H.

Appleby, who had been under-secretary of agriculture and assistant director of the Bureau of the Budget, published three widely read books between 1945 and 1952.[27] A third of the Morstein Marx textbook consisted of chapters about administration's relation to its political settting and to the values and processes of democracy. The objective was understanding of a rich reality, not approximation to exact science. It was Appleby's conception, as Roscoe Martin later observed, that "administration is inseparable from the total process of government; indeed public administration is nothing more (but also nothing less) than a way of looking at government."[28] He invited a reorientation away from universal principles and mere efficiency and toward the more exciting policy-formation processes operative amid the American democracy's pluralistic forces.

Though the issue was not to arise immediately, Appleby and the Morstein Marx collaborators had the clear conviction that, as an Appleby chapter title put it, "Government *Is* Different." Public and private administration could not be fused, for a defining quality of public administration was its publicness, its belonging to government, its inexplicableness if one washed out as irrelevant the democratic system and the political context. This conviction firmly situated public administration in political science. Scholars' commitment to "maintenance" of this relation, Robert T. Golembiewski writes, has precluded due attentiveness to those aspects of the "tasks" of administration that are common to governmental and nongovernmental organizations.[29]

Implied and often explicit among the academics with wartime experience was a conviction that governmental administration must be seen in the contexts of specific policies and programs. This stimulated the preparation and use of case studies of decision making. It reinforced the link between public administration and government regulation, "fields" that were often the academic responsibilities of the same political scientists. It prompted the preparation of monographs about particular agencies and programs, but the emergent pattern was oddly skewed.

The high value set on the experiencing of administrative reality led some to argue, even though it seemed self-serving, that no one should teach public administration who lacked a period of full-time government service. At first a number of students, especially at the graduate level, brought with their GI-Bill benefits their vivid memories of subalternship in military bureaucracies. Experience was something, but nearly everyone's experience was confined to one agency, its oral reporting to others tended to be merely anecdotal, and time's passage dulled memories and audience interest.

The Inter-University Case Program provided in permanent form a range, depth, and contemporaneity of vicarious experience that would otherwise have eluded us. The program began in 1948 under the sponsorship of Cornell, Harvard, Princeton, and Syracuse universities and with the aid of the Carnegie Corporation of New York.[30] Its staff director was Harold Stein, whom Edwin Bock has accurately described as "a man of taste, literary skill, commitment, irony, horse sense, and force," strengths that Bock observes "were fortified (in the eyes of his sponsors) by the high credential that he had never read a textbook on public administration."[31] I had the opportunity to observe him in operation in the War Production Board; he was fascinated by the play of forces in the generation of policy and more by the forces that penetrated an administrative agency from private interests, Congress, the White House, and collateral administrative agencies than by weak interpositions of internal offices that were not themselves exposed to the agency's external environment. This affected his conception of the breadth of public administration's concerns and helps explain why the ICP cases are about important decisions with substantial economic and social dimensions rather than about what he would regard as trivial administrative processes.[32]

Each case focused on a single decision (or set of interconnected decisions) and the emphasis was on behavior of particular organizations, groups, and individuals. Neither individually nor in the aggregate did the cases provide the empirical foundation for scientific generalizations. They were probing but not probative. We had not yet learned to use the scientifically respectable word "heuristic," and so few but the already converted acknowledged that the abundance of hypotheses derivable from the cases helped advance toward a "science" of public administration. And few anticipated that the complexity of factors making each real-life case unique might have cautionary value for scholars eager for grand theories and models purporting to impose a simple order on the multivariate politico-administrative world.[33]

There were other ways of relating administration to the contexts of particular policies and programs. In a field previously indulging in general principles and short of data, this might be a two-stage process: first an accumulation of monographic studies, and, second, a few ambitious efforts to develop taxonomies and to distill from the monographic materials the generalizations appropriate to the respective taxonomic categories.[34] Over the 1946–1960 period we somehow failed to make much progress in these terms. The war-agency histories, together with the few earlier "capture-and-record" studies, were a useful start. But the war-agency histories were, I believe, little used in teaching and research and no one undertook to distill their more generalizable findings.[35]

The literature about peacetime regulatory agencies was given considerable taxonomic order by, among others, Emmette S. Redford and Marver H. Bernstein.[36] However, political-science interest in government regulation and administrative law sharply declined, and those subjects were left largely to the economists and legal scholars.[37]

An astonishing number of political scientists chose to focus on the closely related policy areas of natural resources and agriculture. They were premature ecology buffs, for in the 1946–1960 period their interest seemed oddly placed. The farm population fell from 17 percent to less than 9 percent of the total population. The TVA example did not lead to reproduction of the valley-authority device elsewhere. Though I was a minor participant in this specialized community of scholars, I cannot explain why so many of us—about twenty names of well-known scholars come readily to mind[38]—chose to write in these policy areas when, in retrospect, so many others seem equally inviting. John M. Gaus deservedly had enormous influence, and Roscoe Martin and George Graham induced some younger colleagues to join in collaborative projects in the resources area, but their roles are only a partial explanation.

Interest in natural resources and agriculture persisted throughout the 1946–1960 period.[39] And it may well account for the reserve with which some of these "ecologists" reacted to later-proclaimed "innovations" in administrative analysis. These men had already encountered benefit/cost analysis, and its application to choice among alternative water-resource projects had alerted them to its imperfections. They had fully learned of interagency rivalry—and in its perhaps most virulent form, as exposed by Arthur Maass's classic case study and his published doctoral dissertation[40]—so a "bureaucratic politics" paradigm in the 1970s was unlikely to seem a fresh discovery. The agricultural price-parity index had introduced them fully to the utility and hazards of quantitative formulas for goal-setting and result-oriented feedback on program progress. They knew about "open systems" and organizational interchange with the "environment" through the exposure of the Department of Agriculture to the tender ministrations of the American Farm Bureau Federation. The fate of the Bureau of Agricultural Economics was due warning of the vulnerability of analytical staffs that are bearers of bad news to powerful interests. "Reprivatizing" of governmental functions did not tempt them, for they knew about private utility companies' neglect of rural electrification and the sophisticated modes used to render utility-regulating commissions ineffective. The virtues and problems of clientele, grass-roots, participative decision making had been thoroughly revealed in the agricultural referenda and the elaborate network of farmer-elected committees. No wonder that feelings of *déjà vu* deterred these public-administration students from leaping aboard the succession of bandwagons that were put in motion in the 1960s.

Many other domestic program areas were wholly neglected or were attended to by only one or two members of our community.[41] In the circumstances, we failed to develop an ordering taxonomy despite dissatisfaction with primitive distinctions between autonomous and independent status, collegial and single-headed agencies, regulatory and service activities, and advisory and operating functions.

THE EARLY POSTWAR LITERATURE

In the early postwar years two young men launched remarkably productive and influential scholarly careers by publishing their political-science dissertations. Dwight Waldo's *The Administrative State*[42] appeared in 1948. Reviewing it then, I hailed it as "a major contribution to the literature of public administration . . . stimulating . . . basic . . . pioneering."[43] He articulated the largely inarticulate premises of leading writers on public administration, whether hortatory advocates of "good government," earnest builders of a "science" of public administration, or pragmatists. He did not like much of what he found. I noted, "In Professor Waldo's scale of pleasure-pain values, iconoclasm ranks high in pleasure content." An annotated bibliography, published in 1972, puts it rather sharply, "He wrote this book as an angry young graduate student at Yale University, aiming to destroy certain dogmas in administrative science."[44] Whatever his intentions, his product fitted well with the literature produced by others with wartime Washington experience. He rejected premature claims to a science of public administration oriented to neutrality and a narrowly conceived efficiency, and in this as in his later publications he saw the need to reconcile public administration with democratic values and the governmental context.[45]

Herbert Simon's dissertation, *Administrative Behavior*,[46] appeared in 1947. Reviewing it then, I wrote of "penetrating insight . . . a distinguished talent for abstract thinking . . . an impressive competence" and concluded, "Any student of the theory of administration will henceforth have to start with Simon's analysis of decision-making."[47] But I expressed some reservations, criticizing one large set of distinctions as "scarcely novel," another set for a "formalism" that distanced them from the reality known by those readers who had had administrative experience. Particularly, I was troubled by the fact that, though the reader of that era thought of decision making as almost the same process as policy formation (and Simon's abstract level of discussion did not disabuse him), Simon's examples of decision makers were typically lower-level, professionalized specialists with quite narrow ranges of discretion. After noting this, I concluded the point by writing:

> The reviewer's feeling that the higher reaches of decision-making have at times eluded the author is strengthened further by Simon's discussion of 'the planning process' entirely in terms of an engineer's choice of railroad routes and dam sites and a naval department's designing of a battleship. Important as the planning process is to decision-making in public administration, the whole process is here reduced to physical designing by professionalized personnel rather than treated in the more appropriate terms of policy formation for a great administrative agency.

Some of the tendencies noted were to persist in his future work—for example, a strong concern with "programmed" decision making, which looked very much like the routined procedures that abandonment of the policy/administration dichotomy led political scientists to disdain.[48] The important 1958 book *Organizations*[49] by Simon and James G. March seemed consciously to ignore the relevant public-administration literature. Though both authors are political scientists, their bibliography, listing some 750 authors, includes "only 23 (including the authors) who, by a generous construction of the terms are identified with Political Science or Public Administration."[50] The piquant temptation for the ignored to ignore was not fully resisted.

Waldo and Simon shared a concern for value premises. But Waldo, writing a dissertation in the field of political theory, worried about what the values of public-administration writers had been and what they ought to be in a democratic polity. He sensed, as did Appleby, that values infuse all actions and relationships. Though Waldo was rebelling against orthodoxy, the Waldensian heresies did not include simony. For Simon not only insisted on separating questions of value from questions of fact; he also admonished scholars to concentrate on the efficiency of means for achieving stated ends. What the ends were was an important question of descriptive fact, an essential premise for the analysis of means, but their choice was so shot through with subjective value considerations that it was not the business of "administrative science."[51] He was widely perceived as being in the tradition of the old scientific-management movement and eager to reinstate the concept of administration as a neutral instrument, to revive the policy/administration dichotomy, and to ignore the contextual differences between public and business administration.

A third young Midwesterner, Robert A. Dahl, published a remarkably prescient article in 1947.[52] He identified three obstacles to discovery of general principles of wide validity: (1) "the frequent impossibility of excluding normative considerations from the problems of public administration"; (2) "the inescapable fact that a science of public administration must be a study of certain aspects of human behavior"; (3) the need to take account of "the relationship between public administration and its social setting," for "as long as the study of public administration is not comparative, claims for 'a science of public administration' sound rather hollow." The third point was essentially new; it anticipated by a decade the emergence of the comparative public administration movement.

On the normative issue he argued, consistently with Waldo and Simon, that the student must make explicit the ends or values that he either attributes to society or assumes in his basic hypothesis. But "in most societies, and particularly in democratic ones, ends are often in dispute; rarely are they clearly and unequivocally determined. Nor can ends and means ever be sharply distinguished, since ends determine means and often means ultimately determine ends."

That a science of public administration must take account of human behavior was to Dahl a major obstacle, not easily to be surmounted. To remember man is to be "cursed with his maddening unpredictability"; "too little is known of the mainsprings of human action to insure certitude, or even high probability, in predictions about man's conduct." The assumption that "individuals are dominated by reason ... has been discredited by all the findings of modern psychology," so "we cannot achieve a science by creating in a mechanized 'administrative man' a modern descendant of the eighteenth century's rational man. ..." Hence, the public-administration researcher should learn to use the investigations of the psychiatrist and sociologist.

Norton Long, as was true also of Waldo, Simon, and Dahl, brought to the study of public administration a sure sense of the importance of theory and a solid grounding in theoretical literature extending well beyond that of administration itself. Gifted in literary style and provocatively original, he planted administration solidly in the constitutional and political system and affirmed both the representativeness and the policy-formulating role of the public bureaucracy.[53]

I have dwelt at length on the early postwar publications of this generation of rebels,[54] mostly in their thirties—the Morstein Marx collaborators, Appleby, the founders of the Inter-University Case Program, and Waldo, Simon, Dahl, and Long. I have done so because their rejections of past doctrines and their specifications of new approaches set the course for the whole period to 1960. This is true even though the changes in political science and a sharpened sense of the relevancy of other social sciences were to have great impact.

THE IMPACT OF PLURALISM AND BEHAVIORALISM

The study of public administration soon had to adjust to two developments in its parent discipline, political science: the pluralist "school" and the behavioral movement. At first view the pluralist approach seemed highly congruent with the directions that our field was taking. Pluralism was about government, not about just any kind of organization. We ourselves viewed public administration as interlinked with policy-formation processes, and so with Congress, the White House, and a host of interest groups. Those of us trained in the early 1930s had read the English pluralists and had dismissed the sovereignty of the state, damning it as an obfuscating concept. Many pluralist writers were members of our own group. In 1951 Bertram Gross enthusiastically revived Arthur F. Bentley, and David Truman (whose prewar dissertation had been on administrative decentralization in the Department of Agriculture) published the classic pluralist book, *The Government Process*. And in 1953 Robert A. Dahl's and Charles E. Lindblom's *Politics, Economics, and Welfare* introduced political scientists to "polyarchy."[55]

But in two ways the pluralist school disserved the community of public-administration scholars. The pluralist "hardliners" made extreme claims for the automatism and comprehensiveness with which the calculus of interest-group pressures translated into the substance of policy. This offended our understanding of how policy is made, including the roles of many factors additional to private pressure groups. It also led to a devastating attack on the concept of the public interest, reducing it from a value and an objective to a mere myth.[56] This was dispiriting to a group of people who had experienced the New Deal and the wartime economic-mobilization process as, in their view, a constant battling for the paramountcy of the public interest over selfish private interests.

Secondly, the pluralist school directed scholarly energies to the "input" processes. Many of the brightest scholars concentrated their talents on the legislative process, and the play on it of pressures from members' constituencies, interest groups, and political parties. Some undertook probing studies of the patterns of "community power," setting off a revival, at a sophisticated and policy-concerned level, of the field of local government.[57] On campuses, public administration lost apparent relevance and, so, status. The shift of attention was to be strongly reinforced by the behavioral "revolution."

The behavioral movement struck five blows.[58] First, it depreciated the study of governmental and political institutions and proposed to substitute the study of the behaviors of individuals. A student of public administration could not easily escape the dread label of "institutionalist." Second, it discounted much of what was already known in political science and urged that we become psychologists, sociologists, and anthropologists[59]—or at least master the relevant literatures of the behavioral sciences.

Third, it introduced severe standards of scientific research that demanded rigor (probably the single word of greatest currency), designing of theories and models with strict attention to logical rules, explicitness in definitions and assumptions, operationalism in statement of hypotheses, empirical testing of hypotheses, and the primacy of quantitative methods. Few public-administration scholars were prepared to meet the challenge. Some suffered guilt feelings about their incapacity (they could not even define "public administration"!). Others might have adapted as the behavioral revolution progressed from the enunciatory and denunciatory stages to actual research, but they were dissuaded by some early works in the new mode that fell short of the stated standards and missed elementary aspects of reality.[60]

Fourth, consistently with its emphasis on science, behavioralism proscribed prescription. Yet political scientists specializing in public administration often served as consultants to governments, most prominently with the first Hoover Commission and with the "little Hoover Commissions" in the states. Bureaus of public administration at state universities were conspicuous symbols of the applied-research aspect of our field. Their contributions on larger analytical projects were often lost to view amidst the flow of bulletins and studies on user charges, fire protection, trash collection, and other practical topics, acknowledgment of whose scholarly appropriateness would have to await the era of systems analysts.[61]

Fifth, despite the claimed focus on individual behavior, behavioralists' emphasis on quantitative methods led to the study of designated "populations" as aggregates rather than to the study of single individuals as whole persons. Elections and legislative roll calls automatically yielded officially certified, comprehensive data on voters' and legislators' behavior;[62] the administrative process did not generate comparable data on administrators' behavior. With adequate funding by sympathetic, if not goading, foundations, behavioralists could conduct sample surveys of voters', nonvoters', and legislators' attitudes, a research method most impressively demonstrated by the Survey Research Center of the University of Michigan. The consequence was that, as with pluralism, the behavioral political scientists gave principal attention to input functions—voting and other political participation, public attitudes, and legislators' behavior. Government seemed to have become only a dependent variable[63] and administration an irrelevancy.

Political scientists in the public-administration field varied in their response to the newly regnant orthodoxy. Most who had governmental experience tended not to adapt. Some, recalling the earlier slander that administrative research was "counting manhole covers," hesitated to embrace quantitative methods. They failed to recognize that "*Mene, mene, tekel, upharsin*"[64]—numbered, numbered, weighed, divided—was the handwriting on the wall. Many rejected the "hard-science" model put forth for both theory development and empirical research, and a few suspected that this "behavioral" model was a caricature of how the natural and physical scientists actually behaved. But the students of public administration had no positive alternative to propose, their field was in disarray, and they themselves no longer mentioned "the *science* of public administration" either as accomplished fact or as aspiration.

Nonetheless, adaptation did occur. Textbooks began to incorporate a behavioral approach to public administration. This was especially true of the 1950 text by Simon, Donald Smithburg, and Victor Thompson, and of the 1953 and later editions of the text by John M. Pfiffner and the behaviorally attuned Robert Presthus. Beginnings were made on the quantitative study of administrative elites and of the people's image of the public service; these earliest studies were by sociologist-led teams that included political scientists.[65] Herbert Kaufman sensitively probed how one public agency assured conforming behavior by its field agents.[66]

For the future the important indicator was the surprising ease with which the oncoming generation of political scientists, still in graduate school, accommodated themselves to the often disparate characters of, on the one hand, the public-administration courses and, on the other, the courses fully committed to the behavioral approach. In the department widely supposed to be the most behavioral in the country, those taking graduate courses in public administration between 1953 and 1959 without apparent trauma included, among others: Donald and Sybil Stokes; James Guyot, Herbert Jacob, and Theodore Lowi; Robert Fried, Robert Golembiewski, and Aaron Wildavsky; Fred Greenstein, Nelson Polsby, and Raymond Wolfinger; and Rufus Browning, Peter Savage, Allen Schick, and Herbert Wilcox.[67]

THE IMPACT OF SOCIOLOGY AND
SOCIAL PSYCHOLOGY

The 1946–1960 period brought interdisciplinary approaches into high favor, not least with the grant-bestowing foundations. To the question of which social sciences our discipline should and should not be most attentive to, the behavioral political scientists had clear answers. Certainly not history. And not economics, even though it and political science had overlapping interests in public finance, government regulation, and the substance and formative processes of public policy. Its postulating of self-interested "economic man" had psychological dimensions that might have linked it to behavioral political science, but the opportunity was forgone.[68] Instead, the polygamous marriage proposed for political science was with sociology, psychology, and, though not consummated, anthropology.

Reflecting political science's romance with the behavioral sciences, but also autonomously, the field of public administration interacted extensively with sociology, psychology, and business administration. Ambiguity enshrouded the relationship. Was public administration receiving infusions of insights, theories, typologies, and methods that would strengthen its quality and raise its status? Or was it slowly being nibbled to death? The answer was not clear then and is not clear now.

The first major sociological impact came with the 1946 and 1947 translations of portions of Max Weber's magisterial work.[69] Weber's emphases upon the legitimacy of authority, the rational-legal ideal type, and the attributes of a bureaucracy appropriate to that type had and have great influence within our field. A curiosity of intellectual history is that our disowning of home-grown classical organization theory occurred simultaneously with our cordial reception of the Weberian model that incorporated many of the same values.

Structural-functionalism, whose formulation and elaboration are largely the work of sociologists Talcott Parsons, Marion J. Levy, and Robert K. Merton, had transforming effects on much of social science, most notably political science.[70] My impression is that most students of public administration initially encountered Parsons through intermediaries and adapters, rather than neat, and that the full impact was not apparent until the 1960s.[71]

Of more immediate effect were the writings of sociologists on administration and especially governmental bureaucracies. In 1949 Merton's *Social Theory and Social Structure*[72] included papers specifically on bureaucracy, alerted us to latent functions and to dysfunctions, and consoled us for our lack of comprehensive theory by his advocacy of middle-range theory. In the same year Philip Selznick published *TVA and the Grass Roots*,[73] the classic study of cooptation, which fitted easily with the pluralist approach in political science; later his *Leadership in Administration*[74] afforded fresh perspectives while it seemed confirmatory of our understanding of the nature of organizations. The 1952 *Reader on Bureaucracy*,[75] edited by Merton and others, accelerated our reception of Weber and expanded our appreciation of relevancies in sociological subject matter and styles of analysis. Reinhard Bendix, Peter Blau, and other sociologists staked out interests in the study of organizations, including those in the public sector. But our debts cannot be individually acknowledged here.[76]

The welcome we accorded these sociologists' contributions resulted from several characteristics. They dealt with our scale and category of organization, large-scale and "formal" or "complex" (as they called it), and often with governmental, rather than business or other private-sector, bureaucracies. They focused on problems that we, as they, deemed important, and concentrated more on matter than on manner, that is, more on substance than on methodologies. With a few exceptions they communicated clearly, eschewing the multiplication of neologisms. These "macroadministration" sociologists are to be distinguished from their colleagues, the "microadministration" sociologists whose linkages were with such psychologists and business-administration students as chose to focus on interpersonal relations and individual motivations.

The sociopsychological approach to administration embraced such a variety of scientific concerns and normative enthusiasms that it resists encapsulation. It focused on individual human beings and their face-to-face relations, especially in small work groups. It emphasized informal organization which, because it was natural and organic, seemed more real than formal organization. In fact, formal organization was either ignored or was hypothesized as bureuacratic and, so, hostile to workers' freedom and achievement of their full human potential. It advocated extensive worker participation in organizations' decision making, but largely ignored the role of labor unions in such decision making. Its scientific research methods were generally applied only to persons and groups at lower organizational levels, typically blue-collar factory workers, telephone operators, and clerks, or to college students paid to serve as laboratory subjects. Although the research rarely dealt with business and industrial managers above the foreman level or with government agencies, the writers did not hesitate to extrapolate their findings and theories to such unstudied levels and institutions.

Their confinement to the world of business and industry made them oblivious to the inherent conflict among three versions of democratic, participative decision making (a conflict that any political scientist could have alerted them to): (1) their ideal of worker democracy internal to an organization, say a government agency; (2) the classic ideal and practice of policy making for, and control of, an agency by the electorate and its chosen legislators and political executives; and (3) the ideal and practice of policy making for, and control of, an agency by its clientele.

Ignoring the earlier growth of sophistication in the leadership literature, the bellwether writers of the sociopsychological persuasion primitively categorized leadership styles as good or bad (sometimes modulated to four or five tones), generalized without regard to situational variables, and flatly correlated workers' productivity with their happiness indices.

The sociopsychological approach had and continues to have great influence on our field. The reasons are three. First, in public-administration research, as in that of business administration, human beings had been neglected save in the faceless aggregates of "personnel administration" or at the executive and professional elite levels.[77] So writers about human relations in organizations corrected our tendency to write about organizations without people, even though our correctors tended in turn to write about people without organizations.

Second, the number of students and publications in the sociopsychological tradition was already enormous in the 1950s. Speaking of only one topic in that tradition, Golembiewski wrote, "the bulk of studies of the small group dwarfs the products of any previous analytical preoccupation of the social scientist." The inventory of fourteen hundred items of small-group research already on hand in 1954 rapidly grew, reaching an *annual* output rate of two hundred by the end of the 1950s.[78] On other sociopsychological, administrative topics, the *Administrative Science Quarterly*, which began publication in 1956, offers a wide sample, again with substantial concentration on factory and business settings, or, if in the public and quasi-public sectors, on security institutions such as prisons and mental hospitals. The volume of the research, along with its apparently scientific methodology, impressed our small community as prima-facie important, as too enormous a literature for most of us to master (March and Simon, Golembiewski, and Presthus were the least cowed),[79] and as so fully cultivated a field that we should draw on its fruits rather than ourselves attempt to replicate it in governmental settings.

Third, the "human-relations movement," though it peaked in the 1950s and then ebbed as dienchantment set in, was to revive in later decades amidst a new *Zeitgeist* that stimulated empathic responses from a new generation of public-administration scholars. Proselytizers for human relations, as the later ones for the new humanism, had all the best lines. Our orthodox scholars might insist that so long as men are not angels there will be need for authority, hierarchy, bureaucratic processes, and organization goals. But their vocabulary was chilling when set against such evocative terms as participation, democracy, man's higher needs, self-actualization, job enlargement, and authenticity in interpersonal relations.

SCIENTISM AND PUBLIC ADMINISTRATION

A scientific age induces scholars to search for order in any important field of varied and confusing phenomena. The "New Scientism" of the social sciences in 1946–1960 led quite naturally to grand-scale theorizing about large-scale organizations. As the full flowering was to occur in the 1960s, I indicate here only four early tendencies.

First, nearly every social or behavioral science, basic or applied, contributed directly or indirectly, and the umbrella term for their shared field became "organization theory" or "management science." The term "administration" fell into disuse. The change was not inconsequential for students of public administration.

Second, "organization theory" carried with it the concept of an organization as a system, and systems theory was applied with its full set of concepts. Organization theorists generalized about all kinds of organizations,[80] finding the public analogue to business corporations to be government bureaus. Because systems theory required sharp definition of an organization's boundaries and classed everything outside those boundaries as parts of the organization's environment, the government bureau's department, other bureaus and agencies, the President, the Congress, and government-wide control agencies were indiscriminately—and misleadingly—blended into the environment, along with clients, private interest groups, and the general public.[81]

Third, decision making became the dominant theoretical focus of scholars concerned with business administration. This was, of course, the focus chosen by Simon as early as 1947, and he no doubt influenced the development as he became increasingly identified with the business-administration field.[82] The subject was to be plagued by a built-in antithesis. On the one hand, decision making is done by human beings and its study entails concern with psychological aspects of the decisional behavior. On the other hand, the aspiration is to make decision making rational, and preferably impersonal. Simon attempted to bridge the gap, partly by making concessions to accommodate two facts: that even an intendedly rational "administrative man" may fall short of rationality's demands; and that such a man's self-interested rationality may conflict with organizational rationality. He also sought to reduce the problem by expanding the realm of programmed decision making (automated, that is, by a computer or by cogs-in-a-machine clerks), for a "program" could be rationally designed, monitored, and corrected.

The human-behavior/rational-analysis antithesis remained unresolved in the field of business decision making. Two foundation-sponsored studies of university programs in business administration (both published in 1959) essentially proposed separate but equal accommodations for the two approaches, rather than either integration of the two or subordination of one to the other.[83]

The problem was reflected in the study of public administration. We could not be against rationality or against scientific methods, theories, and models any more than we could be against human beings' finding happiness in their work groups despite assertedly repressive organizational climates. The problem was eased for us by Charles E. Lindblom's now-classic essay, "The Science of 'Muddling Through.' "[84] Simultaneously it established incremental decision making as a rationally defensible alternative model, it reassured active public administrators that they had been speaking prose all along, and it breathed new life into the pluralist tradition of political science. Furthermore, it seemed to experienced scholars to embody an accurate perception of human behavior at the levels where decisions have consequences. In the decade to follow, the incrementalist model was to compete with the markedly ascendant "rational" model of decision making in the public sector.

Fourth, attempts to develop and gain acceptance for large-scope theories and models of organization fell short in two regards. First, because relevant empirical studies were too few, too poor, or simply not taken into account, theorists and modelers relied heavily on deductive logic and imagination. To be sure, assumptions were made explicit, though often set forth as self-demonstrating truths or as mere conveniences of the form, "It is convenient to assume that. . . ." Second, the hypotheses and propositions derived from the assumptions were rarely tested, or, if tested, rarely confirmed by replicative empirical research. My language may seem hyperbolic to some. But published assessments of the organization-theory disciplines and subdisciplines are peppered with complaints about the gross disproportion between theories and facts. The disproportion is of more consequence than misallocation of scholarly resources between speculation and empirical research: empirical researchers themselves wasted energies pursuing lines of inquiry derived from ill-conceived theories and models. The point is not that theorizing is bad. It is absolutely essential. The point is that, in the period we are reviewing, much of the theorizing was inadequately informed.

Students of public administration might have drawn on two stocks of relevant empirical data. Administrative history constituted one stock, and a few of our number not only drew on it but added to it, most notably Leonard D. White with his four-volume administrative history of the United States,[85] but also younger scholars, some addressing themselves to the American setting[86] and some to that of Europe.[87] But the historical approach was uncongenial to behavioral political scientists and its products did not fit easily with the most prominent systemic theories and models.

Comparative public administration promised to strengthen the scientific reputability of our field and, by its attention to development administration, to revive concern with how systems change over time (though few called it "history"). A large body of data was available and rapidly increasing because of governmental and foundation support for foreign-area studies. These data were mostly buried in single-country monographs, whose very number may have discouraged our mining of them. Both these studies of foreign politics and our relating of administration to political, social, and economic development reaffirmed the interrelation of politics and administration[88] and so the distinctiveness of *public* administration at a time when the generic view of administration, regardless of setting, was becoming dominant.

Although the comparative administration "movement" was not in full swing until the 1960s, its beginnings were earlier. Several books had appeared,[89] courses on comparative public administration were introduced in political-science departments,[90] and the June, 1960, issue of the behaviorally oriented *Administrative Science Quarterly* was wholly devoted to the new subject.

These beginnings held promise of building a firmly empirical foundation for generalizations. But many members of the comparative-administration movement seemed responsive to the prestige rewards that attached to invention and elaboration of grandscale theories and models. Few were the scholars who inductively developed comparisons from administrative data for a substantial set of polities and formulated middle-range theories grounded in such comparisons.[91] Comparative-administrative scholars appeared to have adopted William Blake's motto:[92]

I must Create a System or be enslav'd by another Man's.
I will not Reason & Compare: my business is to Create.

LEGACIES FROM THE POSTWAR PERIOD

What legacy did the 1946–1960 developments leave for the future? An heir as eclectic as myself can find many attractive bits and pieces with which to furnish a house. But the legacy does not seem to include a house itself—and certainly not one of architectural distinction.

The following central tendencies of the period stand out (though for each I could note exceptions and qualifications):

1. Basic issues were not settled. Whether public administration should be approached as apolitical, amoral, and ahistorical was as disputed in 1960 as it was earlier.
2. The rapid succession of fashions was a startling feature of social sciences that proclaimed their commitment to rigorous, cumulative, scientific theory and method. Public administration's efforts to adapt to the succession of fashions left it clad in motley in 1960.
3. Changes in the vocabulary were mistakenly taken to symbolize progress. Many who caustically condemned the prewar "principles" of public administration did not hesitate to advance unsupported "propositions" as universal truths.
4. Though we needed to develop self-consciousness about theory and method, this dissensus-generating enterprise unduly diverted energies from solid empirical research. For such research we were surprisingly dependent on published doctoral dissertations.
5. The discounting of "conventional wisdom" gave wisdom it-

self a bad name. And the rise of information-poor approaches to theory formation and of computational research strategies depreciated the value of experience-based insights into administrative reality.

6. We suffered from the lack of large-scale efforts to synthesize what was known about public administration. Between research monographs on the one hand and undergraduate textbooks on the other, the field of public administration produces neither treatises of the Continental European type nor major stock-taking surveys of the field such as are found in sociology, social psychology, and organizational theory.[93] Dwight Waldo is our major resource here, but even his discerning reviews of the field take the form of relatively brief articles.

As the 1960s began, we did not know whether public administration was a field and we did not know how to define an organization. We did not know whether an organization must have a goal, or whether, if it must, the goal is merely organization survival or, instead, is an objective more teleologically energizing, and if the latter, whether the goal is determined by the organization's members or by holders of legitimate authority. We agreed that decisions are important, but their very ubiquity and variety made them an exceptionally diffuse focus. We had two rival models of decision making, one a "rational," benefit/cost, efficiency model and the other an incremental, political-bargaining model. Our colleagues in comparative politics had developed an influential structural-functional model but elaborated the input functions and left output functions, including "rule application," undeveloped.[94]

We were reading, being influenced by, and assigning to the oncoming generation in graduate school literatures of neighboring disciplines that brought into question the foundations laid in the late 1940s.[95] Our problem for the future would be how to discriminate in our borrowings from the behavioral sciences and from economics, how to learn by their errors, and how to adapt their theories, methods, and findings to the distinctive environment in which the public's business is carried on.[96]

NOTES

1. Virgil, *Aeneid*, translated by Allen Mandelbaum (Berkeley: University of California Press, 1971), book 2, lines 7–8.
2. R. G. Austin, in Virgil, *Aeneid* (Oxford: Clarendon Press, 1964), p. 29, note 6.
3. The United Nations and associated agencies had the services of colleagues like Rowland Egger, J. Donald Kingsley, Frederick C. Mosher, and Donald C. Stone in the early shaping of administrative structure and processes and in the first stages of UN technical assistance to developing nations.
4. See Samuel P. Huntington, *The Common Defense* (New York: Columbia University Press, 1961), and Paul Y. Hammond, *Organizing for Defense* (Princeton, N.J.: Princeton University Press, 1961).
5. See Harry Howe Ransom, *Central Intelligence and National Security* (Cambridge, Massachusetts: Harvard University Press, 1958).
6. A major exception is the study initiated by the Carnegie Corporation of New York in 1957. See Edward W. Weidner, *The World Role of Universities* (New York: McGraw-Hill Book Co., 1962). Don K. Price's 1954 attempt to alert us is noted below.
7. Robert H. Connery, *The Navy and the Industrial Mobilization in World War II* (Princeton, N.J.: Princeton University Press, 1951), and, with Robert G. Albion, *Forrestal and the Navy* (New York: Columbia University Press, 1962); James L. McCamy, *The Administration of Foreign Affairs* (New York: Alfred A. Knopf, 1952); Arthur W. Macmahon, *Administration in Foreign Affairs* (University, Ala.: University of Alabama Press, 1953); Frederick C. Mosher, *Program Budgeting: Theory and Practice*, with particular reference to the U.S. Department of the Army (Chicago: Public Administration Service, 1954); John W. Masland and Laurence I. Radway, *Soldiers and Scholars: Military Education and National Policy* (Princeton ,N.J.: Princeton University Press, 1957); Walter Millis, with Harvey C. Mansfield and Harold Stein, *Arms and the State* (New York: Twentieth Century Fund, 1958); Paul Y. Hammond, *Organizing for Defense* (Princeton, N.J.: Princeton University Press, 1961); Harold Stein (ed.), *American Civil-Military Relations: A Book of Case Studies* (University, Ala.: University of Alabama Press, 1963).
8. Rowland Egger, Arthur W. Macmahon, James L. McCamy, Don K. Price, and Harold Stein were consulted by the International Studies Group of the Brookings Institution on its study for the Bureau of the Budget, *The Administration of Foreign and Overseas Operations* (Washington, D.C.: Government Printing Office, 1951); five of the twenty persons more closely involved in the study were students of public administration: Robert H. Connery, Charles S. Hyneman, Wallace S. Sayre, Herman M. Somers, and Clarence Thurber; but only

Connery and Thurber retained a commitment to the special field. About a decade later, only three of twenty-five members of a similar Brookings study's staff and its advisory committee—Harlan Cleveland, Harold Stein, and Donald C. Stone—are recognizable as members of our fraternity. "The Formulation and Administration of United States Foreign Policy," in U. S. Senate Committee on Foreign Relations, *United States Foreign Policy: Compilation of Studies* (86th Congress, 2nd Session, Committee Print) Washington, D.C.: Government Printing Office, 1960), 2 volumes. Only Harlan Cleveland and Stephen K. Bailey of our parish were in the "working group" of nine in the Maxwell School of Syracuse University that prepared "The Operational Aspects of United States Foreign Policy," ibid.

9. U.S. Senate Committee on Government Operations (Subcommittee on National Policy Machinery), *Organizing for National Security:* hearings, studies, reports (86th Congress, 2nd Session, and 87th Congress, 1st Session, Committee Prints) (Washington, D.C.: Government Printing Office, 1960, 1961).

10. Walter R. Sharp, "The Study of International Administration," *World Politics* 11 (October, 1958), pp. 103–117, at pp. 112 f.

11. E.g., Herbert Simon, *The New Science of Management Decision* (New York: Harper & Row, 1960).

12. Morgan Thomas and Robert M. Northrop, *Atomic Energy and Congress* (Ann Arbor: University of Michigan Press, 1956). The Presidential and Congressional lines of responsibility clashed when the AEC and the Bureau of the Budget, responsive to the Eisenhower view of the Tennessee Valley Authority as "creeping socialism," became partners in the Dixon-Yates negotiations that scandalized Congress. See Aaron Wildavsky, *Dixon Yates: A Study in Power Politics* (New Haven, Conn.: Yale University Press, 1962).

13. David L. Sills, *The Volunteers* (Glencoe, Ill.: The Free Press, 1958).

14. Don K. Price, *Government and Science* (New York: New York University Press, 1954).

15. Included in publications of the few are: Herman M. Somers and Anne Somers, *Workmen's Compensation* (New York: John Wiley & Sons, 1954), and *Doctors, Patients, and Health Insurance* (Washington, D.C.: The Brookings Institution, 1961); and James L. McCamy, *Science and Public Administration* (University, Ala.: University of Alabama Press, 1960).

16. Richard E. Neustadt, *Presidential Power* (New York: John Wiley & Sons, 1960). See also Neustadt's articles, "Presidency and Legislation: The Growth of Central Clearance," *American Political Science Review*, 48 (September, 1954), pp. 641–71; and "Presidency and Legislation: Planning the President's Program," Ibid. 49 (December, 1955), pp. 980–1021.

A clue to political scientists' preoccupation with the Presidency was the presumed appropriateness of starting a conversation with anybody at annual association meetings with, "How is your book on the Presidency coming?"

17. Though my focus here is on public events, there were linkages to the academy. Thirty political scientists (including Commissioner James K. Pollock) shared in the work of the first (Hoover) Commission on Organization of the Executive Branch of the Government; see *American Political Science Review*, 43 (April, 1949), p. 352. A number also did studies for the Kestnbaum Commission; and, even if its report did not achieve what Mr. Kestnbaum told me he sought—a distinction equal to *The Federalist* papers—the report was lucid and balanced, partly because of the drafting skills of well-chosen, but anonymous, political scientists.

18. All data shown are for "direct" expenditures, i.e., exclusive of intergovernmental transactions. Aid from the federal government increased only from 11.4 to 13.8 percent of state and local general revenues.

19. E.g., the University of California (Berkeley), University of Michigan, University of Kansas, and the Southern Regional Training Program jointly conducted by the universities of Alabama, Kentucky, and Tennessee. For details of these and other training programs, see Ward Stewart, *Graduate Study in Public Administration: A Guide to Graduate Programs*, U.S. Office of Education Circular 631 (Washington, D.C.: 1961).

20. Municipal Manpower Commission, *Governmental Manpower for Tomorrow's Cities* (New York: McGraw-Hill Book Co., 1962), pp. 1962), pp. 53 f. For a thoughtful analysis of this and other aspects of state and local administration in the 1950s and early 1960s, see York Willbern, "Administrative Organization" and 'Personnel and Money" in James W. Fesler (ed.), *The 50 States and Their Local Governments* (New York: Alfred A. Knopf, 1967), pp. 337–404.

21. Clarence E. Ridley, *The Role of the City Manager in Policy Formulation* (Chicago: International City Managers Association, 1958).

22. Stephen K. Bailey, *Congress Makes a Law: The Story Behind the Employment Act of 1946* (New York: Columbia University Press, 1950). Edward S. Flash, r., *Economic Advice and Presidential Leadership: The Council of Economic Advisers* (New York: Columbia University Press, 1961, 1965); see especially pp. 8–17 for a fuller statement of why, "Although not mutually exclusive in theory and application these sets of expectations [in the Act's language] were so different and opposite in emphasis and ideas as to constitute different standards of conduct and different as well as reciprocal measures of success or failure" (p. 12).

23. Bailey's and Flash's books, both revisions of doctoral dissertations,

are cited immediately above. The political scientists called to testify on how to structure relationships following the 1951 confrontation between the President and the Board of Governors of the Federal Reserve System were Paul H. Appleby, James K. Pollock, Lucius Wilmerding, and Harold Stein, none previously or since a cultivator of this vineyard. Harvey C. Mansfield made important contributions to the report of the Commission on Money and Credit, *Money and Credit* (Englewood Cliffs, N.J.: Prentice-Hall, Inc., 1961), and Michael D. Reagan wrote a valuable article, "The Political Structure of the Federal Reserve System," *American Political Science Review*, 55 (March, 1961), pp. 64–76.

24. In the Bureau of the Budget: Paul H. Appleby, William D. Carey, Bernard Gladieux, George A. Graham, Pendleton Herring, Roger Jones, V. O. Key, Jr., Earl H. Latham, Avery Leiserson, Fritz Morstein Marx, Harold Seidman, Donald C. Stone, and John A. Vieg. In the Office of Price Administration: Merle Fainsod, Harvey C. Mansfield, Norton E. Long, Emmette S. Redford, Wallace Sayre, Donald W. Smithburg, Victor Thompson, Dwight Waldo, and Virgil Zimmerman. In the War Production Board: Robert A. Dahl, James W. Fesler, Lincoln Gordon, and Harold Stein. In the Office of War Mobilization and Reconversion: J. Donald Kingsley and Herman C. Somers. Marshall E. Dimock was in the War Shipping Administration, Charles S. Hyneman in the Federal Communications Commission, Arthur W. Macmahon in the State Department, John D. Millett in the Army Service Forces (Washington), and David B. Truman in the Department of Agriculture. Luther Gulick served in a number of agencies, and some persons listed above served in agencies additional to those with which I have identified them.

25. One indication was the fate of the President's order (drafted by the Bureau of the Budget) that the war agencies should prepare their *administrative* histories. As is evident in the published products, a number of us in charge of the agency histories reinterpreted the order broadly, sometimes rebelliously, as a call for capturing and recording the evolution of *both* policy and administration, with the emphasis on the former, and with the latter interpreted in terms of policy impact.

26. Fritz Morstein Marx (ed.), (New York: Prentice-Hall, Inc., 1946); a second edition appeared in 1959. The authors were (alphabetically) James W. Fesler, George A. Graham, V. O. Key, Jr., Avery Leiserson, Milton M. Mandell, Harvey C. Mansfield, John D. Millett, Fritz Morstein Marx, Don K. Price, Henry Reining, Jr., Wallace S. Sayre, Donald C. Stone, John A. Vieg, and Dwight Waldo.

27. Paul H. Appleby, *Big Democracy* (New York: Alfred A. Knopf, 1945); *Policy and Administration* (University, Ala.: University of Alabama Press, 1949); *Morality and Administration in Democratic Government* (Baton Rouge, La.: Louisiana State University Press,

1952). His books came forth in such short order that when he told me he had just finished a new book, my eyebrows must have lifted. For he qualified his statement by saying, "Oh, I still have to add the grace notes."

28. Roscoe C. Martin, "Paul Appleby and His Administrative World," in Martin (ed.), *Public Administration and Democracy: Essays in Honor of Paul H. Appleby* (Syracuse, N.Y.: Syracuse University Press, 1965), pp. 1–14, at p. 10.

29. Robert T. Golembiewski, " 'Maintenance' and 'Task' as Central Challenges in Public Administration," *Public Administration Review*, 34 (March/April, 1974), pp. 168–76.

30. At first the enterprise was called the Committee on Public Administration Cases; in 1951 it became the Inter-University Case Program. The people other than Stein who were most actively involved in the early stages were Paul Appleby, Merle Fainsod, Oliver Garceau, George Graham, Arthur Macmahon, Harvey Mansfield, Edward Mason, Don Price, and Wallace Sayre.

31. Edwin A. Bock, "Improving the Usefulness of the Case Study in Political Science," in Donald Freeman (ed.), *An Introduction to the Science of Politics* (New York: The Free Press, 1974). Stein's undergraduate major at Yale was in English, a point he enjoyed reminding me of.

32. He set forth his views with persuasive skill in the "Introduction" to Harold Stein (ed.), *Public Administration and Policy Development: A Case Book* (New York: Harcourt, Brace & Co., 1952, pp. ix–xlv); it is reprinted with slight alterations in Edwin A. Bock (ed.), *Essays on the Case Method in Public Administration* (Brussels: International Institute of Administrative Sciences, 1962), pp. 1–38.

33. The value of cases in teaching is so widely accepted that we forget that they were an innovation and that vigorous missionary efforts were necessary to overcome initially sluggish responses by faculty members. The individual cases did not fit neatly into the customary topical segments of public-administration courses, for each case was multifaceted. For a teacher to select the most useful cases called for his reading all the cases, and their number and, often, length were discouraging. The longer, complex cases required close study by the students, so that their assignment meant reluctant displacement of books and articles of analytical value. Further, the cases were problematic. They raised many questions but rarely offered answers. More often they suggested the complexity of real administrative life, the intractability of problems, and the obduracy of men with something to protect. Yet, of course, most of these difficulties also account for the cases' virtues as teaching materials.

34. It has not escaped my attention that there is a chicken-and-egg problem here, and I do not want to be misinterpreted as advocating the

random accumulation of bricks and hoping that they will eventually fit together to build the temple of science.

35. Commercially published studies of individual war agencies had wider currency than those published as government documents. E.g., Herman M. Somers, *Presidential Agency: The Office of War Mobilization and Reconversion* (Cambridge, Mass.: Harvard University Press, 1950), and Victor A. Thompson, *The Regulatory Process in OPA Rationing* (New York: King's Crown Press, 1950).

The following general works did not, as one might suppose, draw substantially on the war-agency histories: U.S. Bureau of the Budget, *The United States at War* (Washington, D.C.: U.S. Governing Printing Office, 1946); Luther Gulick, *Administrative Reflections from World War II* (University, Ala.: University of Alabama Press, 1948); *What We Learned in Public Administration During the War* (Washington, D.C.: Graduate School, U.S. Department of Agriculture, 1949). Some textbooks, it is true, did draw on war-agency histories as well as on the authors' own wartime experience. E.g., Marshall E. Dimock and Gladys O. Dimock, *Public Administration* (New York: Rinehart & Co., 1953); Merle Fainsod and Lincoln Gordon, *Government and the American Economy* (2nd edition, New York: W. W. Norton & Co., 1948); the (third edition with Joseph C. Palamountain, 1959).

36. Especially, Emmette S. Redford, *Administration of National Economic Control* (New York: Macmillan Co., 1952); and Marver H. Bernstein, *Regulating Business by Independent Commission* (Princeton, N.J.: Princeton University Press, 1955). For more particularized studies, see Emmette S. Redford (ed.), *Public Administration and Policy Formation* (Austin, Tex.: University of Texas Press, 1956), Lloyd D. Musolf, *Federal Examiners and the Conflict of Law and Administration* (Baltimore: The Johns Hopkins Press, 1953), and Murray J. Edelman, *The Licensing of Radio Services in the United States* (Urbana, Ill.: University of Illinois Press, 1950).

37. One legal scholar, bearding us in our own den, insisted on our incompetence, especially in the fields of administrative law and government regulation. Kenneth Culp Davis, "Reflections of a Law Professor on Instruction and Research in Public Administration," *American Political Science Review*, 47 (September, 1953), pp. 728–52; see also the exchange between Joseph P. Harris and Davis, Ibid., 48 (March, 1954), pp. 174–85. The dialogue between legal scholars and political scientists was not facilitated by lawyers' substitution of the generic term "administrative" for the special term "regulatory." This was only the beginning of a corruption of our language by disciplines with which we trafficked.

38. Guthrie S. Birkhead, Frederic N. Cleveland, Ernest Engelbert, James W. Fesler, Philip O. Foss, John M. Gaus, George A. Graham,

Charles M. Hardin, Henry C. Hart, Herbert Kaufman, Albert Lepaw-
sky, Grant McConnell, Charles McKinley, Arthur Maass, Hubert R.
Marshall, Roscoe C. Martin, Vincent Ostrom, Egbert S. Wengert,
Norman I. Wengert.

39. I need cite only three collaborative undertakings that together
span the period: James W. Fesler (ed.), "Government and Water Resources: A Symposium," *American Political Science Review,* 44 (September, 1950), pp. 575–649; another symposium, "Water Resources,"
Law and Contemporary Problems, 22 (Summer, 1957), pp. 323–537;
and Roscoe C. Martin, *et al., River Basin Administration and the Dela-
ware* (Syracuse, N.Y.: Syracuse University Press, 1960).

40. Arthur C. Maass, "The King's River Project," in Harold Stein
(ed.), *Public Administration and Policy Development* (New York:
Harcourt, Brace, 1952), pp. 533–72; and Maass, *Muddy Waters: The
Army Engineers and the Nation's Rivers* (Cambridge, Mass.: Harvard
University Press, 1951).

41. E.g., Edward C. Banfield on public housing, J. Leiper Freeman
on Indian affairs, and others cited earlier on other areas. Almost no
1946–1960 program-area studies survived to be among the thousand
books being cited in the late 1960s by even two of the forty "scholars
in public administration broadly defined" whose choices were relied
on for Howard E. McCurdy, *Public Administration: A Bibliography*
(Washington, D.C.: College of Public Affairs, American University,
1972).

42. Dwight Waldo, *The Administrative State: The Political Theory
of Public Administration* (New York: Ronald Press, 1948). See also
Waldo, "The Administrative State Revisited," *Public Administration
Review,* 25 (March, 1965), pp. 5–30.

43. *American Political Science Review,* 42 (August, 1948), pp. 782 f.

44. Howard E. McCurdy, *Public Administration: A Bibliography*
(Washington, D.C.: College of Public Affairs, American University,
1972), p. 80.

45. See, for example, his "Development of Theory of Democratic
Administration," together with spirited comment by Herbert Simon
and reply by Waldo, *American Political Science Review,* 46 (March,
1952), pp. 81–103, and (June, 1952), pp. 494–503.

46. Herbert Simon, *Administrative Behavior: A Study of Decision-
Making Processes in Administrative Organization* (New York: Macmillan Co., 1947), See also Simon's introduction to the second edition
(1957).

47. *Journal of Politics,* 10 (February, 1948), pp. 187–89.

48. Ironically, though, Waldo's chapter for the Morstein Marx textbook was entitled "Government by Procedure." Op. cit., pp. 381–99.
See note 26. Not surprisingly, he made the subject significant.

49. James G. March and Herbert Simon, *Organizations* (New York:

John Wiley & Sons, 1958).

50. Dwight Waldo, "Theory of Organization: Status and Problems," in Waldo, et al., *The Study of Organizational Behavior: Status, Problems, and Trends* (Washington, D.C.: American Society for Public Administration, 1966), p. 17. There were no entries for Appleby, Bernstein, Herring, Hyneman, Long, Maass, or Waldo, or for the war-agency histories, or for the case studies of the Inter-University Case Program. The chapters on "Cognitive Limits on Rationality" and "Planning and Innovation in Organizations" were written on the specific assumption that "empirical evidence of a reliable and persuasive kind is almost nonexistent."

For the 1965 *Handbook of Organizations*, March and an associate checked the citations made in twelve recent works on organizational behavior (including two by political scientists—Robert Presthus and Victor Thompson). To illustrate his point that recent books were the most frequently cited, March noted that in Simon's 1947 *Administrative Behavior* there had been "a fair number of references to a literature that has, for the most part, disappeared from the citation lists; in particular, we find a number of references to research monographs in public administration." James G. March (ed.), *Handbook of Organizations* (Chicago: Rand McNally & Co., 1965), p. xiii. The vanishing act seems to be in part the prestidigative achievement of March and Simon themselves.

51. What Simon was trying to say has been much mooted, and I am not here attempting to add to learned commentary on the matter.

52. Robert A. Dahl, "The Science of Public Administration," *Public Administration Review*, 7 (Winter, 1947), pp. 1–11. See also the comments on the article by Herbert A. Simon in ibid. (Summer, 1947), pp. 200–203, and L. Urwick in ibid., 17 (Spring, 1957), pp. 77–82. All three are conveniently together in Claude E. Hawley and Ruth G. Weintraub (eds.), *Administrative Questions and Political Answers* (New York: D. Van Nostrand Co., 1966), pp. 23–43.

Dahl, as Waldo, wrote his doctoral dissertation under Francis W. Coker at Yale University, but on a political-theory topic distant from public administration. However, he served an internship with the National Institute of Public Affairs and held positions in the Department of Agriculture and the War Production Board.

53. His articles are conveniently assembled in Norton E. Long, *The Polity* (Chicago: Rand McNally & Co., 1962).

54. It is one of life's disapointments that Young Turks became Old Turks. Men now young may doubt that we were ever rebels. Yet it is a historical fact that within the American Political Science Association a number of us were accused of attempting to undermine the Old Guard, to democratize governance of the Association, and to reorient the *American Political Science Review*.

55. Bertram M. Gross, in *American Political Science Review*, 44 (September, 1950), pp. 742–48; David B. Truman, *The Governmental Process* (New York: Alfred A. Knopf, 1951); Robert A. Dahl and Charles E. Lindblom, *Politics, Economics, and Welfare* (New York: Harper & Co., 1953).

56. See, especially, Glendon A. Schubert, *The Public Interest* (New York: The Free Press, 1960). I am aware that the term "myth" has both a neutrally descriptive and a denigrative meaning. In practice, I now believe, writers and teachers cannot dissipate the deprecatory aura surrounding the term in ordinary language.

57. For a critical assessment of the established approaches to local government, see Lawrence J. R. Herson, "The Lost World of Municipal Government," *American Political Science Review*, 51 (June, 1957), pp. 330–45. Leading examples of the new pluralist approach are: Robert A. Dahl, *Who Governs? Democracy and Power in an American City* (New Haven, Conn.: Yale University Press, 1961); Nelson W. Polsby, *Community Power and Political Theory* (New Haven, Conn.,: Yale University Press, 1963); and Raymond E. Wolfinger, *The Politics of Progress* (Englewood Cliffs, N.J.: Prentice-Hall, Inc., 1974). The Polsby and Wolfinger books are revisions of doctoral dissertations.

58. The classic, nonpolemical assessment is Robert A. Dahl, "The Behavioral Approach in Political Science: Epitaph for a Monument to a Successful Protest," *American Political Science Review*, 55 (December, 1961), pp. 763–72.

59. Even before the behavioral revolution took hold, Herbert Simon wrote, "We cannot accept Mr. Dahl's reassuring answer that it is unnecessary for the student of public administration to become a psychologist and that merely he 'must be capable of using the investigations of the psychiatrist and sociologist'. . . .

"The research worker in administration must consider himself not merely a person whose work *is related to* social psychology, but a person who *is* a social psychologist concentrating in a particular special area of human behavior." "A Comment on 'The Science of Public Administration,' " *Public Administration Review*, 7 (Summer, 1947), pp. 202 f. (emphasis in original).

60. Early encounters may not be representative. Mine were: as reader of a thesis that ranked the authors of public-administration textbooks on their valuation of democracy by frequency of their use of the term itself; as commentator on an annual-meeting paper that ranked subordinates' influence on a superior in a government bureau by frequency of each subordinate's conferences with the superior (ignoring range and significance of matters discussed); and as reader of dissertations whose first chapter's promise of rigorous methodology and important findings must have been penned before the authors ex-

perienced disappointments in field research and found that critical gaps in analysis occurred when attempted correlations failed tests of significance. As late as 1966 the American Political Science Association's Committee on the Leonard D. White Dissertation Award reported that "there is something to be said for advising students to write their first chapter last."

Senior political scientists published behavioral research that was generally of a much higher quality, perhaps because they were more eclectic than the juniors, were well grounded in history and the classics of political theory, and had enough experience to be more tentative than dogmatic.

61. Actually, even before systems analysts rediscovered such topics, they received fitful attention from highly sophisticated scholars. Both Herbert A. Simon and William J. Gore devoted substantial attention to local fire departments: Simon, et al., *Fire Losses and Fire Risks* (Berkeley, Cal.: Bureau of Public Administration, University of California, 1943); Gore, *Administrative Decision-Making: A Heuristic Model* (New York: John Wiley & Sons, 1964), which draws on his eighteen-month study of the Lawrence, Kansas fire department. Note also Clarence E. Ridley and Herbert A. Simon, *Measuring Municipal Activities* (Chicago: International City Managers' Association, 1940; 2nd edition, 1943); and Simon, et al., *Determining Work Loads for Professional Satff in a Public Welfare Agency* (Berkeley, Cal.: Bureau of Public Administration, University of California, 1941).

In contrast to bureau directors of the how-to-do-it orientation, Roscoe C. Martin conceived, and the University of Alabama's Bureau of Public Administration sponsored, the research project by V. O. Key, Jr., and Alexander Heard that resulted in the notable *Southern Politics* (New York: Alfred A. Knopf, 1949).

62. The advantage was relative, not absolute. State and local election and legislative data were often unpublished, unavailable, or unreliable. As Lindsay Rogers observed, the statistical records of baseball were far more complete and reliable than those of politics. The first of the biennial data volumes, *America Votes*, prepared by Richard Scammon, appeared in 1956.

63. Most behavioral scholars were initially ahistorical, addressing themselves to interpreting, or to developing models from, the most recent opinion surveys, elections, and Congresses. Yet if it is true, as the incrementalists were to argue, that current governance rests on the accumulation over time of policies and programs and that new decisions alter that inherited corpus only marginally, then the behavioralists were focusing not on the government's principal course but on slight and often temporary adjustments of that course. This was curable. V. O. Key, Jr. was never ahistorical (as his theory of critical

elections attests) and, as its data bank grew, the Survey Research Center undertook longitudinal studies.

64. Daniel 5, verses 25–28.

65. Morris Janowitz, Deil Wright, and William Delany, *Public Administration and the Public: Perspectives Toward Government in a Metropolitan Community* (Ann Arbor, Mich.: Bureau of Government, Institute of Public Administration, University of Michigan, 1958); W. Lloyd Warner, Paul P. Van Riper, Norman H. Martin, and Orvin F. Collins, *The American Federal Executive* (New Haven, Conn.: Yale University Press, 1963), based on data collected in 1959.

66. Herbert Kaufman, *The Forest Ranger* (Baltimore: Johns Hopkins Press, 1960).

67. Each set of students (marked off by semicolons) were in Yale University's basic graduate public-administration seminar at the same time, except the last set who were together in a graduate seminar on regulatory administration. The list is incomplete (even as a selection of now familiar names), as it is drawn from my course lists and so does not include other students taught by my colleague Herbert Kaufman.

68. However, economics in this period (a) served as a model for political science, (b) deemphasized its fields that had traditional linkages to political science. The major advances in macroeconomics stood as standing rebukes to political science's backwardness in both theory and data manipulation. The rise of macroeconomics in turn led to decline in the status of the economic-history and business-regulation fields, to further distancing of economics from business administration, and to public-finance courses' shifting of interest to the role of fiscal measures in management of the whole economy.

69. *From Max Weber: Essays in Sociology,* translated, edited, and with an introduction by H. H. Gerth and C. Wright Mills (New York: Oxford University Press, 1946); *The Theory of Social and Economic Organization,* translated by A. M. Henderson and Talcott Parsons, edited with an introduction by Talcott Parsons (New York: The Free Press, 1947).

70. A concise and typically lucid treatment is Martin Landau's "On the Use of Functional Analysis in American Political Science," in Landau, *Political Theory and Political Science* (New York: Macmillan Co., 1972), pp. 103–21.

71. But note Talcott Parsons, "Suggestions for a Sociological Approach to The Theory of Organizations," *Administrative Science Quarterly,* 1 (June and September, 1956), pp. 63–85, 225–39.

72. Robert K. Merton, *Social Theory and Social Structure* (Glencoe, Ill.: The Free Press, 1949; 2nd edition, 1957). Note especially "Bureaucratic Structures and Personality" and "Role of the Intellectual in Public Bureaucracy."

73. Philip Selznick, *TVA and the Grass Roots* (New York: Harper & Row, 1949).
74. Philip Selznick, *Leadership in Administration* (New York: Row, Peterson, 1957).
75. Robert K. Merton, et al., *Reader in Bureaucracy* (Glencoe, Ill.: The Free Press, 1952).
76. An excellent conspectus is W. Richard Scott, "Theory of Organizations," in Robert E. L. Faris (ed.), *Handbook of Modern Sociology* (Chicago: Rand McNally & Co., 1964), pp. 485–529.
77. E.g., Joseph E. McLean (ed.), *The Public Service and University Education* (Princeton, N.J.: Princeton University Press, 1949); John J. Corson, *Executives for the Federal Service* (New York: Columbia University Press, 1952); American Assembly, *The Federal Government Service*, edited by Wallace S. Sayre (Englewood Cliffs, N.J.: Prentice-Hall, Inc., 1954; 2nd edition, 1965); Paul T. David and Ross Pollock, *Executives for Government* (Washington, D.C.: The Brookings Institution, 1957); Marver H. Bernstein, *The Job of the Federal Executive* (Washington, D.C.: The Brookings Institution, 1958); and the Task Force reports on personnel for the first and second U.S. (Hoover) Commissions on Organization of the Executive Branch of the Government (Washington, D.C.: U.S. Government Printing Office, 1949 and 1955).
78. Robert T. Golembiewski, "Small Groups and Large Organizations," in James G. March (ed.), *Handbook of Organizations* (Chicago: Rand McNally & Co., 1965), pp. 87–141, at p. 87.
79. James G. March and Herbert Simon, *Organizations* (New York: John Wiley & Sons, 1958); Robert T. Golembiewski, *The Small Group* (Chicago: University of Chicago Press, 1962), and *Behavior and Organization* (Chicago: Rand McNally & Co., 1962), both drawing in part on his 1958 doctoral dissertation; Robert V. Presthus, *The Organizational Society* (New York: Alfred A. Knopf, 1962) and his chapters in John M. Pfiffner and Presthus, *Public Administration* (New York: The Ronald Press, 3rd edition, 1953, and 4th edition, 1960).
80. I refer only to what became dubbed "formal, complex organizations," with full-time employees as the members, although some writers generalized across them *and* voluntary membership organizations such as clubs and associations.
81. Here, as elsewhere in this paper, I must speak about general tendencies, without noting the more percipient scholars who modified or rejected such tendencies. "Open" systems theory developed as a lowerer of organizational boundaries, but did not address itself to the peculiarities of the public sector. The relatively recent realization (!) that other organizations in frequent interchange relations with a particular organization should be regarded as more salient than just

"everything out there" in the environment does not meet the problem directly. "Constraints" and "parameters" limiting an organization's autonomous decision making are helpful concepts, though their inadequacy seems clear from any of a number of more complex case studies of governmental decision making.

82. His academic posts, beginning in 1942, were at the Illinois Institute of Technology and in the Graduate School of Industrial Administration at the Carnegie Institute of Technology (later Carnegie-Mellon University). James G. March, whose first eleven faculty years were at the California Institute of Technology, referred to March and Simon's *Organizations* as "a recent book dealing extensively with business organizations." March, in Austin Ranney (ed.), *Essays on the Behavioral Study of Politics* (Urbana, Ill.: University of Illinois Press, 1962), p. 191.

83. Robert A. Gordon and James E. Howell, *Higher Education for Business* (New York: Columbia University Press, 1959); Frank C. Pierson, et al., *The Education of American Businessmen* (New York: McGraw-Hill Book Co., 1959). Gordon and Howell write: 'By *management analysis* we mean an explicitly rational approach to the making of decisions about the allocation of resources within the firm. . . .

"The methods available for a scientific or rational approach to managerial decision-making can be viewed broadly or narrowly. Broadly considered, they include any techniques that help the decision-maker to discover and evaluate alternatives and to make that choice which seems, in the light of given objectives, to be most rational.

"In a narrower and more technical sense, management analysis . . . draws on such fields as statistical decision theory, mathematical programming, inventory theory, and motion economy, and includes much of what goes under the heading of operations analysis.

"*Organization theory*, or 'theory of administration,' is concerned with the scientific study of human behavior in organizations. It deals with how human beings function in organizations, with what conditions are necessary to secure effective action within organizations, and with the problems that arise in connection with making and implementing decisions in an organizational context." Gordon and Howell, *Higher Education for Business*, pp. 179 f. Note that "decision making" figures in both the rational-analysis and human-behavior fields of study.

84. Charles E. Lindblom, "The Science of 'Muddling Through,'" *Public Administration Review*, 19 (Spring, 1959), pp. 79–88.

85. Leonard D. White, *The Federalists* (1948), *The Jeffersonians* (1951), *The Jacksonians* (1954), and *The Republican Era* (1958), all published in New York by the Macmillan Company.

86. Lynton K. Caldwell, *The Administrative Theories of Hamilton*

and Jefferson (Chicago: University of Chicago Press, 1944); Paul P. Van Riper, *History of the United States Civil Service* (Evanston, Ill.: Row, Peterson & Co., 1958); Herbert Kaufman, "The Growth of the Federal Personnel System," in American Assembly, *The Federal Government Service*, edited by Wallace S. Sayre (New York: Columbia University, 1954), pp. 7–69; and Kaufman, "Emerging Conflicts in the Doctrines of Public Administration," *American Political Science Review*, 50 (December, 1956), pp. 1057–73.

87. Carl J. Friedrich, *Constitutional Government and Politics* (1937, 1941), and *Constitutional Government and Democracy* (1946, 1950, 1968, the last published at Waltham, Massachusetts by Blaisdell Publishing Co.), especially the classic chapter, "Bureaucracy: The Core of Modern Government"; Fritz Morstein Marx, *The Administrative State* (Chicago: University of Chicago Press, 1957).

88. E.g., Alfred Diamant, "The Relevance of Comparative Politics to the Study of Comparative Administration," *Administrative Science Quarterly*, 5 (June, 1960), pp. 87–112.

During the 1950s, financial support for foreign-area studies and extensive involvement of American scholars in public administration abroad both focused on what were at first called "backward," "undeveloped," or "underdeveloped" countries. This skewing (a necessary correction of an earlier skewing) may have had intellectual consequences we have not yet calculated. Within the Comparative Administration Group in the 1960s, Diamant was largely responsible for establishment of a Europe Committee—considerably after committees had been set up for the less-developed continents. In the decade of the 1950s, the scholarly contributors on European administration were mostly identified with the "comparative government and politics" field —e.g., Friedrich, Morstein Marx, Taylor Cole, Henry Ehrmann, and Samuel Beer. Cole's contributions in that and earlier decades remarkably dealt with bureaucracy in Switzerland, Germany, Italy, and Canada.

89. Albert Lepawsky (ed.), *Administration* (New York: Alfred A. Knopf, 1949); William J. Siffin (ed.), *Toward the Comparative Study of Public Administration* (Bloomington, Ind.: Department of Government, Indiana University, 1959); Ferrel Heady and Sybil L. Stokes, *Comparative Public Administration: An Annotated Bibliography* (Ann Arbor, Mich.: Institute of Public Administration, University of Michigan, 1960); Fred W. Riggs, *The Ecology of Public Administration* (New York: Asia Publishing House, 1961).

90. The first such course at Yale University, introduced in 1955/56, was jointly taught by Herbert Kaufman, Fred W. Riggs, and Walter R. Sharp.

91. These observations are not, as some might suppose, a criticism of Fred W. Riggs. He had a natural, not an induced, taste for theoriz-

ing and had a formidable command of the descriptive literature on a large number of politico-administrative systems.

92. William Blake, "Jerusalem," in *The Portable Blake*, edited by Alfred Kazin (New York: Viking Press, 1946), p. 460.

93. The only comprehensive survey of the literature to my knowledge is Robert L. Peabody and Francis E. Rourke, "Public Bureaucracies," in James G. March (ed.), *Handbook of Organizations* (Chicago: Rand McNally & Co., 1965), pp. 802–37.

I have commented earlier on our failure, at a lower level of generality, to distill the findings of American agency histories and of monographs on individual foreign nations.

94. Gabriel A. Almond, "A Functional Approach to Comparative Politics," in Almond and James S. Coleman (eds.), *The Politics of Developing Areas* (Princeton: Princeton University Press, 1960). For a discerning, critical assessment of the utility of the structural-functional approach in comparative studies, see Joseph LaPalombara, "Parsimony and Empiricism in Comparative Politics: An Anti-Scholastic View," in Robert T. Holt and John E. Turner (eds.), *The Methodology of Comparative Research* (New York: The Free Press, 1970), pp. 123–49.

95. An important evidence of this is Dwight Waldo, "Organization Theory: An Elephantine Problem," *Public Administration Review*, 21 (Autumn, 1961), pp. 210–25. Six books are reviewed; none of the authors is a political scientist and, to revive an earlier theme in my paper, none, as I read the review, is familiar with our literature. Waldo comments, ". . . those concerned with organization theory are denying themselves a source of insight and even, I venture to think, of scientific conclusions and hypotheses when they scorn the traditional literature of social and political theory," p. 225.

96. Informed and critical reviews of trends in the study of public administration are numerous. I chose the odd strategy of not reading them again while preparing this paper, believing that that exercise would be discouraging ("It's all been said before") and might result in my quoting and paraphrasing them, instead of making my own interpretations. Eleven such reviews published between 1950 and 1956 were listed in my "Administrative Literature and the Second Hoover Commission Reports" (itself such a review, in part), *American Political Science Review*, 51 (March, 1957), pp. 135–57, at p. 135, and I shall not repeat the citations here. Among later reviews that include the 1946–1960 period in their coverage are: André Molitor, *The University Teaching of Social Sciences: Public Administration* (Paris: United Nations Educational, Scientific, and Cultural Organization, 1959); Martin Landau, "Political Science and Public Administration: 'Field' and the Concept of Decision-Making," in Sidney Mailick and Edward H. Van Ness (eds.), *Concepts and Issues in Administrative Behavior*

(Englewood Cliffs, N.J.. Prentice-Hall, Inc., 1962), pp. 1–28; Thomas J. Davy, "Public Administration as a Field of Study in the United States," *International Review of Administrative Sciences*, 28 (1962), pp. 63–78; Robert L. Peabody and Francis E. Rourke, "Public Bureaucracies," in James G. March (ed.), *Handbook of Organizations* (Chicago: Rand McNally & Co., 1965), pp. 802–37; Lynton K. Caldwell, "Public Administration and the Universities: A Half-Century of Development," *Public Administration Review*, 25 (March, 1965), pp. 53–60; Keith M. Henderson, *Emerging Synthesis in American Public Administration* (New York: Asia Publishing House, 1966); Dwight Waldo, "Public Administration," *International Encyclopedia of the Social Sciences* (New York: Crowell, Collier and Macmillan, Inc., 1968), and numerous journal articles; Alan A. Altshuler, "The Study of American Public Administration," in Altshuler (ed.), *The Politics of the Federal Bureaucracy* (New York: Dodd, Mead & Co., 1968), pp. 55–72; Peter Self, *Administrative Theories and Politics* (London: George Allen & Unwin, 1972), especially pp. 19–54; Howard E. McCurdy, *Public Administration: A Bibliography* (Washington, D.C.: College of Public Affairs, American University, 1972), especially pp. 9–28; Robert T. Golembiewski, "Public Administration and Public Policy: An Analysis of Developmental Phases," in Robert N. Spadaro (ed.), *Toward Understanding Public Policy* (Lexington, Mass.: D. C. Heath & Co., 1975). I have omitted from this selection the numerous reviews of trends in special fields, such as organization theory and comparative public administration.

4. The Trauma of Politics: Public Administration in the Sixties

ALLEN SCHICK

It was the best of times. It was the worst of times. It was a time of hope. It was a time of despair. It was a time of bringing together. It was a time of tearing apart. It was a time of doing. It was a time of not knowing what to do.

Amidst all the contradictions, it was throughout a period of turbulence. The 1960s were never at rest, driven always by exigencies of the moment or aspirations for the future. The decade began with confidence and vigor, expressed by John Kennedy on May 25, 1961, when he placed before the American people, "the goal, before this decade is out, of landing a man on the moon and returning him safely to the earth." So typical in promise, this was one of the few to be achieved during the decade. Other new frontiers were no less venturesome, closer to home, but further from realization when the decade ended on a different theme. Poverty did not cease from the face of the land, slums still sprawled where cities were not yet rebuilt, black and white did not yet stand on level ground. Richard Nixon closed the decade with a plea "to lower our voice." "America has suffered from a fever of words; from inflated rhetoric that promises more than it can deliver."[1] The decade bequeathed to America the legislative harvest of a Great Society and the searing heritage of Vietnam and Watts.

Out of the decade came an overwhelming sense of bewilderment as statistics of success clashed with verdicts of failure. Most of the conventional measures were favorable: The GNP escalated from $500 billion to the brink of a trillon-dollar economy; substandard housing dropped from 8.4 million to 4.7 million units; college enrollments soared from 3.7 million to 8.5 million; Ph.D. production tripled from 9,800 to 29,800; households owning television sets rose from 45 to 60 million.[2] The tangible fruits of an affluent society were available to more Americans than ever before: more dishwashers, more second cars, more vacation homes, more . . .

Where statistics once produced understanding and consensus, they now spawned new confusions. James S. Coleman triggered intellectual strife with his 1965 claim that the enrichment of educational inputs does not significantly improve school performance.[3] A team of RAND analysts canvassed the vast literature of educational innovation for the President's Commission on School Finance and reported its dismal conclusion: "research has found nothing that consistently and unambiguously makes a difference in student outcomes . . . research has not discovered any educational practice (or set of practices) that offers a high probability of success over time and place."[4]

The sense of failure infected older programs such as urban renewal and newer ones such as model cities, new towns, and home-ownership. A bewildering array of manpower programs—JOBS, WIN, CAMPS, CEP, etc.—did not markedly expand the work opportunities of the poor. LEAA did not make the streets safe and during the decade the incidence of violent crimes zoomed from 159 to 397 per 100,000 population. Even when the statistics showed real improvement—such as a sharp decline in infant mortality rates or a narrowing of the gap between black and white incomes—they did not seem to impact on the public consciousness. "Quality-of-life" indicators were coming into vogue at the end of the decade, as many Americans questioned the value of economic growth and the comforts it brought to them. Things that were not measured (for example, satisfaction with one's neighborhood) came to be regarded as more vital and relevant than things that were measured (such as the availability of indoor plumbing).

Agenda for the Nation, issued by the Brookings Institution, pointed to "the central paradox of American society in 1969: on the one hand, we are a nation which sees itself as wracked and divided over problems of poverty, riots, race, slums, unemployment, and crime; on the other hand, we are a nation which is clearly enjoying high prosperity, rapid economic growth, and a steady diffusion of affluence at a rate almost unimaginable a decade ago."[5] The Brookings group acknowledged that "the paradox cannot be simply resolved," but it urged further action rather than pause or stocktaking: "In a setting so turbulent, it is always a tempting option to postpone decision making, in the hope that the passage of time will bring greater certainty; but this is a luxury which governments are often denied."[6] Nevertheless, the Nixon administration sponsored few program innovations and though it was unable to reverse most of the initiatives of the 1960s, it sought a lower federal profile.

ANOTHER HOPE, ANOTHER DISAPPOINTMENT

PPB was another attempt at innovation that began with exciting prospects and ended in disappointment. Perhaps the major administrative innovation of the decade, its architects were not public administrators but economic and systems analysts newly come to governmental power. When Planning-Programming-Budgeting was launched on a government-wide basis in August, 1965, President Johnson spoke with the same optimism that infected his Great Society initiatives:[7]

> This morning I have just concluded a breakfast meeting with the Cabinet and with the heads of Federal agencies. I have asked each of them to immediately begin to introduce a very new and very revolutionary system of planning and budgeting and programming throughout the vast Federal Government—so that through the tools of modern management the full promise of a finer life can be brought to every American at the lowest possible cost.

PPB did not succeed, at least in terms of reorientating federal budgeting from a routine for financing public bureaucracies to an analytic determination of the purposes of American government. After several years of moribund existence, PPB was quietly discarded in June, 1971.[8] Elements survive in some agencies, particularly in the Defense Department and HEW, though nowhere with the salience and expectations it possessed at the start.

When PPB was started, government confidence in its ability to liquidate hard-core social and human problems was pervasive. During the peak Great Society years of 1964 and 1965 scores of new programs sprang into being with little or no pretesting. Program planners were sure that they could rebuild cities, end poverty, bring educational opportunity to all. The problems would be as tractable in health care as in military hardware, the objectives as reachable in urban construction as in space exploration. All that was required was the right combination of political will, program resources, and analytic know-how. The new analytic elite ("the best and the brightest") possessed an arrogance of intellect that swept aside all doubt. They could fine-tune the economy, specify in advance the cost and performance of a C-5A with contractual exactitude, predict what each incremental dollar would buy in lower mortality or accident rates. They were the answer men of American bureaupolitics, carrying their specialized skills and outlooks from Defense to HEW, to all government.

PPB turned out to be one of the closing episodes of the Great Society. By the summer of 1965 almost all of the new programs had been formulated, much more as the products of legislative frenzy than of analytic search. Only weeks before PPB was announced, American ground forces took over prime responsibility for fighting in Vietnam, and Watts exploded.[9] Once these fateful events escalated to their awesome impacts, America no longer was certain it had the answers. Nor did it have the money or the will for social innovation. Thus by the time PPB had moved from press release to budgetary realities, the conditions that spawned it had vanished. As the urban conflagration spread to additional cities, the war on poverty settled for precarious tokenism (keeping OEO alive and the summers cool), and the market for bold analysis dried up.

There was an affinity between the failure of PPB and the failure of domestic programs. The technology for choice could not be successful if the choices themselves were not. Both budget reform and program innovation were change-oriented, though both accepted—and ultimately were judged by—conventional definitions of success. Both were burdened with the task of accommodating to the institutions they sought to change.

WHAT WENT WRONG?

After the decade was over, there was an abundance of explanations of what had gone wrong. Some thought that the problem was a classic case of expectations growing faster than real gains, that what de Tocqueville wrote of the *ancien régime* had afflicted American society. *Toward a Social Report* (the first fruit of the social-indicators movement) issued in the last days of the Johnson regime sided with this viewpoint: "It has been wisely said that the conservatism of the destitute is as profound as that of the privileged."[10]

Some attributed the turbulence of the 1960s to exogenous factors such as the Vietnam debacle or the extraordinary growth in the youth population.[11] Others were less optimistic and found a social or economic determinism that cannot be uprooted by conventional governmental intervention. Banfield wrote of a lower class that is unable to defer immediate gratification in favor of future gain and that misuses the resources and opportunities granted by a beneficent government. For Edward C. Banfield, the chief lesson of the 1960s was the helplessness of government: "If what is, in general, feasible is not acceptable, the reverse is also true: what is acceptable is not, in general, feasible."[12] Using an entirely different methodology, Jay Forrester came to a similar conclusion, the cities are driven by an economic dynamic that renders their intuitive responses to urban poverty counterproductive. He argued that the very steps taken to meliorate the plight of the poor will condemn them to even greater poverty.[13]

Peter Drucker found a fundamental error in the policies of the 1960s: governments cannot do; they only can govern: "Any attempt to combine governing with 'doing' on a large scale, paralyzes the decision-making capacity. Any attempt to have decision-making organs actually 'do,' also means very poor 'doing.' They are not fundamentally concerned with it."[14] Drucker preached "reprivitization" to get government out of the business of doing. Coming to the same conclusion from different premises, Milton

Friedman implied that the federal government could efficiently handle the distribution of money (through a negative income tax) but would fail if it ventured into program operation.

Some thought that the government had not committed sufficient resources or support. While domestic spending climbed sharply in the 1960s, it never reached the heights expected by some Great Society planners. Despite the guns-and-butter rhetoric of a beleaguered President, the poor got much less than they wanted. If the gap between authorizations and appropriations is used as a measure of the shortfall, social expenditures in the late 1960s were billions of dollars below the target.[15] *Counterbudget,* published by the Urban Coalition in 1971, advocated a tripling of income-maintenance expenditures along with substantial boosts for health, education, and job training.[16]

Some thought that the problem wasn't money but knowledge about what to do with it. Moynihan castigated social scientists for preaching community-action programs based on social ideology rather than on social science.[17] Most of the major programs formulated during the first part of the decade underwent little prior analysis. But after the legislative ferment had cooled, during the second half of the decade, there was explosive growth in program analysis, particularly of the stern cost-effectiveness variety. As a consequence, there was widening awareness of program deficiencies. "What has changed," Alice Rivlin suggested, "is our *perception* of our ignorance. We now know that we do not know. The analysts who have addressed themselves to the problems of producing social services have been partially responsible for exposing this ignorance. They have raised new questions, and revealed the lack of answers."[18]

America was in a hurry during the 1960s, never possessed of sufficient patience to wait for results in the next decade or the next generation. Hard core human problems had to be eradicated in the ten months of the school year or the two years of a political term. In retrospect there is reason to believe that the decade produced substantial achievements. There have been notable gains in the equalization of opportunities and in civil rights. Health care has been made more widely available, though the cost has been astronomical. The number of persons below the official poverty line has dropped markedly since the early 1960s. Even the precipitous climb in AFDC rolls could be interpreted as an indicator of success: public assistance finally reached millions of previously excluded persons.

On the whole, success seemed to come easier when the government had full command of a program than when its activities merely were inputs into other social processes. In the category of success, surely one of the most distinguished was the achievement of the space mission set early in the decade. The moon landing—and the many important antecedent activities that were essential for it—was facilitated by the stretching of administrative science and practice to accommodate the new large-scale enterprise. There was the same bold use of contractors that had characterized the atomic energy program two decades earlier, imaginative use of project-management concepts, and a breaking away from conventional budgetary and personnel controls.

But regardless of the ultimate verdict, in the heat of the 1960s there were few who claimed success for the billions of dollars and the policy initiatives dedicated to social change.

ADMINISTRATIVE FAILURE

In official quarters, much of the blame was placed on the administrative infirmities of American government. Breakdowns had occurred in the "delivery" system, a term which suggested that there was no fault with the purpose or the policy but that good programs were not being properly administered. The delivery theory was appealing because it explained why money and energy pumped in at the national end was not getting results at the local level. Social services were not getting through to their intended clients, health care was not reaching the indigent, compensatory education was not being served the disadvantaged. The long supply lines from Washington to the community were being disrupted by intergovernmental and interdepartmental barricades.

According to the delivery theory, public administration was well prepared for conventional operations in which policymaking and implementation are joined in the same government or agency.

But in the 1960s, as programs spilled over their political and organizational boundaries, it became difficult to deliver the right benefit to the right client. The spillovers also reached to the private sector as extragovernmental institutions (such as community-action agencies) were established to assist those who were not being adequately served by the administrative structure. Many of the basic problems were not new but were rooted in the character of federalism or in the tension between the field and the center. But the problems were compounded by the enormous increase in grant programs, each with its own eligibility rules, funding arrangements, administrative procedures, etc.

Delivery is a special case in the problem of implementation.[19] It does not concern the full range of POSDCORB activities, but it addresses the relationship between the administrator and the client. In most instances, problems in delivery arise because the administrator is unable to reach the client or cannot establish a satisfactory rapport with him. Stated this way, delivery essentially is a political problem that has to do more with class and power than with administrative procedures. In anticipation of these problems, many Great Society programs were designed to vest political power in disadvantaged groups by opening up the administrative process to their participation. Community action and model cities provided new channels of representation and leadership. The strategy was to give power to the poor, and with that universal currency they could acquire status, wealth, self-esteem, organization, and the other essential possessions of a pluralist society. This required a tearing down of any barrier between political and administrative practice. Elections, representation, advocacy—the heart of the political process—were to be introduced into the administrative arena. Federal assistance programs were proliferated in order to give the poor their own programs and their own administrative units in the same manner that "interest-group liberalism" customarily provided political and administrative power to the advantaged sectors of the American polity. Project grants were favored because they enabled federal agencies to function on behalf of groups that were stronger in Washington than in their own communities. The federal government forged more direct grant-in-aid relationships with cities, bypassing the states (which still were dominated by rural interests) in order to reach the areas where the problems were concentrated.

But if the delivery mechanisms of the 1960s were intended to redress the powerlessness of the poor and the weak, they also generated a great deal of administrative disarray. A catalog of administrative deficiencies would have included: too many categorical grant programs; overlapping planning requirements; lack of information; insufficient field authority to approve projects; overlapping regional boundaries; unrealistic federal standards.[20] In most instances, the problems appeared to be conventional (inadequate coordination); so, too, were many of the remedies sought. Cabinet status was accorded to Housing and Urban Development and to Transportation, but proposals to realign existing departments made little headway.[21] Nothing was done about Health, Education, and Welfare, the domestic conglomerate that one secretary wanted to split among its three functional constituencies and another wanted to convert into a superdepartment.[22] Interagency committees and agreements were popular but rarely successful: between 1961 and 1966, at least seventeen executive orders provided for the coordination of intergovernmental programs.[23] Convenor authority was given to HUD for urban affairs and to Agriculture for rural policy, but it proved difficult for an administrative agency to lead its peers. Modest steps were taken toward grant consolidation (Partnership for Health) and proposals were advanced for grant simplification and joint funding, yet the number of domestic-assistance programs continued to climb. At the local level, authority for regional planning and coordination was seeded in the Demonstration Cities and Metropolitan Development Act of 1966 and in the Intergovernment Cooperation Act of 1968.[24]

Problems of intergovernmental and interdepartmental management escalated to the Presidential level as White House functionaries took over tasks previously handled by operating agencies. But the Presidency which had operated with task force frenzy during the formative years of the Great Society lacked the staying power to move its programs through the bureaucratic labyrinth. The President promised to build a neighborhood service center in every ghetto, but the participating agencies wrangled endlessly over finances and purpose. The President had an idea to turn surplus federal lands into new towns, but years later the land was still vacant.[25] The administrative-management section in the Bureau of the Budget had become a "depressed area" and lacked the standing it had held two decades earlier.[26] The Budget Bureau requested funds to reestablish field offices (which had been terminated in 1953), but it was turned down by Congress, which was unwilling to lodge a presidential presence in the field. President Johnson convened a Task Force on Government Organization that (in an unpublished report) urged the placement of a coordination staff in the White House to function as presidential "eyes and ears" in the field. Nothing came of this or other recommendations as the energies of the administration were diverted to international affairs.

The administrative legacy of the 1960s spilled over into the next decade as the Nixon administration sought to strengthen political control over the bureaucracy. Standard regional boundaries were drawn and a federal council was set up in each region. Administrative management was upgraded in the Offices of Management and Budget, though it could not attain parity with the budget function. Efforts were made to extend the political reach of the White House through the new Domestic Council and the conversion of high administrative positions into political appointments.[27] General revenue sharing, which had been advocated in the 1960s as a means of redistributing government wealth, was transformed into a justification for redistributing governmental functions. Special revenue sharing was promoted as a means for withdrawing from local concerns and for divesting federal bureaucracies of control over intergovernmental programs.

In buildup and in retreat, the 1960s attested to the domination of administration by politics. However, public administration had become associated with an approach to politics that was itself under challenge in the 1960s; hence, political confrontation also affected the study and practice of administration.

PUBLIC ADMINISTRATION AND POLITICAL POWER

Public administration always has served power and the powerful. It came of age at the turn of the century with the emergence of the chief executive as the most important powerholder in American government. In the name of efficiency and rational government, it promoted the augmentation of executive power through a succession of reform instruments; the short ballot, administrative rerognization, the executive budget. When public power began to gravitate from city halls and state capitols to Washington, D.C., the geographical focus of public administration also shifted.

The service of power was *pro bono publico*, to help power holders govern more effectively. The presumption was that everyone benefits from good government, and so it was unnecessary for public administration to examine the consequences of its cherished norms. The constant concern with power was masked by the celebrated dichotomy between politics and administration. But the dichotomy, rather than keeping them apart, really offered a framework for bringing politics and administration together. As I have explained elsewhere,[28] the dichotomy provided for the ascendancy of the administration over the political: efficiency over representation, rationality over self-interest. The subservience of politics to administration furnished a theoretical basis and practical guidance for the extension of these administrative values to the political sphere. The reformer could use the same arguments in support of fewer elected officials or fewer units of government that he used to justify fewer administrative agencies. Thus, it was not a false separation but a dominant political theory that guided public administration during its most successful period.[29]

In the end, the dichotomy was rejected not because it separated politics and administration but because it joined them in a way that offended the pluralist norms of postwar political science. I shall leave for a later section of this essay a discussion of the relationship between political science and public administration, considering here the relevance of pluralism for administrative practice.

The coming of pluralism brought considerable strain for public administration. Beholden to the concept of one powerholder, public administration now had to reckon with multiple centers of power. In this environment, it was not easy for a practitioner to profess absolute neutrality on behalf of the common good. One of the early adaptations to the pluralist challenge was to regard the administrator as an arbiter of conflicting forces, powerful but still neutral and with no political stake of his own. This conception, however, was at variance with the experiences and observations of the young public administrationists who returned to academic life from wartime service no longer certain of the differentiation of the administrative from the political. With the politicization of public administration and the penetration of dominant political values into the administrative process, the administrator had to be regarded as a political force in his own right, not merely as the loyal agent of a powerful executive.

As a partisan, however, the administrator worked with power and for the powerful. Whatever the dislocations provoked by the triumph of pluralism, it did not require public administration to give up its service in behalf of power. What had changed were the number and variety of interests that had to be served, but as Schattschneider and others who followed him noted, it was pluralism for the blessed, not for those of low political caste. This exercise of power was legitimized by vague notions of representative bureaucracy, of an administrator who speaks for client interests. Reality, of course, was much more complex, as administrators formulated and lobbied for legislation, criss-crossed the country to organize clienteles, gave powerful interests preferred access to their organizations, and made conflict of interest an everyday administrative problem. It was no longer possible to demark who was the representative and who the represented. Public administration came to be a dialogue between the powerful and the powerful.

Public administration could be silent, even indifferent, about the outcomes of this relationship because it held to its chronic confidence in the goodness of government and because pluralism assured that each partisan would be the guardian of his own interests. Given the tenets of pluralism, it was convenient to believe that if an outcome was not wanted, it would not have been adopted. This pluralist blind spot fitted well with the fixation of public administration on the processes of government, presuming that a good process would yield a favorable outcome. Hence despite the "who gets what" rhetoric, there were few studies of political outcomes.

The enthronement of pluralism occurred during a period marked by the ascendancy of executive leadership as a dominant value of American public administration.[30] As Dahl found in New Haven, an "executive centered coalition" welded the various centers of power into a cohesive structure.[31] For from being antagonistic to the workings of pluralism, executive leadership was the "glue" that held the process together.

THE REDISTRIBUTION OF POWER

"Doing good" has long been a vital part of the public-administration ethic. One need not subscribe to Frederickson's speculation that "maybe public administrators (generally) are social revolutionaries"[32] to recognize that many administrators are predisposed toward change, want to side with the poor, and have committed themselves to the betterment of society. The New Deal was a massive mobilization of administrative power on behalf of the underprivileged and it pulled into the public service many thousands who were dedicated to doing good for the have-nots of America.

However, two of the working conditions of public administrators make it difficult to sustain this commitment. One is their everyday contact with the powerful; the other, their everyday utilization of value-concealing techniques. The policy administrator rarely has much to do with those who lack the leadership, organizational strengths, and other resources that make for success in a pluralist polity. Once he moves from the street level to the executive suite, the administrator's primary contacts are with powerful interests bent on leveraging their public access for private gain. Out of sight, out of mind, the powerless have paper identities as numbers in a statistical series or as cases in operational reports. A public-interest perspective could not withstand the pressures of special interests, not because the administrator takes private gain from this relationship but because he has a public dependence upon the powerful for the success of his agency.

The powerless are distant not only politically, but administratively as well, walled off from awareness by the value-free curtain of budgets, personnel forms, the techniques that (as Sayre warned many years ago) dominate over purpose. It is hard to keep in mind the effects of administrative action on the disadvantaged when the effects are masked in line-item detail, civil-service procedures, or even computer wizardry.

In the heat of the 1960s, many public administrators probably believed that their profession had served even-handedly, that it faithfully mirrored the political values of the American people, and that change would have to be initiated through the political process rather than in the administrative arena. But the politicization of public administration rendered it untenable to deploy the old dichotomy in behalf of administrative neutrality. Public administration had become a political arena.

Looking back at the noble aspirations of the past decade, this writer is drawn to several conclusions. (1) Grass roots do not readily grow on urban soil; it is impossible to resurrect the small town in a mass society. The problem of scale, which Plato confronted in *The Republic* and Dahl in his APSA presidential address,[33] is a barrier to neighborhood government in the megacity. (2) Notwithstanding Paul Appleby's wisdom that power must first be centralized before it can be decentralized, it is difficult politically and administratively to break up large governmental units. (3) To the extent that community control and action would have meant a genuine redistribution of power, it was thwarted by entrenched powerholders. Maximum feasible participation never was permitted to grow into a transfer of power to the weak. (4) It is still an unsettled question whether political power precedes or derives from the acquisition of socioeconomic status. In the 1960s, the debate was over an "income" versus an "opportunity" strategy. One need not accept the argument that the poor would have been better off if they had simply been given money to recognize that the redistribution of power is an even more difficult task than redistributing wealth.

Perhaps the most important and yet conventional means for giving administrative power is to assign a client interest its own administrative organization. The strategy had worked for labor, business, agriculture, and after a hard fight it was extended to urban interests. Bureaus, divisions, etc., were given to or captured by their clients. Why not do the same for the politically deprived?

The 1960s showed that it is one thing to institutionalize power for those who already possess it; quite another to vest client status in those who are weak or disadvantaged by public organizations. A weak clientele breeds a weak agency, a condition that is common to antipoverty agencies and to correctional systems. Moreover, the poor already were the clients (anticlients might be a better term) of bureaucracies that confronted them on the "street level"; the police, the social worker, the teacher.[34] These may be more responsive to their larger political environments than to their immediate clients. Efforts to sensitize "hostile" bureaucracies to the needs of their dependents probably bore more fruit (at least in the case of welfare programs) than did the creation of mendicant agencies.

THE FIELD OF PUBLIC ADMINISTRATION

The first parts of this essay have depicted the political condition in the 1960s; the remaining parts relate to the intellectual development of public administration during the decade. I have proceeded thus far without declaring the premise that I hope gives thematic unity to the essay: politics is the existential imperative of public administration—not just one of the factors to be reckoned with, but the situation that defines the administrative enterprise. "The Trauma of Politics" title announces my overriding concern with matters of political power. My focus on politics allows me to exclude much of the 1960s from this account, but it also requires that the intellectual side be considered largely within a political context.

American public administration entered the decade in disarray and left in disarray. It was not a productive period as the promises opened up by the postwar attack on administrative orthodoxy proved to be more paralyzing than realizeable. There were fewer "soul-searching" articles in the *Public Administration Review* than there had been in the preceding decade, but the drop was due to the futility of the search rather than to satisfaction with the state of the discipline.

The eclecticism that marked public administration after its breakaway from old commitments proved to be little more than ambivalence and confusion. Matters that were unsettled a generation earlier remained unsettled. Public administration had come apart and could not be put together again.[35] The many sources of fragmentation included: the separation of politics from administration; the tension between study and practice; the smashing of old administrative norms; the abortive striving for scientific status; the faddish reaching out to exotic specializations; the conflict between organizational and individual actualization. None of these strains first appeared in the 1960s, but none were healed during the decade.

One indicator of the entropic tendencies was that no new textbooks were published, though old ones were substantially recast from edition to edition in futile efforts to be both fashionable and familiar. A text helps to shape a field, giving it boundaries and some sense of unity. Sometimes a text gathers together the conventional wisdoms of the field; sometimes it marks out new directions. When neither of these functions is served, the sense of discipline is diminished. John Pfiffner and Frank Sherwood's *Administrative Organization* appeared in 1960, accommodating to the diversities within public administration by pyramiding various "overlays" upon its basic organizational framework. A decade later, Ira Sharkansky's *Public Administration* sought to package policy analysis into a systems design. During the intervening years, some collected readings and a few introductory essays were issued, but not a new text.

"Is there a 'field' of public administration?", Frederick Mosher asked in 1956. "If so, what is its scope, its rubric, its method? I am not sure that either question can be answered?" Mosher found vigor and opportunity in this eclecticism:[36]

It has cross-interests with virtually all the other social sciences.
... In fact, it would appear that any definition of this field would
be either so encompassing as to call forth the wrath or ridicule
of others or so limiting as to stultify its own disciples. Perhaps it
is best that it not be defined. It is more an area of interest that a
discipline, more a focus than a separate science.

Writing in 1962, Martin Landau insisted that public administration could not flourish without "organizing assumptions, the
concepts and definitions that underlie any systematic inquiry.
These are the elements that provide a field with coherence and
relevance."[37] Landau cautioned that unless public administration is
properly defined, it "can result in a scope of interest so unlimited
as to produce a subject matter that defies discipline and order as it
reflects babel and confusion."[38]

However, the critics had destroyed too well, and any effort at
definition only left public administration enfeebled by its own am-
bivalences. Dwight Waldo, who had contributed brilliantly to
the tearing down of the old structure and valiantly tried to
breathe vigor and meaning into many of the new directions, acknowledged in a 1968 article on "Scope of the Theory of Public
Administration" that the difficulties remained:[39]

> Both the nature and boundaries of subject matter and the meth-
> ods of studying and teaching this subject matter became prob-
> lematical. Now two decades after the critical attacks, the crisis of
> identity has not been resolved satisfactorily. Most of the impor-
> tant theoretical problems of public administration relate to this
> continuing crisis, to ways in which it can be resolved, and to the
> implications and results of possible resolutions.

Waldo proposed that public administration abandon its striving
for disciplinary status and that it make a virtue of necessity by
adopting a professional perspective that "gives unity while permit-
ting diversity."[40]

> What I propose is that we try to act as a profession without
> actually being one, and perhaps even without the hope or inten-
> tion of becoming one in any strict sense.... The professional
> perspective or stance is the only one broad and flexible enough to
> enable us to contain our diverse interests and objectives, yet firm
> and understanding enough to provide some unity and sense of
> direction and purpose.

No more paradigm problem, no more crisis of identity, no more second-class academic status, no more political-science problem. But what of the positive side of professionalism? What does this new identity add to the study and practice of public administration? It does not suffice to claim professional standing merely as an escape from the dilemmas of discipline. A profession, after all, exacts a high standard of shared purpose. A mature profession, ideally, establishes and enforces its own code of behavior, effectively controls entry into its ranks, and permits practice only by those who satisfy its standards. Clearly, these conditions do not prevail within public administration, a field in which there is little shared purpose among the legions of practitioners who are united primarily by the fact of working for the same type of employer. Perhaps these inadequacies of public administration *qua* profession are why Waldo hedged his suggestion with the caution that public administration ought not have the hope or intention of becoming a real profession.

I believe that the seeking after professional recognition is an effort to establish an identity apart from political science rather than a means of accommodating to the diversities within the field. The lack of a paradigm is not what tears public administration apart, nor is it the diversities that pull scholars in so many directions. There are at least as many diversities within political science (and most other major disciplines) as there are within public administration. Political science does not have a unifying paradigm and there is little intellectual contact among its disparate specializations. The problem of public administration is its place within political science, the relationship between politics and administration.

PUBLIC ADMINISTRATION AND POLITICAL SCIENCE

Throughout the years of separation, public administration was one of the most active and esteemed fields of American political science. Frank Goodnow, one author of the dichotomy, was the first president of the American Political Science Association, and public administration supplied a fair share of APSA notables during this period. In terms of governmental service and influence, these years were also the best for public administration. From President Taft's Commission on Economy and Efficiency (1912) through President Roosevelt's Committee on Administrative Management (1937), reform-minded leaders of the discipline supplied a stream of proposals for governmental betterment.

It is instructive that the opening of public administration to political norms coincided with a depreciation of public administration by the parent discipline. The destruction of the dichotomy also destroyed the unifying ethic of public administration and rendered it impotent to integrate political realities into its core values. The political shock was damaging because the pluralist norms were sharply at variance with classic administrative ideals. In place of form and order, there was muddling through and the babble of competing interests. Hierarchy gave way to bargaining, rationality to group demands. Means were to be preferred over ends, a fragmented view considered superior to comprehensive plans. All these were not mere suboptimization or acceptance of the "second best"; they were articles of faith for a pluralist polity. It was difficult for public administration to retain both its orthodox notions of rationality and the tenets of pluralism. In his 1968 article recommending a professional posture, Waldo argued that:[41]

> It is now unrealistic and unproductive to regard public administration as a subdivision of political science.... The truth is that the attitude of political scientists (other than those accepting public administration as their "field") is at best one of indifference and is often one of undisguised contempt or hostility. We are now hardly welcome in the house of our youth.

My own view is that public administration can no more escape political science that it can escape politics. For various reasons it might be convenient or fruitful to locate public administration in a separate department, or even in its own professional school, but the intellectual ties with political science cannot be severed. All attempts to conjoin public administration with other disciplines have failed because its special relationship with political science cannot be abandoned. Until it makes peace with politics, public administration will wander in quest of purpose and cohesion. To paraphrase what Wildavsky has written of budgeting: perhaps the study of administration is just another expression for the study of politics. If this is so, it will require a theory of politics to resolve the intellectual crisis of American public administration.[42]

THE NEW PUBLIC ADMINISTRATION

It was in quest of a new political theory, that "new public administration" became a self-conscious enterprise in the late 1960s. Gathered at Minnowbrook under the stimulating patronage of Dwight Waldo, some of the best of the younger generation of scholars challenged the doctrine they had received. *Toward a New Public Administration* and a companion volume, *Public Administration in a Time of Turbulence*,[43] display the wrath of intellectual Luddites intent on tearing down the "givens" of orthodox public administration and pluralist political science.

Virtually all the contributors to these two publications were young political scientists specializing in public administration. For most of them, the crisis was not the lack of a paradigm but a refusal to accept either the classical or the pluralist version of administrative politics.

The new public administrators adopted as their own Wallace Sayre's remark that "public administration is ultimately a problem in political theory."[44] As restated by Peter Savage, the battle cry became: "politics first, administration afterward."[45] Yet these angry young men could not abandon their quest for an administrative theory. Perhaps their academic associations with public administration impelled them to continue in this direction. A better explanation offered by Orion White is that public administration is a crucial part of the political problem:[46]

> Public administration ... is currently the most relevant and immediate context for the problem because it is mostly through public administrative institutions that the requisites of technological society are expressed to human communities—and hence it is here that the conflict begins and is felt most intensely.

The countercultural wrath of the new public administrators was inflamed by their ideological conviction that the bureaucratic instruments of power utilized by the political establishments and

studied with academic detachment by the intellectual establishments are among the most oppressive institutions of American
society. For them, confrontation with the bureaucratic state represents the channeling of political protest through public administration.

New public administration literature stressed four themes: relevance, values, equity, and change.

Relevance. Public administration always has worshipped at the
altar of relevance. It came of age and prospered as an effort to improve governmental performance. A feeling that public administration has become irrelevant for these times was widely expressed
at Minnowbrook. The first chapter (after the introduction) in
Toward a New Public Administration is "The Recovery of Relevance in the Study of Public Organizations." It was the publication of the Honey Report on Higher Education for Public Service
in November, 1967, that sparked the feeling that public administration had little to say about contemporary problems and issues
and led to Minnowbrook.

Many of the new public administrators had recently completed
graduate education and had taken their first teaching jobs. These
young teachers wanted a policy-oriented public administration,
not one hiding behind procedure. They had tired of personnel administration, budgetary technique, organization form. They
wanted a curriculum that deals openly with the political and normative implications of administrative action.

What they found lacking in the curricula was substantially
a result of their own perspectives. They were political scientists
specializing in public administration. Few of the protesters were
involved primarily in training for public employment; they were
not engaged in Masters or midcareer programs for persons facing
everyday administrative routines.

Another dimension to the cry of irrelevance came from those
who raised the old question "knowledge for what?" in order to
attack the employment of administrative knowledge in behalf of
political power. Among the items on the Minnowbrook agenda
were the following questions:[47]

(a) What standards of decision do we use to select which questions ought to be studied and how to study them? (b) Who defines our questions and priorities for us? (c) To what extent are we aware of the social and moral implications of knowledge in Public Administration? (d) What are the uses of Public Administration as a social and political science? (e) Does Public Administration presently yield knowledge useful to certain institutions in society (usually the dominant ones) and not to others?

Seeking after relevance is a fashionable endeavor. But as fashions change, so too do notions of what is relevant. As the protests of the 1960s faded into the comparative calm of the 1970s, public administration continued to serve its traditional uses. Enrollments soared (primarily in Masters and midcareer education) as employers and employees coveted the relevance that has been marketed by public administration since its inception. However, the protest left its imprint on graduate education and more attention is now given to urban administration, public policy, and program analysis.

Values. New public administration is openly normative. It rejects the value-concealing behavioralism of contemporary political science as well as the procedural neutrality of orthodox public administration. The willingness to espouse values springs from two convictions: that value-neutral public administration (or political science) is impossible; and that public administrators ought to be advocates for disadvantaged interests.

New public administrators believe that it is not possible to escape values, to be indifferent about the moral consequences of one's acts. They argue that only if normative issues are explicitly discussed and decided will be it possible for administrators to avoid complicity in immoral actions. The expectation is that openness about the values that are being served will have a significant impact on administrative outcomes, for it no longer would be acceptable to obscure inequitable outcomes behind the mask of neutrality.

Normative public administration probably would be more comfortable as a profession, rather than as a discipline. But the new public administrators wanted to retain academic respectability even as they warred against dominant societal norms. As stated by George Frederickson in his summing up of the creed, the new public administrator:[48]

> is less "generic" and more "public" than his forebear, less "descriptive" and more "prescriptive", less "institution oriented" and more "client-impact oriented", less "neutral" and more "normative", and it is hoped, no less scientific.

Social equity. Once it opts for partisanship, the new public administration must decide which values are to be served. On this question, the chorus is virtually unanimous, at least when the issue is cast in general terms. Public administration must be vitally concerned with the distributive functions and outcomes of governmental institutions; it must come to grips with who wins and who loses in political confrontation. But new public administrators appear to be divided on the extent to which it is appropriate to engage in compensatory in contrast to equity-maximizing behavior.

The equity-maximizing position is expressed by Todd LaPorte in a neo-Benthamite formula:[49]

> The purpose of public organization is the reduction of economic, social and psychic suffering and the enhancement of life opportunities for those inside and outside the organization.

LaPorte wants public administrators to be objective on behalf of social equity, a role that probably comports with the idealized self-perspective of many public employees. But it would be necessary to devise an interpersonal benefit-cost calculus in order to implement LaPorte's rule.

A bolder social-equity viewpoint, arising out of the special-interest accomodations of pluralist political science, is expressed by Frederickson:[50]

> A Public Administration which fails to work for changes which try to redress the deprivation of minorities will likely be eventually used to repress those minorities.

In this formulation, public administration is called upon to withstand the power of the powerful, to compensate for the wrongs of society. Does this mean that majority will must be rejected by the administrator if it is contrary to his own view of the right source of action? The logical answer is "yes," but this presents grave political and moral difficulties and is not sustainable in administrative practice.

Change. The achievement of social equity requires the active promotion of change by public administrators. The status quo, after all, works to the advantage of dominant interests. But reading the new public administration literature, one gets the feeling that change is sought for its own sake, as a means of rejecting administrative tradition, an affirmation of youthful integrity, a refusal to allow enslavement to permanent institutions. Change is necessary to prevent public administration from once again coming under the dominance of powerful interests. Permanent institutions become corrupt institutions; whatever noble purpose may have inspired their creation, such institutions become self-perpetuating power centers.

The new public administrators regard change as a constant fact of administrative life. *The Temporary Society* possibly was the most frequently cited book by the Minnowbrook participants, as they sought ways of institutionalizing change and avoiding the bureaucratic tendencies of large organizations.

Blending stability and change is like growing mature while remaining young. It is not likely that the new public administrators will be the first to succeed.

The rhetoric and logic of new public administration is a bundle of paradoxes and contradictions—antinomies might be a better term—reflecting the value conflicts within the movement. Waldo's concluding essay in *Public Administration in a Time of Turbulence* soberly warns new public administrators that they have demanded too much of their field:[51]

> Public administration cannot conveniently "compose" the world in order to solve its own problems. And while it can hope, without danger of hubris, to have some part in determining the destiny of the whole, its destiny rests with the whole, not in its own hands....
>
> The problem of adjustment and synthesis, to which some of those self-consciously seeking to develop a "new" public administration

have committed themselves, will nowhere present greater difficulties than in the manner of relating politics and administration.

PUBLIC ADMINISTRATION AS MANAGEMENT

During the period in which the new public administration struggled to devise a political theory in harmony with its countercultural ethic, public administration was pulled away from politics by what has come to be known as the generic approach. The simple idea of the generic approach is that core administrative activities are the same in public and nonpublic organizations and that while "public" adds something to the administrative enterprise, it is more productive for research and training to concentrate on the common elements of all administrative activity. In effect, the genericists would leave the "public" dimension to political science, thereby interposing a new dichotomy between politics and administration.

Public administration was launched on a generic course by Woodrow Wilson in 1887 and the idea achieved its postwar formulation in Simon's *Administrative Behavior*. But the generic concept was in eclipse during the 1950s and most of the 1960s as the politics of administration dominated the field. The resurgence of generic administration has been a case of relationship following reality. In the 1960s, many business schools became involved in public-sector activities. Their students were taking government jobs, their faculties, government grants and contracts. Management consulting firms were selling the same wares to public and private clients. A few schools (such as Cornell's Graduate School of Business and Public Administration) were already attuned to generic thinking; many, however, accommodated to the new style by adding public-sector courses and faculty. On some campuses, public and business administration were merged into schools of management.

The popularity of the generic concept was due in part to the feeling that standard public-administration courses do not equip students with the competences necessary for the management of large organizations. The conventional curriculum had ceased being a wellspring of administrative innovation; it was oriented to basic personnel, budgeting, and administrative practices and did not give adequate attention to modern analytic and informational technologies. The generic schools, by contrast, provide a heavy dose of problem solving, decisional strategy, and business-school staples such as management by objectives plus training in the use of statistics and data.

ADMINISTRATION AS PUBLIC AFFAIRS

For almost a hundred years the generic approach has vied with political science for dominion over public administration. The contest is not yet ended, as the "political" approach to public administration has gravitated toward schools or programs in public affairs, policy studies, policy sciences, and similar policy approaches. The trend began in the late 1960s under the same impulse that spurred the establishment of generic schools: dissatisfaction with the core curriculum as an aid to public policymaking. Both the generic and policy-oriented schools concentrate on statistical analysis and the use of informational technologies, though the policy schools seem to be more enraptured by economic analysis. The key difference between the two schools is the place of politics, and this often is concealed by similar terminologies and methods. For example, both emphasize the determination of program objectives. However, in the generic school, the objective is a "given," to be PERTed and pursued; in the policy schools, the objective is grist for the analyst's mill. In one, the objective is a problem to be solved; in the other, it is the policy to be decided.

It may be that the principal differences between public administration and public policy relate to style and freshness, though the latter tends to be more comfortable with political science and other disciplines.[52] The policy approach shares public administration's positive thinking about government. Policy is good, wanted, helpful. It suggests an active government, in line with recent growth. It retains the old promise that research and science can produce governmental rationality. It comes with none of the encumbrances of public administration. It is explicitly multidisciplinary; it is receptive to politics; it is at home with the dazzling new techniques of science.

The new policy disciplines demand less disciplinary cohesion than was required in public administration. The bands are matters of convenience. The sociologist is brought together with the economist by a shared interest in a particular policy or problem. Neither is required to abandon its primary disciplinary association. Thus they have less vulnerability to come apart because they insist on much less commonality.

The policy approach may offer an alternative to the professional identity sought by Waldo. Policy is not the paradigm, but it is a unifying force. As Mosher has noted, "the primary and unique feature of the school of public affairs is explicit in the key word of its title: *public.*"[53]

Between the pulls of genericism and policy, it may be difficult for public administration to retain identity or status. My own view is that public administration will opt for a political partnership. This alliance is reflected in the establishment of the National Association of Schools of Public Affairs and Administration.

COMPARATIVE ADMINISTRATION AND ORGANIZATION THEORY

Thus far I have considered the three new trends that emerged in the 1960s: new (normative) public administration; management sciences; and public policy. What of the "new" public administrations that had been developed in the postwar period? The two that attracted the most interest probably were comparative administration and organization theory. The former represented a broadening of public administration to other cultures and environments, the latter, a broadening to other social sciences. In both subfields, there was a conscious effort to break away from the categories and method of American public administration.

Comparative administration blossomed as an offshoot of the American foreign-aid program, which in the mid-1950s was concentrated on third-world countries. When foreign assistance waned a decade later, so too did interest in comparative administration. This focus on underdeveloped areas helps to explain why comparative administration had a greater impact on the literature of political development than on writings in public administration.[54] American public administration always has been distinctly American (in part, I think, because its teachers often also carry courses in American government) and comparative administration could not separate it from its cultural ties and norms.[55] One might speculate that comparative administration could have left a stronger mark if it had been oriented to western experience, but this was not the path it took.

In its prime, comparative administration was much given to modelbuilding at a high level of abstraction and with attention to the full range of social and political processes that impact on administration. It may be that scholars examining other societies were able to perceive more clearly what American public administrators have been telling themselves for a generation: that administration is a political process. Accordingly, even less than when they looked at their own society were they able to avoid the preemption of administration by politics. Comparative administration moved away from public administration and became comparative politics. The outcome is summed up in a forceful question by Keith Henderson: "What, it can be asked, is *not* within the scope of comparative Public Administration?"[56] The answer: nothing in the field of political science was excluded from comparative administration.

In the 1960s, organization behavior probably was the most popular subfield within public administration.[57] The study of organizations brought public administration back to its historic concern with structure and control. The organization theorist could wrestle with the big issues: hierarchy, bureaucracy, decision making, rationality, communication. The organization was a forum, short of the political process itself, in which power was exercised and could be studied. The concept of organization gave the discipline scientific respectability as well as a manageable context for the conduct of empirical research. Organization brought a commonality of interest with sociology, psychology, economics, business management and was in accord with the electic strivings of the discipline.

But for all its utility and excitement, organization theory revealed the intellectual difficulties of the discipline. One tipoff was that the literature was not a literature of public administration but rather a literature that attracted the interest of public administration researchers and teachers. With the exception of Herbert Simon, few persons identified with public administration contributed actively to the study of organizations. None of the six books reviewed by Waldo in his "Organization Theory: An Elephantine Problem" was written or edited by a public administration researcher.[58] Few of the many articles on organization behavior in *Administrative Science Quarterly* are the product of public-administration research. Organization theory is a conscious repudiation of classic administration theory.[59]

The fascination with organizations brought to the fore again the unresolved question of the relationship between the individual and the collectivity in which he works. From Mayo to McGregor, resolution was sought through "human relations" engineering in which the individual could be made more productive, happy, and cooperative if he were given some opportunity to participate and shape his activity on behalf of the organization.[60] This neo-Taylorist discovery of the individual was purely exploitative and calculated to make the workers a more responsive and efficient tool of the organization. Participation was to be contrived and controlled in the interests of the organization, not for any self-realization by the participants.

This instrumental manipulation of the individual came under severe attack in the 1960s, though some of the basic statements predate the decade: Maslow's early writings on personality and self-actualization, Whyte's expose of *The Organization Man* and Kafka's *The Trial*.[61] The alienating effects of organization on human behavior were strongly argued by Robert Presthus: "Man, in effect, is made for the organization. *He may succeed and prosper within it, but the organization always defines the terms of success.* Yet, given his dignity as a human being and his capacity for reason, man ought not to be viewed as an instrument."[62]

The reconciliation of man and his organization has proved to be an essential but perhaps hopeless task. Either the individual is autonomous or the organization is dominant, for the very notion of individualism wars against even benevolent organization. For almost two decades, Chris Argyris has resisted his own findings that organization demands and individual needs are incongruent, and he still labors to develop models of compatibility.[63] Breaking away from the human-relations movement, Warren Bennis preaches the withering away of the bureaucracy and the emergence of "adhocracies," temporary organizations rooted to specific tasks.[64] In one the few public-administration writings on the subject, Larry Kirkhart proposes a "consociated model," 'in which diversity, tolerance, and ambiguity are tolerated.[65] But Kirkhart acknowledges that "every empirical study and most theoretical summaries explicitly or implicitly rest on Weberian concepts of formal organization."[66] Kirkhart's is a prescription for "consciousness III" communes, not for large-scale, mainstream organizations.

PLANNING, ECONOMICS, AND LAW

During the 1960s, three fields (two professions and one discipline) became more active in administrative practice. Planning, economics, and law are "political" fields in the sense that they deal with the distribution of values in society; they also are "administrative" fields in the sense that they provide models of order and rational behavior.

Planning has a reputation almost the opposite of that held by administration. Planning is change-oriented; people or governments plan in order to make possible a future different from that which would otherwise occur. The planner starts with a bias against keeping things as they are. He is an interventionist and therefore is not apt to remain a center of power for more than a brief period.

Deserved or not, the image of administration is of stability and continuity. One need not embrace the inertia theory of bureaucracy to sense permanence in government organizations. The cycles of reroganization attest to striving for change but difficulty in achieving change. The administrator is at the center of power and he cannot hold on to this status and yet act as a force for change.

Planning had a revival in the 1960s. Not since the halcyon years of the National Resources Planning Board had the federal government been such an active sponsor of planning and planners. At the urban level, the profession that had received a head start in land-use control and zoning was broadened to cover the full range of social programs. Hundreds of intergovernmental assistance programs called for plans of one sort or another. Planning rode the crest of the Planning-Programming-Budgeting movement in the 1960s and it was fully compatible with the doctrines of systems analysis: Both preached looking ahead and being comprehensive. Planning received the ultimate governmental recognition, a big governmental subsidy program of its own—"701" comprehensive grants.

As might be expected, planning came to mean and be different things; with planners taking over all but the routine POSDCORB functions, moving into policymaking and staff roles, trespassing on the work space of budgeters, and becoming an administrative class of sorts. The ferment of the decade opened up a lively debate within the pages of the *Journal of the American Institute of Planners* and forced the institute to modify its examination standards for admission to full membership. In an article that reminded this reader of the Friedrich/Finer exchange on administrative responsibility, Martin Rein identified four sources of legitimacy for the planning of social change: expertise, political support, client support, and professional values.[67]

"Advocacy planning" was an issue for the profession during the decade. Raised in a provocative 1965 article by Paul Davidoff and practiced by some urban and regional planners, advocacy meant giving a voice and representation to interests and values that would otherwise be neglected in a pluralist society. Taking a position that is similar to that of new public administration, Davidoff insisted that "appropriate planning action cannot be prescribed from a position of value neutrality" and he went on to argue "that the planner should do more than explicate the values underlying his prescriptions for courses of action; he should affirm them; he should be an advocate for what he deems proper."[68] By the end of the decade, forms of advocacy had been applied to community action, legal services for the poor, and model cities.

Advocacy for the underrepresented, whether by the planner or the administrator, is a perennially vulnerable enterprise. The advocate cannot build a permanent power base on the support of weak interests, and advocacy planning has gone the way of new public administration.

Economics. For a few camelot years in the mid-1960s economics enjoyed public esteem and trust. There was overwhelming confidence that the economy could be fine-tuned and kept on a high-growth, noninflationary course. It was expected that the economist would deliver annual increments of economic expansion and the fisal dividend from which government could draw resources for expansion without taking more from the private sector.

Economics meant the exaltation of quantitative and analytic specialization and the depreciation of the administrative generalist. Public administration always had been ambivalent about government-by-expert; the economist was the expert who could apply his cost-effective tools to defense policy one day, health programs the next, converting the axioms and values of his discipline into the universal language of public policy.[69]

Economics had its greatest impact on the most specialized of the POSDCORB functions. The budget came to be regarded increasingly as an instrument of economic policy rather than as a process for funding government agencies. The budget totals came to have an importance of their own, apart from the policies and programs comprising them. In matters of fiscal policy, the economist claimed a near monopoly of intelligence, and a succession of budget directors in the 1960s came with graduate degrees in economics. With regard to the distributive effects of the budget, the economist offered data to answer the "Who gets what?" questions that had gone unanswered for so many years.

The appeal of economics left its mark on administrative study and research. Governmental studies were downgraded at the Brookings Institution and economic research gained preeminence. Many public-policy curricula and degree programs had a substantial economics content. When the United States government sent promising young employees back to school for training in systems analysis, it turned mainly to business schools or to graduate departments in economics, rather than to public-administration programs.

In organization theory, there was something of a shift from the sociological to the economic, reflecting in part the growing involvement of economists in public affairs.[70] This shift paralleled the displacement of public-administration generalists by economists in high governmental posts such as the United States Bureau of the Budget as well as the introduction of new management technologies.

The advance of specialization is a characteristic of modern societies. Once public administration was regarded as a discipline that promoted the infusion of vital skills into the public service. Now it is among the least specialized of the social disciplines, and this position is one of the issues it must face.

Law. Once an active concern of public administration, law was molded in the postwar period into an effective instrument of pluralist policy. Rule-of-law problems seem to have been put to rest by enactment of the Administrative Procedures Act, which brought due process into the administrative arena. The establishment of formal procedures for notice, hearings, and other elements of fairness provided sufficient protection for the interests that had standing and power in American society. The regulating agency and its regulated client could engage in an administrative process in which the trappings of judicial procedure were replicated. Some questions might be raised about the independence of the regulatory agency ,or about the invitation to conflict of interest opened by the interdependence of regulated and regulator. By and large, however, the quasi-judicial procedures had brought law to the twentieth-century administrative state and were regarded as one of the finest accomplishments of American public administration.[71]

Different questions were raised in the 1960s about unrepresented parties and interests, about the networks of advisory groups, about the privileged access of certain interests to the administrative process. *Ex parte* dealings flourished in the form of premerger clearances by the FTC, no-action letters by the SEC, advisory rulings by the IRS. The Administrative Procedure Act itself stood as a barrier to open disclosure of these portentious relationships, for it imposed a stern need-to-know test that could be satisfied by the regulated client but not by third parties. Nor did such parties have a right to participate in either administrative or judicial proceedings involving their vital interests.

Much was changed in the 1960s under the onslaught of Naderite attacks on administrative policies and the aggressive use of legal power to compel administrative change. The Freedom of Information Act entitled ordinary citizens to administrative records previously withheld from them; advisory committees were opened to public scrutiny; class-action suits were allowed in certain proceedings; environmental and consumer interests were vested with standing. In a reversal of the historic court/agency relationship, in which administrators were told what they must not do, courts began to instruct governments as to what they must do. For example, court rulings in the welfare area required administrators to provide benefits to indigents who did not satisfy local residence requirements and to give financial assistance above the levels enacted by the state legislatures.

The astounding spiral in law-school enrollments is a well-known phenomenon. The effect has not only been the siphoning away from public administration of potential graduate students but the reinforcement of governmental bias to employ lawyers in generalist positions that might otherwise be given to individuals trained in public administration.

COPING

Public administration will not wither away—not any more than will the state which it serves. It is my sad belief, however, that the discipline will not recover its past glory. The "New Public Administration" offered honesty, excitement, and fashion—all appealing attributes for a discipline in trouble, but not enough to give it a sense of self or direction.

In the 1960s, American government moved from muddling through to coping. So did public administration. This is the best we will be able to do until we answer the challenge raised by our teachers in the 1940s and our contemporaries in the 1960s. And the answer will have to accommodate the political while preserving the separate identity of matters administrative. As the twenty-five-year search has shown, this may be an impossible task.

Notes

1. Inaugural Address of President Richard M. Nixon, January 20, 1969.
2. Most of these statistics are taken from U. S. Office of Management and Budget, *Social Indicators 1973* (Washington, D.C.: Government Printing Office, 1973).
3. For a recent assessment of the Coleman Report, see Frederick Mosteller and Daniel P. Moynihan, *On Equality of Educational Opportunity* (New York: Vintage Books, 1972).
4. Harvey A. Averch and others, *How Effective is Schooling: A Critical Review and Synthesis of Research Findings* (Santa Monica: The RAND Corporation, 1971), p. xi.
5. Kermit Gordon (ed.) *Agenda for the Nation* (Washington, D.C.: The Brookings Institution, 1968), p. 5.
6. Ibid., p. 10.
7. Lyndon B. Johnson, "The President's News Conference of August 25, 1965" in *Weekly Compilation of Presidential Documents*, vol. 1, p. 143.
8. See Allen Schick, "A Death in the Bureaucracy: the Demise of Federal PPB" *Public Administration Review* vol. 33, (March/April, 1973) pp. 146–56.
9. On July 28, 1965, President Johnson announced a boost in United States Vietnam troops from 75 to 125 thousand. The Watts riots broke out on August 12, 1965.
10. U. S. Department of Health, Education, and Welfare, *Toward A Social Report* (Washington, D.C.: U.S. Government Printing Office, 1969), p. xii.
11. Moynihan has pointed out that the age 14–24 population grew more in the 1960s (13.8 million persons) than it had in the preceding 70 years (12.5) See "Peace—Some Thoughts on the 1960's and 1970's" in *The Public Interest* (Summer, 1973).
12. Edward C. Banfield, *The Unheavenly City* (Boston: Little, Brown & Company, 1970), p. 239.
13. Jay Forrester, *Urban Dynamics* (Cambridge: The M.I.T. Press, 1969).

14. Peter F. Drucker, *The Age of Discontinuity* (New York: Harper & Row, 1968), p. 233.

15. See U. S. Advisory Commission on Intergovernmental Relations, *The Gap Between Federal Aid Authorizations and Appropriations* (June, 1970).

16. The National Urban Coalition, *Counterbudget: A Blueprint for Changing National Priorities* (New York: Praeger Publishers, 1971).

17. Daniel P. Monihan, *Maximum Feasible Misunderstanding: Community Action in the War on Poverty* (Glencoe: Free Press, 1969).

18. Alice Rivlin, *Systematic Thinking for Social Action* (Washington, D.C.: The Brookings Institution, 1971), p. 69.

19. "Implementation in recent years has been much discussed but rarely studied . . . except for an excellent book by Martha Derthick, we have not been able to locate any thorough going analysis about implementation." Jeffrey L. Pressman and Aaron Wildawsky, *Implementation* (Berkeley: University of California Press, 1973), p. xiii.

20. See U. S. Senate, Subcommittee on Intergovernmental Relations, *Hearing on Creative Federalism*, 89th Cong., 2nd Sess.

21. During the Johnson years, proposals were made to merge Labor and Commerce into a Department of Economic Affairs and the concept of a department of natural resources was a perrenial favorite.

22. See George D. Greenberg *Governing HEW* (unpublished Ph.D. dissertation, Harvard University, 1972).

23. See *Hearings on Creative Federalism*, p. 425.

24. For the early development of substate regionalism, see James L. Sundquist, *Making Federalism Work* (Washington, D.C.: The Brookings Institution, 1969); a later and expanded view is contained in U.S. Advisory Commission on Intergovernmental Relations, *Regional Decision Making: New Strategies for Substate Districts* (October, 1973).

25. The story is well told in Martha Derthick, *New Towns In-Town* (Washington, D.C.: The Urban Institution, 1972).

26. See Allen Schick, "The Budget Bureau That Was: Thoughts on the Rise, Decline, and Future of a Presidential Agency" in *Law and Contemporary Problems*, (Summer, 1970), pp. 519–39.

27. In particular, political functionaries were placed in high positions in OMB and regional offices while career positions at the assistant secretary level (for legislation, administration, and public affairs) were turned into political jobs. See National Academy of Public Administration, *Watergate: Its Implications for Responsible Government* (March, 1974).

28. Allen Schick, "Coming Apart in Public Administration," *Maxwell Review*, vol. 10, no. 2, pp. 13–24.

29. This is a principal motif of Dwight Waldo's *The Administrative State*.

30. See Herbert Kaufman, "Emerging Conflicts in the Doctrines of

Public Administration," *American Political Science Review*, vol. 50 (1950) pp. 1057–73.

31. Robert A. Dahl, *Who Governs? Democracy and Power in an American City* (New Haven: Yale University Press, 1961).

32. Quoted in Peter Savage, "Contemporary Public Administration: The Changing Environment and Agenda", in Dwight Waldo (ed.) *Public Administration in a Time of Turbulence* (San Francisco: Chandler Publishing Company, 1971), p. 46.

33. Robert A. Dahl, "The City in the Future of Democracy", *American Political Science Review*, vol. 61 (December, 1967), pp. 953–70.

34. See Michael Lipsky, "Street-Level Bureaucracy and the Analysis of Urban Reform", in Virginia B. Ermer and John H. Strange (eds.) *Blacks and Bureaucracy* (New York: Crowell, 1972) pp. 171–84.

35. For a fuller elaboration, see "Coming Apart in Public Administration."

36. Frederick C. Mosher, "Research in Public Administration", *Public Administration Review* (Summer, 1956), p. 177.

37. Martin Landau, "The Concept of Decision-Making in the Field of Public Administration", reprinted in Landau, *Political Theory and Political Science* (New York: The Macmillan Company, 1972), p. 178.

38. Ibid., p. 192.

39. Dwight Waldo, "Scope of the Theory of Public Administration", in The American Academy of Political and Social Science, *Theory and Practice of Public Administration: Scope, Objectives, and Methods*.

40. Ibid., p. 10.

41. Ibid., p. 8.

42. This is what Vincent Ostrom tries to develop in *The Intellectual Crisis in American Public Administration* (University: The University of Alabama Press, 1973; rev. ed., 1974).

43. While it is not a "new public administration" document, *Public Administration in a Time of Turbulence* considers many of the issues raised by new public administration.

44. Wallace Sayre, "Premises of Public Administration: Past and Emerging" *Public Administration Review*, vol. 18 (Spring, 1958), p. 105.

45. Savage, "Contemporary Public Administration . . . ," in Waldo (ed.), *Public Administration in a Time of Turbulence*, p. 56.

46. Orion White, "Organization and Administration for New Technological and Social Imperatives", in Waldo (ed.), p. 152.

47. Frank Marini (ed.) *Toward a New Public Administration* (San Francisco: Chandler Publishing Company, 1971), p. 7.

48. H. George Frederickson, "Toward a New Public Administration" in Marini, ibid., p. 316.

49. Todd R. LaPorte, "The Recovery of Relevance in the Study of Public Organization", in Marini, ibid., p. 32.

50. Frederickson in Marini, ibid., p. 311.

51. Dwight Waldo, "Some Thoughts on Alternatives, Dilemmas, and Paradoxes in a Time of Turbulence", in Waldo (ed.), *Public Administration in a Time of Turbulance*, p. 266.

52. This and the next paragraph are adapted from "Coming Apart in Public Administration," in *Maxwell Review*, vol. 10, no. 2, pp. 13–24.

53. Frederick C. Mosher, "The Public Service in the Temporary Society", in Waldo (ed.), *Public Administration in a Time of Turbulence*, p. 255.

54. See, for example, Joseph LaPalombara (ed.) *Bureaucracy and Political Development* (Princeton: Princeton University Press, 1963).

55. Dwight Waldo, "Public Administration and Culture", in Roscoe C. Martin (ed.) *Public Administration and Democracy* (Syracuse University Press, 1965), pp. 39–61.

56. Keith M. Henderson, "A New Comparative Administration", in Marini, *Toward a New Public Administration*, p. 242.

57. In the latest (1973) Biographical Directory of the American Political Science Association, more than half of the entries under "Public Administration" appear under "bureaucracy," "organization and management analysis," and "organization theory and behavior." But inasmuch as many names are listed under more than one of these subfields, fewer than half—though certainly more than for any other subfield—regard organization study as a main interest.

58. *Public Administration Review*, vol. 21 (1961), p. 225.

59. See James G. March and Herbert A. Simon, *Organzations* (New York: John Wiley & Sons, 1958), especially chapter 2.

60. Among the more important books in this genre are Elton Mayo, *The Social Problems of an Industrial Civilization* (New York: The Viking Press, 1945); Douglas McGregor, *The Human Side of Enterprise* (New York: McGraw-Hill, 1960); and Rensis Likert, *New Patterns of Management* (New York: McGraw-Hill, 1961).

61. These writings were assigned by me in public administration courses during the 1960s, but I have no basis for claiming that they were widely used.

62. Robert Presthus, *The Organizational Society* (New York: Vintage Books, 1965), pp. 25–26.

63. See His *Personality and Organizations* (New York: Harper & Rowe, 1957) and *Integrating the Individual and the Organization* (New York: John Wiley & Sons, 1964).

64. Warren Bennis, *Changing Organizations* (New York: McGraw-Hill, 1966).

65. Larry Kirkhart, "Toward A Theory of Public Administration", in Frank Marini (ed.) *Toward A New Public Administration* (San Francisco: Chandler Publishing Company, 1971), pp. 127–64.

66. Ibid., p. 144.

67. "Social Planning: The Search for Legitimacy", *Journal of the American Institute of Planners*, vol. 35 (1969), pp. 233–44.

68. Advocacy and Pluralism in Planning", *Journal of the American Institute of Planning*, vol. 31 (1965), pp. 331–38.

69. One congressional subcommittee issued a delightful selection of fables, anecdotes, homilies, and reflections under the title *Specialists and Generalists*, leaving little doubt that it much preferred the wisdom of the generalist to the sharp skills of the specialist. See U. S. Senate, Subcommittee on National Security and International Operations, *Specialists and Generalists: A Selection of Readings*, 90th Cong. 2d Sess.

70. Two leading works on organization theory by economists are Anthony Downs, *Inside Bureaucracy* (Boston: Little, Brown & Company, 1967) and William A. Niskanen, *Bureaucracy and Representative Government* (Chicago: Aldine-Atherton, 1971).

71. One of the few works on this subject, by its preeminent authority is Kenneth Culp Davis, *Discretionary Justice* (Baton Rouge: Louisiana State University Press, 1969).

5. Education for Public Anministration in the Seventies

DWIGHT WALDO

This essay, as its title states, is primarily about education for public administration in the 1970s—or more specifically, from the sixties to 1974—but I hope to be forgiven if I encroach somewhat on the territory of my colleagues. For it appears impossible to address the four years of the 1970s without copious reference to the past or to discuss current developments without some speculation about the future.

The subject will be addressed in three parts. First, I shall discuss the "ambience," the conditioning environment of ideas, values, perceptions, and events. Second, I shall report on some recent and current educational activities, responses, and initiatives. Third,

---

*This essay was drafted in January, 1974. A few changes were made in July, 1974, to add later data and further documentation; but the essay was not "rethought" in the light of six months of further history and the presentations of my colleagues in this series. I acknowledge with thanks the assistance of Eldon Steeves, particularly with the documentation.

In this essay I follow a practice I have recently adopted to help cope with the fact that "public administration" is a slippery term. I use Public Administration when the reference is clearly to the self-conscious activity—teaching, research, etc. I use public administration when the reference is (a) to the activity "out there," that is, the object of the teaching, research, etc., or (b) to the total complex of phenomena and activities, public-administrative institutions, activities, teaching, research, etc. For the purpose of consistency, I use the capital letters in referring to other academic fields.

I shall reflect upon some problems and prospects of the educational enterprise in and for public administration.

THE AMBIENCE: HERITAGE, EVENTS
AND VECTORS

The "surround" of education for public administration in the seventies is complex beyond any possible complete identification of its parts, much less of accurate determination of their relationships. This "surround" is the total of historical deposits and current events, of things material and ponderable interacting with ideas and sentiments ordinarily conceived as imponderable. Indeed, what "surround" is and what "it" is turns out, on close inspection, to be a matter of perspective, of convention and convenience.

In an attempt to put education for public administration in the seventies into context I shall, somewhat arbitrarily, address three subjects: (1) certain aspects of the heritage carried forward into the sixties and seventies; (2) the dislocations and ferment of the sixties; and (3) the events and movements of the seventies that appear of greatest relevance.

The Heritage. It is (I am prepared to argue) quite impossible to understand the accomplishments and problems of education for public administration in the seventies without the perspective of history. Therefore, I wish to refer to some aspects of the history of self-conscious Public Administration. While some of the aspects to which I call attention are generally well known (and are discussed elsewhere in this volume), my reasons for reiteration and emphasis will, I hope, be justified in the sequel. I shall be brief, as "telegraphic" as I can force myself to be.[1]

While of course a great deal of importance for Public Administration took place before the twenties and became a part of the heritage, self-conscious Public Administration came into being in the twenties, as heralded and symbolized by the L. D. White and W. F. Willoughby textbooks. White's textbook proved much the more influential, going into a second and then a third edition, and being extensively used through the midcentury decades.

The crucial fact of importance is that White "created" Public Administration by a formal joining of Political Science and "management." White was of course a professor of Political Science and a great deal of the theory and values of American Political Science was woven into the book. But the "tilt" toward management (and away from law) was deliberate—and influential.

Corollary premises included: (1) that management is a single process wherever found; (2) that administration can reasonably aspire to move from art toward science; (3) that problems of administration are now and will remain the central problems of modern government; and (4) that the objective of public administration is efficiency.[2]

White was a cautious man as well as a learned one. He knew that reality is not simple, and he made no dogmatic statements on what came to be called the "politics-administration dichotomy." But that he contributed substantially (ironically, in view of much of his later career) to a theoretical framework for public administration that could be so epitomized seems warranted on the evidence.

By definition, so to speak, this theoretical framework, this "tradition," placed very important matters outside of Public Administration. While Public Administration, thus conceived, devised "working compromises" with the Constitution and the three branches of government, it had only rather simple and problematic formulae with which to deal with the tremendous problem of reconciling the realm it had claimed for itself and the institutions and values known as democracy. In accepting—and emphasizing—an instrumentalist role it denied itself philosophy. Thus it was handicapped in trying to devise or adapt a "theory of politics," in dealing with problems of formulating public policy, in coming to grips with problems of ethics, in devising a theory (theories) of change appropriate to its tasks, in developing a rationale for having and exercising influence and power, and in developing a realistic and inspiring self-image.

Of course, I have simplified, perhaps oversimplified, to make my points. In any event, it should be recognized that numerous writers—both "in" and "out" of Public Administration—created in the thirties, forties, and fifties a more diverse and "inconsistent" literature than has been suggested. Paul Appleby, Marshall Dimock, John Gaus, Pendleton Herring, Norton Long, and Wallace Sayre are but outstanding representatives of those who enlarged and enriched the heritage. If, individually and even collectively, they did not redraw the basic "map" of Public Administration, they nevertheless changed it in significant detail.

In the thirties and early forties the basic postulates of Public Administration were occasionally (and increasingly) under critical attack. But after World War II these basic postulates were subjected to severe and extremely damaging critiques. The critiques, on the one hand, challenged both the method and the product of its "science" as presented in "principles" and, on the other hand, denied that its instrumentalist, value-neutral[3] stance was in accord with present realities or future possibilities.

The most notable of the critiques, that by Herbert Simon in *Administrative Behavior* (1947), was accompanied by a prescription for reform. Simon argued that the subtle apparatus of logical positivism, substituted for an uncritical positivist-pragmatism, would "save" the essentials: Science is indeed possible, and efficiency is indeed the objective. But there must be a reordering of the intellectual map; a distinction between (but a joining of) fact and value in all decisions must replace crude and unrealistic dichotomies, whether logical or institutional.

For whatever reasons, the Simon reformulation, though it gradually gained converts and became influential with the years, did not succeed in remaking the intellectual map of Public Administration. Rather, it became but one of various competing perspectives or "approaches," which included the case method, bureaucratic theory from Sociology, human relations, and comparative administration. Meanwhile, of course, though intellectually wounded, the basic postulates survived and continued to be influential through the fifties and sixties. In truth, they remain influential today, related as they are to major currents in American life (e.g., efficiency, productivity, science), and serving as they do to make pragmatic adjustments between an eighteenth-century constitution and a late twentieth-century world (e.g., in the idea of a competent and neutral civil service).

In the fifties, observers of the Public Administration scene began to comment on the openness and pliability of Public Administration, its great receptivity to ideas and techniques of varied provenience, accompanied by an inability—or at at least a disinclination—to address central problems of intellectual reconstruction posed by the postwar critiques. In the sixties—and into the seventies—this situation continued and was accentuated: a constantly greater mass and an increasing heterogeneity of what was putatively a part of (or importantly related to) Public Administration, together with failure to achieve and agree upon a new intellectual map. Some writers borrowed from Psychology the concept of an "identity crisis" and applied it to the discipline (subdiscipline? profession?): Public Administration is suffering from an identity crisis, having enormously expanded its periphery without retaining or creating a unifying center.

Such concerns were those of a minority, however; most Public Administrationists, challenged by the work of the day and fortified by a belief in its importance, seemed content to leave the "big issues" to others. Or to History.

The Sixties. The sixties are, of course, outside the scope of my assignment, and have been examined at some length by my immediate predecessor. But since the first years of the seventies are a mystery unless seen in the context of that extraordinary decade I wish to note, for my own purposes, some of its salient features.

The Cold War perhaps gave the dominant tone to the decade. Certainly this is true if the hostilities in southeast Asia may be regarded as the propensity of the Cold War to become, from time to time, "hot" at its margins.

The first years of the decade were marked by portentous confrontations, particularly in Berlin and in the Caribbean, and the mid- and later years were dominated by the Asian conflict, which threatened from time to time to become a world conflagration. The superpower status of the United States, given the Cold War, meant an extraordinary allotment of resources to military and (more generally) defense-related purposes. Our superpower concerns continued both to stimulate and to color an interest in international affairs and in the so-called Third World. The space race, begun in the fifties, was a Cold War product ("sublimation") that was prominent through the decade.

The economic expansionism and seeming prosperity of the postwar period continued into the sixties, faltering only in its final years—this despite the large military-defense outlays (and of course in some respects because of them). This acceleration in the production of "wealth," without historical precedent or contemporary equal, was transforming our landscapes and our living styles. At the same time, however, economic and social "distance" between different part of the population was increasing, and this increasing distance was increasingly perceived and became a stimulus to social-political action.

The forces and movements that accompanied the military-defense and economic motifs, which somehow reinforced them, sprang from them, arose in reaction to them, or at least somehow interacted with them, are beyond cataloguing, much less analyzing. A naming of some of the more prominent must suffice. A national war against poverty mounted by the dominant political party of the early and middecade, an effort that raised expectations that could not be (or at least were not) fulfilled. A movement for equal civil rights, which broadened into (or stimulated in reaction) a search for and assertion of ethnic identity, not only of blacks but of other components of the national mosaic. An "urban crisis" with seemingly endless facets: employment, race, housing, transportation, crime, drugs, taxation, planning, federalism, and so forth. The rise of civil disobedience, and beyond that, of increasing crime and violence, peaking in riots and the assassination of prominent public figures. An accelerated growth of science and, especially, science-related technology. A sharp upward movement in the number of students in educational institutions, and the level of their formal attainment. A sharply increasing awareness, particularly at the decade's end, of environmental costs, problems and dangers. The rise of the New Left (or reactivation of an *old* Left) and the strong assertion of a Counterculture. The continued growth of a "gray" area (or Third Sector) greatly complicating patterns of interaction between Public and Private as these have been perceived; and a concomitant "graying" of federal-state-city interrelations. A "turning inward" to address domestic problems, the growth of a mood of what has been termed neo-isolationism.

This listing is of course only suggestive, omitting, for example, the consumer and women's liberation movements and the surge of unionization in public administration. Nor does it seek (as does, for example, the literature of postindustrialism) to probe underlying tendencies or currents that might make sense of seeming diversity and tumult verging—it sometimes seemed—on the breakdown of the social order.

Elsewhere I have tried to "make sense" of the sixties by picturing several pairs of opposing forces in conflict, with resulting turbulence and irony.[4] Thus a revulsion against "governmental solutions" and a movement for "reprivatization" has been faced by a seemingly inevitable turning to government for solutions, with a continued growth in government expenditures and personnel. Thus the movement for equality in terms of rights and material goods has found itself confronting the implications of the renewed concern for resources and "environmental quality." Ultimately, however, one risks hubris if he presumes to understand the causes or the consequences in a societal panorama so full, so varied, so confused.

The above-listed phenomena impact public administration in innumerable ways, presenting problems for solution, narrowing or broadening the boundaries within which problems must be solved, supplying or denying tools for problem solution. They thus affect self-conscious Public Administration, which takes as its mission improvement in decision making and decision execution in the administrative world "out there." But there is a realm of less visible events and movements, of which Public Administration is also a part and to which it is also responsive: the world of intellectual currents and fashions, of academic economics and politics, of disciplinary shifts and fissions, of career opportunities and perceptions. To be sure, this "less visible" realm is closely joined to the world of widely noted public events and is not a separate realm; the distinction is one of convenience, of perspective. No attempt will be made here to discuss this less visible, less public, realm.[5] But various aspects of it will become relevant, and will become a part of the account and analysis, in what follows.

The Seventies. Four public-affairs "events" of the seventies strike me as of overriding importance for their actual or potential impact upon public administration: the ending of the Vietnam War, détente with China and Russia, the Watergate-related exposés and investigations, and the Arab-Israeli war of 1973 with its aftermath of energy shortages.

The catalytic factor that made the mid- and late sixties a period of extraordinary ferment and dislocation was unquestionably the Vietnam War. With American direct participation diminishing, and then formally ending in early 1973, one might expect a leveling off, perhaps even a sloping off, of some of the phenomena that were the subject of major news coverage in the late sixties and early seventies. This did indeed occur. Notably, campus and campus-related disturbances, and civil-disobedience episodes, declined sharply. Race-related violence declined (its role in prison violence apart). The strident, even ominous note sounded by various "causes" gradually diminished. With each year the New Left and the Counterculture seemed less likely to effect swift and drastic changes in established institutions and conventional values.

Patently, however, there has been and will be no "return to normalcy." One need not accept all the analyses and prognostications of *Future Shock*[6] to conclude that the present is, and the proximate future will be, characterized by rapid social, economic, and political change accompanied by a high level of ferment and stress. By and large, the causes and movements of the sixties have not vanished; they have adapted to altered circumstances and adopted strategies and tactics appropriate for longer time expectations. In so doing, their "radical" nature is seemingly diminished. Paradoxically, this may serve, by disarming resistance, to increase the long-range effect of some "causes." One must recognize, too, that much that once seemed new and threatening has had its edge dulled by time and familiarity. Further, one must appreciate that the partial success of various causes now brings them partially within the "establishment": civil rights, racial equality, environmental protection, consumerism, women's liberation, and other causes have changed laws and created new administrative arrangements to advance toward their goals. In short, the rules of the game have changed, but not the essential game.

The détente with China and Russia may prove in retrospect to have been the major event of the decade, of decisive import for the future of the nation, indeed of the world. If this proves to be true, public administration will have been profoundly affected, even though the effects on public administration to date are slight. On the other hand, the détente (with respect to either or both) may prove to have been but a temporary easing of tensions in a long-term confrontation. The future will instruct us on this portentous matter.

With respect to the various exposés and investigations for which "Watergate" is the sign, the situation is quite different. While the long-range implications of Watergate can only be speculative, obviously it is a complex of events of great import for public administration. Some of the results were apparent almost immediately: for example, delay or abandonment of plans for reorganization of federal administration. Others are "in process." They pertain to such fundamental matters as control over federal administration by *any* effective means, relative Presidential-Congressional-Judicial control of administration, the balance of powers and functions in the federal system—what shall be done, where, by whom, and how.

Clearly, not just the President but the Presidency has been wounded by Watergate. While much of what has and still may transpire goes far beyond "public administration" in any immediate sense, everything is still of a piece. The chief executive in general and the President in particular are potent symbols in and for public administration. And not only symbols: If our thories of cause and effect are correct, they are potent actors. Whatever, then, affects their functions and powers in the political system is of import for public administration.

Some of the possible implications for public administration, and for education in Public Administration, will be suggested below. For the present let me comment on but two points. The first is that Public Administration (allying itself with and relying upon strong currents in American life, in and out of academia) has placed much faith in the idea of a strong President, seeking both to draw upon that strength *and* to contribute to it. Perforce, the "alliance" must now be reassessed.

The second point is that a result of Watergate may be simultaneously to increase the power of administrative agencies ("the bureaucracy") and to diminish their prestige. As to the latter, Watergate clearly seems to have magnified a widespread belief that government generally is untrustworthy, inefficient, dishonest. While the "regular" bureaucracy might seem, to the close observer, almost to play a "hero" role in recent events, it is not likely that the general public makes such fine distinctions. *But* to turn to the government for solutions, for action, even though its prestige sinks, is a paradoxical fact of contemporary life. If the power of the executive to control is diminished, that of Congress and the judiciary is not thereby necessarily increased. The bureaucracy may be the "beneficiary." If so, this sharpens and (or) changes old questions of administrative power, policy and morality.

The fourth major public event of the seventies, the Arab-Israeli war of the autumn of 1973 is important chiefly for its aftermath, yielding neither a decisive military result (though its indecisiveness may, ironically, prove crucial) nor a definite test of the détente with Russia. The oil-related phenomena—embargoes, shortages, price increases, inflation—triggered by that conflict appear to have major national and indeed international importance. Magnifying an already-existing general energy problem, the oil embargoes and price increases clearly have impacted American public administration significantly in a very short period of time, and all signs point to a significant long-range effect.

What follows in the next section is an attempt to "fine down" from the rather grand, but necessarily sweeping or superficial, generalizations above. I wish to indicate how (beyond the few dicta above) I think the events and movements reviewed—in interaction among themselves and with other factors—provide context for and give shape to some aspects of public administration; and thus, actually or potentially, to education for public administration. (No significance attaches to the order of treatment. Nor is any attempt made to relate one item to another—which would mean a considerably extended treatment.)

CONTEXTUAL INFLUENCES AND IMPERATIVES: SOME OBSERVATIONS, EXTRAPOLATIONS— AND GUESSES

Socio-Economic Programs. The reference here is to programs, chiefly "people" programs, that were embraced (some inaugurated) under the ensign of the Great Society. The "retreat" here began before the end of the Johnson administration and was accelerated after the Nixon inauguration in 1968. Program failures, in fact or in perception, were both cause and effect in the retreat; and the retreat has been both cause and effect in whatever "return to normalcy" has occurred in the seventies. But—there has been and will be no return in expectations, programs, and administrative arrangements to the early sixties. The experimentation of recent years leaves a permanent residue of altered expectations and perceived options.

The prospect for the proximate future might be designated an "uneasy stalemate" arising from a balance of political forces; or one might think of it, more positively, as a period of digestion, reflection, gestation. In any event, a "crippled" President is little likely to be able to force major changes in a "conservative" direction; conversely, there is no indication that the Democrats (or anyone else) are prepared to lead in some "thrust forward."

Federal-State Relations: Functions and Powers. President Nixon's well-publicized intent to shift functions and powers from the federal government to the states (how much this means to local governments, or to "the people," is very cloudy) has been arrested by Watergate and its repercussions. Additionally, it will be arrested or even reversed if disruptions caused by the energy crisis bring crisis-type national programs; for crisis situations seem of necessity to bring vigorous national, i.e., federal, action.

Again, however, recent events will not be reversed. Revenue sharing and other aspects of the New Federalism have now created machinery and expectations that cannot be simply "turned off." Probably there will be further experimentation, but at a reduced level.

The Public-Private Balance/Mix. For reasons adduced for the previous two items (i.e., a balance of political forces and the lack of a national climate conducive to radical change) I do not sense or foresee any significant change in the public-private balance and mix.

There are of course long-range and deep-thrusting forces at work here, forces reaching far back into American history and related to industrialism and an alleged movement into postindustrialism. These forces and the artifacts they create are not easily changed—not by the "program" of a political party, no matter how great its so-called mandate, or in a few years by any possible force short of catastrophic crisis.

Contending forces "churn": antigovernment sentiments and movements press for market control, small government, "reprivatization"; but these are countered by requests, even loud demands, for governmental solutions to problems perceived as pressing. The result is the creation of an incredibly complex interlacing of the public and the private, the further erasure of a line already indistinct, the further growth of a "gray" area.

This "graying" will continue, and it will accentuate. The study of administration, whether "public" or "private," must reckon with this fact.

Neo-isolationism. This term came into use in the late sixties to designate a change in national mood (felt or expressed in different ways across the political spectrum) in the direction of concentration upon our own problems. The United States cannot, or ought not, to "police the world," or try to solve the social, economic, or political problems of other peoples. Morally, we have no warrant; practically, we have neither the knowledge nor the resources: we need to concentrate on our own serious problems.

To the extent that neo-isolationism has been a mood and a movement, qualifying if not reversing policies and programs of the fifties and sixties, it continues. Only the gravest of international crises (e.g., a serious worldwide depression caused by energy shortages) could bring large, new extranational expenditures, significant new extranational programs.

The import for Public Administration? The proximate future is not likely to see any spurt in the study of foreign administration or of "aid" mechanisms. "Funding," both public and private, now bends attention (in teaching and research) toward our own problems. The recent and still echoing cry for "relevance," ironically, meets with and enforces old, conservative tendencies *for* economy and *against* foreign ventures. This is a potent combination.

Science and Technology. The sixties and early seventies witnessed an upwelling of sentiment against science and technology. The sources were many, from the philosophical (even "spiritual") to the intensely practical, and the manifestations were many—from, say, the call (at M.I.T.) for a national day of scientific repentance and meditation to Luddite-spirited attacks upon "the machine." (Despite official acclaim and celebration, the moonwalks, when they occurred, took place in a subdued, almost apologetic atmosphere.)

Again, I do not expect the sentiments and events of recent years simply to be erased: there will be a permanent effect on our scientific and technological enterprises. But science and technology are writ so deeply into the record of the United States that they are not likely to be seriously curtailed, however much they may be refined or redirected by social mechanisms. New crises—energy, transportation, food—will emphasize the contribution (even if only *alleged* contribution, in the judgment of some) of scientist, engineer, researcher, technologist.

Prediction: the present close and growing interrelation of the scientific/technical enterprise with the governmental/administrative will continue. Opinion: it deserves increasing attention.

Urban-Metropolitan: A Withering Away? Here is a paradox: the more urban, the more metropolitan, the United States becomes, the less relevant to problem identification and problem solution such designations may become—this because, in a country overwhelmingly urban and increasingly metropolitan, such terms designate nearly everything and exclude hardly anything.

The sixties was a decade of popularity for urban-metropolitan approaches: in public discussion, in public policy, in special programs, in research and teaching. Presently, however, there would appear to be a two-way erosion. On the one hand, particular problem areas (e.g., transportation, crime, planning) are "factored out" for attention on their own; that they exist in an urban context is deemed important, of course, but they are not seen as "city" problems in a differentiating sense. Rather they are viewed as national or general problems. On the other hand, the rise of general "policy studies" poses a jurisdictional threat to urban-metropolitan study centers: in a highly urbanized society most of the policies to be studied are "urban" policies.

These remarks are not to be taken, of course, as a judgment on the product of the urban-metropolitan programs. Nor am I arguing there are not city problems "as such" and worthy of attention as such. Rather, I am trying to discern forces and trends; and I judge "urban-metropolitan" to be sloping off as an organizing or programmatic designation.

Productivity—A Revival? A number of currents in the sixties moved in the direction of criticizing "production" or of minimizing the importance of productivity: ours has become a "throw away" society, our obsession with production is despoiling the earth, materialism (linked with dire forces such as capitalism and imperialism) has taken over. With the maturation of industrialism, the problem of production has been solved, and with emerging postindustrialism other problems supersede this age-old problem.

Such currents still move strongly today, but in the seventies they have been met by strong countercurrents. These countercurrents have had several origins, e.g., the economic recession of the late sixties and early seventies, budget stringencies and "tax rebellions," a growing concern with foreign competition, the energy crisis, inflation.

Reflecting such matters in public administration, there has been in the seventies a considerable concern for "productivity." In important respects this is but a new name for an old central concern: issues of economy and efficiency.

The renewed emphasis upon productivity does not bring its proponents into direct confrontation with those who see issues of "equity" as the central ones of contemporary public administration; "both sides" would claim a substantial interest in the other's central concern. But the renewed interest in productivity (a) gives "economy and efficiency" a new importance, and (b) complicates problems of emphasis and "mix" in education for public administration.

Professionalism/"Credentialism." The overall increase in information, the rapid growth of "new" knowledge (particularly scientific and technical knowledge), multiplication and division of fields of knowledge, increasing specialization—these are matters that have received much attention in recent years. The related rise of scientific, technical, and professional organizations, and analysis of their implications and impact, has likewise received much attention. One of the most notable additions to our literature in recent years is Frederick C. Mosher's *Democracy and The Public Service* (1968), which examines the implications of increasing professionalism for the public service.

A theme prominent in the ferment of the sixties was that specialization had proceeded too far (producing narrow, warped human beings) and that professionalism had become selfish and self-defeating. The more affluent and the socially privileged, it was charged, were creating a new guild-feudal system: degrees, certificates, credentials were being used not to prove true competence but to gain privileged status and higher income—and to exclude those deemed "undesirable" in terms of family, ethnic origins, social status. This theme, combined with others, such as the charge that higher education had become formalistic and remote ("mandarin") and needed to be made "relevant" to the urgent problems of society, was pressed with considerable vigor. And with some success: educational systems, civil service systems, labor organizations and professional societies made concessions in response to the criticism.

At present, the protest against "credentialism" seems to be waning, the strong forces of specialization and professionalism again ascendant. But the situation is complicated, and—as with the matters noted above—some effects of recent and contemporary protest will be long-lasting if not "permanent."

Patently, the issues in contention are of prime importance for public administration. They bear upon "civil service" philosophy and techniques generally. It would appear that *both* increasing professionalization and the protest against "credentialism" pose threats, the former against traditional civil-service authority and control, the latter against the "merit principle" (i.e., against the way it has been interpreted and applied). Centrally involved, also is the question whether public administration is (totally or by parts) a "profession" for which curricula can be prescribed, educational programs accredited, and so forth. This perennial question is about to be addressed with renewed seriousness.

Other Contextual Complexes, Vectors. This attempt to indicate the environment of recent and contemporary education for public administration can appropriately end with the admission that, in addition to the errors and limitations of the foregoing discussions, the treatment is limited by its lack of completeness. Nothing has been said (other than perhaps a mention in passing) of such important matters as public-service unionism, consumerism, client-centered administration, affirmative action. And there is the problem noted above, namely, over much of the terrain of interest to us, how does one realistically distinguish between "context" and "public administration"?

THE EDUCATIONAL SCENE: DIRECTIONS, ACTIVITIES, MOTIFS

My objective now is to convey information about recent and contemporary education for public administration—trends, rationales, methods, and so forth.[7] I shall first address some overall factors and trends; then trends in the organization and presentation of education for public administration; then some trends in curriculum content and rationale; and finally some trends in the intellectual-conceptual map. I shall try to reserve for the concluding section personal analysis and speculation, centered on what are perceived to be central problems and crucial choices.

Some Overall Factors and Trends. Recent and contemporary trends in education for public administration display and accentuate its propensity to enlarge its perimeter, to increase both in mass and diversity, without, however, moving decisively toward an agreed upon intellectual paradigm or well articulated "public philosophy." A fateful question seems posed: does Public Administration, by becoming "everything in general," thereby become "nothing in particular"? Whether, and in what ways, the present situation is a reason for pessimism or optimism depends upon the viewpoint and the mood of the observer. But the *facts* of increasing mass and diversity are clear.[8]

Public Administration moves outward in diverse directions or, if one chooses to view it differently, is impacted or invaded from diverse quarters. In some sectors it seeks to move toward science, while in other sectors it seeks philosophy and (or) a closer alliance with "values." In some sectors it continues to respond to historic impulses and objectives, while in other sectors it bends its efforts to accommodate impulses from the New Left and the Counterculture, or at least from recently fashionable intellectual currents. In some sectors it tries diligently to maintain and even improve the traditional filial relation with Political Science, while in other sectors this has become a meaningless (perhaps even an undesirable) objective.

The increase in the mass or size of Public Administration seems clear. This is true on a "strict construction" of Public Administration, in terms of teaching staff, students in courses and programs, degrees awarded. If a "broad construction" is used, and Public Administration is taken to mean teachers, courses, and so forth, in courses that are Public Administration "in fact" if not in

name, then the recent increase in size is the more impressive. To
be sure, only a fraction of 1 percent of those entering the public service work force each year are products of Public Administration programs—or of Public Affairs or similarly named programs. But there has never been any aspiration to put a Public
Administration label on the great majority of public employees,
only a hope to prepare enough able persons to make an important
difference in the "administrative" component of public employment. The measure of recent growth is best taken by comparing
Public Administration with other programs, and viewing recent
absolute increases against the budgetary stringencies and "cut
backs" in academia during recent years.[9] Public Administration
has been sustained and increased in part simply in response to the
fact that public employment has continued its secular upward
trend.[10] But in part it is the beneficiary of the events and accompanying sentiments of the sixties and early seventies. Public administration has (widely, not universally, of course) been perceived as "relevant," as a place where "concerned action" can be
taken. This has been a frequent student perception; and while it
might be said to be a normal belief of Public Administration faculty, this normal belief has in recent years been abnormally strong,
especially among younger faculty members. Concurrently, with
the economic stringencies of the recent period and with some fad-
ing of the impulses from the sixties and early seventies, there is a
renewed interest in "practical," if not exactly "traditional," mat-
ers. The result is a new mix of the altruistic and personal, of the
idealistic and practical/professional.

The attenuation of the historic connection with Political Science—Public Administration being thought of as a "field" thereof,
as a subdiscipline of a discipline—continues. The reasons for this
are varied, but they include the following. Older Political Science
is strongly imbued with the "liberal arts" tradition, and the interest of Public Administration in practical affairs ("counting manhole covers") and vocational training rendered it suspect from
the start.[11] Newer Political Science, the behavioral wave following
World War II, has viewed Public Administration as a backward
area of the discipline, as its adherents were more interested in

applied science (at best) than in research seeking (in the "proper way") to advance scientific frontiers. Sensing the disinterest or disdain, but convinced of the importance of their enterprise, Public Administrationists have been inclined to withdraw from Political Science connections, informal or formal. Any tendency to withdraw on such grounds has been greatly accentuated by other important circumstances. One is that Political Science gave scant help with matters of importance; that is, if Political Science is conceived as the source of the theory (scientific or other) that is to be applied in governmental administration, then it failed badly. Other disciplines and "foci," on the other hand, were judged as capable of supplying data and theory of great utility. Thus among the other disciplines, especially Economics, Sociology, and Social Psychology; and thus among foci, systems theory and computer science.

Though evolution steadily diminishes the Political Science-Public Administration bond, the bond remains important.[12] Well over a third of the programs in Public Administration are formally within Political Science departments, and many teachers, young as well as old, have their advanced degrees in Political Science and give this designation their primary allegiance. Still, the trend seems clear. Many programs located in a department of Political Science are so located because there is no feasible alternative, given history and available resources. The number of teachers coming from independent (or at least non-Political Science) programs is increasing (certainly in absolute and probably in relative terms). And the proportion of Political Science based courses compared to courses based in other disciplines or specialties, beyond question, has been and is diminishing.

Trends in Program Organization and Presentation. Trends in the organization and presentation of education for public administration somewhat resemble those evident with regard to courses, ideas, and so forth: up to this point there is great, and increasing, diversity. This is evidenced dramatically in the membership roster of the National Association of Schools of Public Affairs and Administration. Membership has grown rapidly in recent years, now totaling 125 "domestic" members. The designations of members are highly diverse: schools, departments, programs, institutes, and so forth, provide nouns; while adjectives and adjective phrases include not only public affairs and public administration, and political science, but various more specialized, programmatic designations. (The decision on the name itself—to include Public Affairs as well as Public Administration—was of course significant, indicating a lack of confidence that Public Administration is precise or strategic.)

Some of the trends in program organization and presentation move, in a formal sense, in opposite directions. Whether this signifies complementarity or contradiction is a matter of interpretation.

One trend is toward increasing the amount and diversity of postentry education. Centrally involved is the knowledge explosion, with its implications for the obsolescence of knowledge learned in youth in professional schools, and for shifts in career channels, particularly from another specialization to administration. But there are other sources of support. One is increasing attention to adult or continuing education generally, a movement to follow pedagogy with "androgogy."[13] Another is the criticism (prominently a part of the ferment of recent years) of the rigidity and formalism of the academy, and the resulting movements to "deschool" education: to create "universities without walls," to substitute work experience for classroom instruction, to set up educational ventures in nonacademic locations, to experiment with new learning techniques.[14]

On the other hand, there is some tendency for education for public administration to move downward, evidenced by more numerous, and larger, programs that award a bachelor's degree in Public Administration. Some of these programs are specialized by level or function of government; and in some cases instruction in Public Administration merely becomes a part of occupational preparation nominally in some other area (perhaps resulting in a certificate rather than a degree). While in a formal sense this movement "downward" is at odds with the movement "upward," in fact both movements have something in common. Both are (or at least may be) responses to the criticism that educational forms are traditional and rigid, and do not permit learning (and employment) at the times and places that are most appropriate for both individual and society.[15]

Recently two related trends have been important. One is for schools of business administration to introduce or expand programs in preparation for public administration—"public-sector management."[16] Movement in this direction has taken place partly in response to a perception that many graduates will be going into public-service, or public-service-related, employment. (Many already are, and with the "public sector" constantly enlarging and with an increasing "gray area," a prudent business sense, so to speak, would dictate that attention be given to producing a suitable and saleable product.) In part, the movement in this direction has come from signals on the "supply" side, i.e., the recruitment of students: To youths accustomed to affluence, a career in business does not have the strong appeal it once did. This may or may not be a secular trend, but certainly the ferment of recent years produced a search for "relevance" or "social engagement" that led many youths to reject what their fathers had earnestly sought.

Related to the growth of public-sector programs in schools of business is the movement toward "generic schools": schools of administration or of management without a qualifying adjective. Movement in this direction takes place in two ways. One is the establishment *de novo* of such schools; the other is the renaming of established schools, i.e., the "school of business" becomes a "school of management."

As the idea that management or administration is essentially the same wherever found (no matter the function of the particular organizations in which it is performed) has been with us for decades, perhaps the wonder is that there was not earlier, and greater, experimentation in this direction. Be that as it may, experimentation has now begun, and schools of management as well as schools of business now concern themselves with education for public-sector employment. The trends reinforce: A "school of management" has a logical appropriateness, as well as greater psy-

chological appeal, if the mission is expanded beyond business.
Again, at least in a formal sense, there is a countertrend. As
against the "generic" idea, there is a trend toward the establishment of programs focused upon particular functions, i.e., toward
specialization in preparation for some "part" (program, level or
tool) of public administration. This specialization, for example in
economic analysis, social-services administration, urban affairs,
health administration, judicial administration, may be comprehended in a school or program of Public Administration; but it
may also now be established on an independent or quasi-indepen-
dent basis. To be sure, specialization is not new—witness, for example, long-established programs preparing for city management
or for personnel management. But the normal bent of modern
society toward specialization has been reinforced, rather paradoxically, by reform currents critical of "establishment" ways.[17]

Still again, parallel and overlapping countermovements: There
is a movement, on the one hand, toward schools, centers, institutes,
or programs of policy study, policy analysis, or policy science.
Whatever the formal designation, the motivating idea is that policy, in general or "as such," is the proper focus for sustained attention, including research and teaching—some of which, at least, can
prepare for careers in public bureaucracies. Typically, a policy
"center" is—whatever else—interdisciplinary, drawing persons
from various disciplines into some kind of working relationship.
The "mix" will vary, but economists are likely to be the most
highly visible, and quantitative and formal analytic tools are likely
to be stressed.[18]

On the other hand, it appears that a considerable number of
specialized (i.e., specialized by function or field) institutes, centers, and programs that emphasize "policy" are also being established. These overlap or blend into the special programs noted
above, especially if preparation for a career on the "outside" is
stressed. But the stress may be on policy or analysis, in which case
the "flavor" tends to be that of the general center, even if the
ambition is sectoral rather than global.[19]

Trends in Curriculum Content and Rationale. In speaking to recent and contemporary trends in curricula it is appropriate, first, to stress a point already made. I refer to the attenuating connection with Political Science and the complementary inclination to draw upon other disciplines and foci. The favored disciplines are Economics, Sociology, and Psychology (especially Social Psychology). Business Administration and Management Science are less clearly "disciplines"; but however they may be designated, subjects and techniques characteristic of them are often drawn upon— especially of course in programs located in schools of business or management. Some foci of intellectual-scientific interest it seems most appropriate to regard as interdisciplinary or nondisciplinary. Thus statistics (though if occasional departmental status establishes a disciplinary claim, then the claim can be made), computer science, organization science, and systems theory and techniques of analysis. Whatever their origins and affiliations, they are now drawn upon extensively in choosing, naming, and constructing courses.[20]

The decline of Law continues. Constitutional Law receives slight attention, and even administrative law is little stressed—in fact, even a single course therein may not be required in a master's program.[21] Interest in and use of the case method of inquiry and education in Public Administration probably peaked in the sixties. But the case method continues to be used extensively, and in the seventies there is no evidence to suggest a sharp decline and fall.

Three major traditional curriculum "areas" continue in popularity, but continue also to be transformed. These areas are personnel, budgeting, and organization. Some, I fear, believe that Public Administration is mired in tradition because it continues to instruct under these rubrics—or more accurately, some variation on them. But this is misperception, and an unfair conclusion, at least for the great majority of the programs in Public Administration.

In content and spirit these three areas have been deeply altered through the years, as a comparison of the teaching materials and methods of the thirties and the seventies graphically illustrates. Personnel administration has been vastly altered by the Human Relations vogue and by later researches and movements, as well as by the equal-rights movements of the sixties and seventies. Budgeting has been transformed by, first, the Performance Budgeting movement, and then by the Planning, Programming, Budgeting System complex of ideas and techniques, which rose to high popularity in the late sixties; and by a liaison with Economics and the policy analysis movement. Organization has become a vast field in which "traditional" organization theory is only an introduction (or a curiosity), a field with a heterogeneous literature arising in (or connected with) Sociology, Social Psychology, systems theory, management science—or (allegedly) organization science per se.

These generalizations are suggestive only.[22] It would necessitate a substantial essay for each area to do justice to a generation of change.

Indicative of a trend toward professionalization, the (foreign) language requirement for the master's degree has all but disappeared and a minority of programs require a master's thesis in the scholarly mold. In some cases a "thesis-size" exercise in administrative analysis or problem solving (perhaps a group enterprise) takes the place of the traditional thesis. On the other hand, internships are frequently required or at least are optional. No doubt they would be more widely required were they not so demanding of scarce faculty time and so difficult to administer properly. There is some disposition to solve the "experience" problem by requiring an administrative work record prior to matriculation. The great majority of masters programs have a "program requirement" in basic statistics, and many have also program requirements in more advanced quantitative/mathematical techniques, data processing, and computer science.

Trends in the Intellectual-Conceptual Map. The matters to which I am about to speak certainly are trends in (or affecting) the teaching of Public Administration, but it seems appropriate to regard them as matters that are not solely "curricular," however much they bear upon the curriculum.

One of these concerns the political, in general and with special relation to public administration. What has been happening with reference to—in the words of the cliché—"the breakdown of the politics-administration dichotomy"?

What can be reported is that, at least on the empirical side, a great deal of progress has been made. For decades now a varied and rewarding literature has been building—essays, monographs, cases, research reports—that treats the interaction of the political and the administrative (the effect of politics on administration, the politics of administration, etc.). The past few years have witnessed notable additions to that literature—works of depth, sophistication, balance. We now "know" that administration is a process or function that takes place in, and in conjunction with, a political process or function; we have a great deal of information on what takes place, how, and why, and we have adapted our emotional responses and our professional expectations to this knowledge.[23]

The situation on the normative side is not so happy, if clear articulations of political theory and ethics rather than pragmatic adjustments to the "facts of life" are the criteria. Of this, more below.

"Policy" is of course closely related to politics, as etymology alone suffices to indicate. (It is a relevant circumstance that some languages closely related to English have only one word for the "two things.") But by convention we tend to draw the two apart. While recognizing the close interaction of politics and policy (making and execution), we have rather different cognitive maps and emotional responses in the two cases. These differing responses, one suspects, are deeply rooted in a general national experience and are reinforced by certain intellectual and professional orientations. "Policy" (we believe) is somehow better, less tainted and dangerous. The right of an administrator to engage in "policy" is clearer; indeed, he may be perceived as having no choice but to do so. Since he should, or must, then he needs help; and fortunately (we believe), he can be helped by the apparatus of scholarship and science.

There is, then, a differential response to politics and policy, however close the two may be interwoven. On the empirical side we are probably not as good—that is to say, as responsive—to the recognition that policy can no more be separated from administration than politics. But on the normative side we are better; we may not be ready with substantive advice in various policy areas (though there is some of this), but we certainly believe that we can help with the *process* of policy making, by supplying (for example, and depending on circumstances) historical perspective, conceptual clarification, theoretical frameworks, quantitative measures, analytical tools, and guiding values.

I do not mean to suggest that empirical studies of policy making in administration are lacking or of poor quality. A moment's reflection suffices to cast up monographs, cases, analyses, of note and in number; in fact—remembering that Pendleton Herring's signal work in this area preceded World War II—it is obvious that for decades there have been good empirical studies of administrative policy making. But recent years have not witnessed any upwelling; this has not been an active area of scholarly-scientific work.

On the normative-prescriptive side the picture is very different, as the above noted burgeoning of policy-centered programs, institutes, centers, and schools indicates. In the sixties, one looking for a "growth stock" in academia would have done well to put his capital on something with "policy" in its name; this probably would *still* be a good risk, for there is no visible diminution of interest in policy studies. While policy study tends to be an important aspect of Public Administration, the majority of the institutes, centers, programs, and so forth, are organizationally outside of Public Administration entities. But they are relevant to the future of public administration, and of course relevant to the future of Public Administration.[24]

It is characteristic of recent and contemporary Public Administration that both "hard" and "soft" methodologies are advancing. In a formal sense this appears to be a paradox. But while the situation does make for occasional anomalies and ironies, the two seemingly contrary trends not only coexist but perhaps are moving toward some kind of synthesis.

Perhaps "technologies" would be better than "methodologies." Anyhow, I refer to a wide spectrum of means by which the social world is apprehended and changed, some based on what are regarded as well-established science but some regarded as humanistic and exploratory. These means, these methodologies—consisting of collections of data, bodies of theory, methods of inquiry, congeries of norms, personal and interpersonal skills—are (by intention) passed to the student as his professional endowment.[25]

On the "hard" side the folowing can be discerned: (1) The impact of the post-World War II behavioral wave in and flowing from Political Science. The impact has been relatively light, as noted above, and it was delayed. But still there has been and is an impact. (2) A greater emphasis upon statistics and quantitative analysis. This comes from a "market" analysis and from a reading of the "competition," as well as from a disinterested conclusion that such skills are useful in administration. (3) The pressing in of, and the borrowing from, other disciplines and foci: Economics, Sociology, systems theory, and others. Both tools of research, in an academic sense, and techniques for application in administration have been sought. (4) The effects of the development of the computer and of "information science," bringing training in computer programming, data processing, and so forth. These various strands of "hard" methodologies are not discrete, of course, but meet and meld in various ways.

On the "soft" side the following can be discerned: (1) The lingering influence of the liberal arts-humanist heritage from Political Science: This, it may be correct to say, is occasionally refreshed or augmented by influences from the Counterculture. (2) Impulses stemming from the ferment of the sixties. Some of these are New-Left, more are of Counterculture, derivation—however attenuated the derivation. They are associated with the so-called New Public Administration. They find expression in various ways, including an attempt to find and implement equalitarian norms ("social equity") and a search for modes of human interaction to replace bureaucratic formalism. (3) The human-relations movement, as broadened and deepened by new influences, chiefly from Social Psychology. The "names" here are, prominently, Abraham Maslow, Douglas McGregor, Warren Bennis, Rensis Likert, Chris Argyris. (4) The sentiments, objectives, techniques and experiments designated by Organization Development. The taproot here runs (probably) to the National Training Laboratory; but there is now a varied set of impulses and a considerable variety of techniques aimed at changing, correlatively, organization and personality. (5) Impulses toward philosophical restructuring. There is a desire in some quarters to reject logical positivism and interpretation of the enterprise of science associated with it and to accept other philosophic groundings, prominently the view(s) designated by phenomenology. Again, these "soft" currents are not to be viewed as discrete; they meet and mix in many subtle ways.

If this attempt to depict a "hard" and a "soft'" component of contemporary Public Administration evokes a vision of two forces in frontal engagement this is an erroneous vision. While there are militants of various persuasions, the "mix" of ideas, persons, programs, and movements is much too complicated to be pictured thus. In fact, what may be the most significant characteristic of the situation is that not only do methodologies of varying provenience and purpose coexist with relatively little overt disharmony, there is a remarkable mingling of hard and soft technologies—sometimes in the psyche and professional activities of a single individual. This *may* have something to do with the "applied" objective of Public Administration, an impulse to get on with the "mission"—which makes Public Administration less prone than (say) Political Science to engage in academic disputation and factional warfare. Some may (and do) view the resulting situation as one of intellectual sloth and flabbiness; but arguing from pragmatic and situational premises (indeed, even from highly regarded epistemological and scientific bases) a favorable rather than unfavorable construction is possible.

PROBLEMS AND PROSPECTS: SOME REFLECTIONS

In this concluding section I wish to direct attention to certain critical problem areas with respect to education for public administration. In doing so I shall move overtly and intentionally from "reporting" to "analysis." Beyond analysis, I shall in some cases indicate my guess as to future developments. Until I reach the final sections I shall stop short of "prescription," though no doubt some of my preferences will be indicated.

A useful perspective in beginning the undertaking is provided by recurring to the framework for Public Administration set forth by L. D. White. I shall say something with respect to each premise reviewed above, and then move beyond them.

The Joining of Political Science and Management. The considerations that led L. D. White to "marry" Political Science and the New Management appear in retrospect to have been reasonable, if not persuasive beyond challenge. Small as they seem in retrospect, by the twenties governmental functions had grown tremendously since the Civil War, and problems presented in public administration were serious. In the search for remedies, where would one turn for ideas and techniques? Political Science, as W. F. Willoughby (in the preface to his textbook, which followed White's by a year) observed, simply did not address the new area of administration; whereas the scientific-management movement at that time was so vigorous that it even drew the praise of the premier Bolshevik, Lenin. But to regard Public Administration as *formally* an aspect and subdivision of Political Science was eminently reasonable—and all but necessary for a professor of Political Science. Where else might it "belong"?

In retrospect—I believe it is proper to speak thus—it is clear that the union was a marriage of convenience. Public Administration certainly could not make its own way in the world, and it had no other place to go; and the marriage did serve some purposes for both parties. For Public Administration departmental status and disciplinary inclusion were substantial benefits; and Public Administration contributed to the union in various ways—after all, its image as "Useful" has, innumerable times, served Political Science well at budget time. However, Public Administration never was fully accepted by and integrated into Political Science. To change the metaphor, it was rather like a grafted organ. Its applied mission and its "alien" technology stimulated antibodies that constantly acted to reject the transplant.

What is the future of the relationship? Conceivably (as suggested above) certain changes in Political Science might operate to reverse the attenuation. I have in mind such possibilities as the following: The movement (arising in the ferment of the sixties and paralleling New Public Administration) for a "new" Political Science, one that is "relevant" to today's problems, becomes influential enough to change the agenda and tone of Political Science. The vigorous movement toward a "new" Political Economy becomes strong enough to carry Political Science generally in that direction. The policy-studies movement proves strong enough to reconstruct the social-science map, bringing Political Science generally into a new posture. These three movements, especially the second two, are somewhat related; individually, and especially collectively, it is possible that they would so reconstruct the disciplinary-professional map that what we know as Public Administration would be again closely joined with Political Science (whatever name(s) might be given to the result).[26]

While I do not judge that we will move far in this direction in the proximate future, I do not want to be understood as arguing the irrelevance of Political Science for Public Administration. Quite the contrary: Political Science is *logically* the central disciplinary contributor to a profession (or the professions) of Public Administration, just as Biology is the central disciplinary contributor to a profession (or the professions) of Medicine—to anticipate an argument made below. Medicine is not Biology, but without Biology it is an absurdity or a fraud; Public Administration is not Political Science, but without that which by definition Political Science *should* contribute, it is an absurdity or a fraud. If Political Science fails to contribute what is needed, then it must be "self"generated, or perhaps borrowed—with more or less adaptation and even distortion—from other disciplines and foci.

Management Is a Single Process. The proposition that management or administration is the same phenomenon, no matter the enterprise in which it is found, not only has survived, it has thrived. In fact, one can say that in the generic school the full logic of the proposition is finally realized. Rather ironically, what was to White the basis upon which the legitimacy of Public Administration could be argued can become the basis upon which it can be denied.

Is the proposition "correct"? This is a complicated matter, the exploration of which is far beyond the scope of this essay. Suffice it to say that, on the one hand, given the parameters and purposes of those who have made the argument, the proposition can be argued cogently and persuasively: there *are* uniformities in large-scale cooperative endevaors over a wide spectrum of the human experience, and one can profitably study and generalize about them. On the other hand, if one chooses not to accept certain premises and purposes, the case is weaker and, perhaps, collapses in ruins: the "generic" argument is time- and culture-bound, an attempt to universalize certain values and techniques of the modern West and (or) an attempt (even if not seen as such) to constrain the human future within a limited set of possibilities

At all events, the generic school is now with us. It is, I believe, an experiment worthy of the investment of considerable resources. It may well prove to be the best "solution" in some circumstances, the optimal way to "put things together" to achieve certain results. Conceivably it may prove to be *the* organizational form of the future fifty years hence it may seem quaint that there were once separate schools and programs of administration. On the other hand, the generic school, however persuasive its logic, faces substantial practical problems, and these may prove decisive. These pertain to the optimal size of educational units, to the diversity of the habitats and functions of administration, and to the forces of specialization and professionalization in the university and in society. It is easy enough (well, there may be some arguments . . .) to specify a curriculum common to all who wish preparation for administration: quantitative methods, organizational sociology and social psychology, systems theory and analytical techniques. But how is the "common core" to be bridged over to the different functional areas; how is it to be adapted to the pulls and demands of specialization and professionalization? To these practical problems there are practical responses; the generic schools develop separate programs or options, such as business administration, public administration, health administration, educational administration. Such responses "make sense." But they also make generic schools vulnerable to the charge that the change is nominal and not substantial; that to keep things on a proper scale and in a convenient location, and to adjust to "habitat," it makes (at least) equal sense to have the "generic" subjects taught in separate schools or programs.[27]

Administration as Science. The proposition that administration can aspire to move from art toward science has fared well. In fact, it is much more widely credited today than it was in the twenties. We have come a long way. The arguments of the twenties and thirties about "art" and "science" now strike us as quaint. We view them as failures to identify referents and to use proper terminology, as attempts to impose simplistic or erroneous categories on the administrative world. We are, generally, willing to admit a certain truth in the "art" argument—*after* qualifications are made, new terminology is used, the relevant universe is specified. Here the distinction between theoretical and practical science (as set forth, for example, in the appendix of Simon's *Administrative Behavior*) has proved useful; it helps in determining where differences of opinion are genuine, not illusory.

On the other hand, beliefs that we have already arrived at firm scientific "principles," even that we are about to achieve them, have fared badly. Almost, it could be said, the firmer the conviction that scientific method is the road to Truth and that one day we will have "genuine" scientific knowledge about administrative phenomena, the more doubtful and apologetic about present knowledge. But the faith is strong, and the total of resources devoted to increasing scientific knowledge of things administrative is very substantial. Comparatively little of the research (by most understandings of the term) is in or supported by Public Administration; it borrows and adapts, for the most part, and this situation is not likely to change in the immediate future. The reasons why this is true have been suggested and, while they are several, differential access to resources is certainly prominent among them.

What will be most significant for the immediate future is the result of reformist and humanist forces generated or accentuated by recent (and "present") history acting upon and interacting with the secular drive to make administration more scientific. While no doubt there are real antinomies, I commented above upon the possibility of syntheses; contrary to what sheer logic might seem to dictate, "hard" and "soft" approaches have a way of melding.

Beyond administration, beyond social science, are events and movements that are ultimately decisive. For example, the strength and direction of the recent "revolution against science" is yet unclear. What is possible or impossible in administration cannot be divorced from the deepest currents that move society and its thoughtways.

The Centrality of Administrative Problems. What of the proposition that it is problems of administration that are the central problems of modern government? The first thing to note is that while, almost by definition, the Public Administrationist believes this to be true, Political Scientists generally (in the several other fields or subdisciplines) have not and do not believe it to be true—which is both cause and result of the diminishing relationship. On the other hand, and ironically, to judge by their scholarship, a significant number of persons identified with other disciplines believe that the proposition is true. If we extend the relevant universe beyond *public* administration to administration generally, and beyond modern *government* to modern *society*, then the number of persons in other disciplines who work in this spirit is greatly extended.

As one widens the circle of attention beyond academia, one encounters puzzles, baffling contradictions. At base is the contradiction, the churning, commented on above. On the one hand, forces—historical, institutional, ideological—making for "small government" are massive and powerful. On the other hand, there is a steady movement toward increasing governmental (which means administrative) functions; and even those opposed, theoretically or "in general," to increasing the functions of government are likely, as a practical matter, to contribute to this secular movement.

What results might—unhappily—be summarized thus: the people will the ends of public administration but not the means. They have a generalized dislike of governmental administration—"bu-

reaucracy." They would like public administration to be efficient
—or would they, remembering "Good government is dangerous.
Efficient government eats holes in our liberties"? In any case, they
are not prepared to take much interest in public administration or
to commit substantial resources to improving it.

In the background looms a very substantial matter: the large
and increasingly large "gray" area where the conventional categories of public and private are mingled in intricate new ways;
and related thereto the trends that are usually discussed as a movement from industrialism to postindustrialism. Where, in what
ways, does the question "Are public administration problems the
central problems of modern government?" cease to be a meaningful question, because it is not clear what "*public* administration"
or "government" *is*? Do the forces in operation here, by melding
old distinctions and creating new relationships, increase the plau-
sibility of the generic approach?

Efficiency as the Objective of Public Administration. The idea
that efficiency is the objective of public administration, and thus
central to Public Administration, has had a troubled and tortuous
history, but remains vigorous and, in the main, respectable today.

The barest acquaintance with the history of Public Administration gives awareness that efficiency, together with the close-linked
matter of economy, has been criticized, qualified, refined, and
redefined at length. (One probably would not, today, speak of
efficiency as the "objective" of public administration, but he
would speak of it as a "criterion," or perhaps a "value.") The
history of critical attack and defense, of demolition and reconstruction, cannot even be sketched. What warrants noting is only
that out of the protest and ferment of the sixties came a new
assault upon efficiency. Efficiency, it was asserted, is a covert
ideology; it is an alleged "neutral" mask hiding a preference for
establishment values, for actual waste in the pursuit of private
profit, for an inequitable distribution of national income, and so
forth. Moreover, in the transition from industrialism to postindustrialism, it is becoming increasingly irrelevant. Only habit abetted
by greed drives us toward increased productivity; the problem of

productivity has been "solved," and problems of distribution and social equity now are central. However, questions of efficiency were not so easily put aside. Economic recession plus political realities brought to prominent attention "productivity" in public administration, and "productivity" proved to be largely a matter of "economy and efficiency."

Additionally, it should be observed that questions of economy and efficiency are (were?) obviously at the center of the Planning, Programming, Budgeting System, even though a different terminology was customary. They are also involved in the current concern with "evaluation." The more complex governmental programs become, the more intangible the products of public administration, the more difficult it is to judge success, the more important it is to measure results. In the attempt, it would seem that the considerations historically designated by the terms "economy" and "efficiency" cannot be ignored, no matter how humanitarian the objective, no matter how humane the administration.

What is implied for directions in education for public administration? What is suggested, certainly, is that the enterprises—Business Administration, Economics, "management science"—that have made considerations of economy and efficiency central in their concerns have an important contribution or even an active role. But at the same time it needs to be recognized that these enterprises do not have the "answers." If they did, PPBS would still be tracing an ascending line, "productivity" would not be a matter of controversy, and "evaluation" would not so often seem an impossibility.

POLITICAL-ETHICAL PROBLEMS

Reflecting on the recent development, present posture, and future possibilities of education *in* Public Administration in relation to education *for* public administration, I think I discern two major "clusters" of problems. Since—as will be clear—these two clusters interrelate and there is some arbitrariness in my assignment of matters between them, perhaps my clustering represents more an attempt to order my own psyche than an "objective" ordering of events and ideas. Be that as it may, I shall conclude by addressing, first, "Political-Ethical Problems" and then "The Paradigm Problem."

By political-ethical problems is meant the cluster of problems created for Public Administration when it became clear that politics and policy cannot be separated from public administration and that a science of administration based upon the premise that administration has only an instrumentalist role is impossible. The problems involved are not neatly sorted and catalogued, and someone could do us a service by "surveying and mapping" the terrain. But they include, to illustrate, the following: What meaning, if any, can properly be ascribed to the concept of a "neutral" civil service—if at least certain kinds of neutrality are impossible? How can a *non*neutral public administration be justified in, and adapted to, the Constitutional system? Whence should an administrator get norms for official decision making and official-related personal conduct, so far as these are neither given to him by Constitutionally derived sources (or these sources conflict!) nor flow "inexorably" from technical-scientific sources? Regardless of provenience, how can such norms be *justified*?

The first and crucial thing to do is to recognize the magnitude of the problem, for the problems in the cluster are aspects of one large problem. In an overall way *the problem is probably insoluble*, given as parameters major facts of American history, culture, and political system as developed under the Constitution. If this is true, then to blame Public Administrationists for failing to "solve" it, that is to say, to replace the neat formulae of the instrumentalist model with other neat formulae, is rather like blaming geometricians for inability to square the circle or physicists for failure to invent a perpetual-motion machine. Let me put it as a question: How *could* public administrationists, given a Constitution that does not even contain the word administration (or management), justify and rationalize the exercise of substantial independent power? The public administrationist, in trying to "solve" the problem, is in a dilemma. In one direction is the Constitution, the institutions and expectations created under it. In the other direction is the complex of sentiments and expectations, historically derived, we know as democracy. To go in either direction risks bloody impalement. The "bureaucrat" is a subordinate or "derived" actor under the Constitution, and there seems to be no way to give him legitimate unambiguous power (assuming that to be desirable) following the Constitutional route. But unless elected (in which case technically, of course, he is not a bureaucrat) he cannot clearly claim the legitimacy that is given by the Democracy that has grown upon and supplements the Constitution. (Theories by which we "attach" administration to the Executive represent attempts to solve the problem by moving in the Constitutional direction. Theories of "representative bureaucracy" represent attempts to solve the problem by moving in the direction of democracy.)

If it is granted that creating a new political theory and, correlatively, establishing new constitutional arrangements, are legitimate and desirable tasks (and of course many would not so grant) then it must be observed, secondly, that these are tasks that run far beyond the competence and responsibility of those identified with Public Administration; and to regard the small number of public administrationists as having "failed" because they have not accomplished such labors in a generation is unfair, indeed absurd. The problems involved run to the boundaries of contemporary science, philosophy, and ideology, to the foundations of our social order and governmental system. Short of cataclysm, "reconstruction," if it takes place, will take a long time and result from many and diverse labors.

Some observations, briefly, on three problem areas.

Political-Administrative Power—The Inward Dimension. One of these concerns the extent to which, and the means by which, administrative powers, functions, and authority are to be conceived as having a special relationship of mutual support with the powers, functions, and authority of a political chief executive. Watergate and its aftermath pose this matter for renewed and urgent consideration.

The "fit" between administrative-bureaucratic theory and the notion of a political executive exercising administrative power on behalf of the polity and the people has both a logical and a historical dimension. Logically, there is complementarity, congruency. Both administrative theory as shaped in the "management movement" and bureaucratic theory à la Weber favor a single executive at the top of an administrative-bureaucratic structure. Historically, most of the framers of Public Administration argued in effect that the need of administration for unified direction is—fortunately—met and matched by the need of an executive, if he is to govern effectively on behalf of the people, to exercise control over an administrative apparatus.

This political theory (as I regard it) had been moving toward coherence for decades before the twenties; indeed, some of *The Federalist* writings are plausibly cited in its support. But it was the events of the thirties that made the political theory into something of an administrative dogma, particularly at the federal level: the events that led, especially by way of the report of the President's Committee on Administrative Management, to an emotional joining of support for the President as "tribune of the people" with the theories and techniques of (in Weber's terms) the monocratic form of bureaucracy.

I simplify, of course. There have always been doubters, even heretics. But in the main Public Administration theory and sentiment supported a strong President not only through the first postwar Republican Presidency (Eisenhower) but through the second up to—Watergate. There were contradictions and ironies aplenty with the passage of time, when the strong "liberal" sentiments of most public administrationists did not necessarily march with Presidential politics, but in the main the "union" held. In a formal way, White House operations in the first months of 1973, and the President's scheme for departmental reorganization, were consonant with the mainstream of administrative theory.

Watergate may, and certainly should, provide the occasion and the stimulus for a rethinking of all the matters involved. The task will be one of extreme difficulty. The "answers" must be sought in a complex and constraining context—of law, institutions, political sentiments, and so forth. To what extent is executive direction of administration proper/optimal? What is the proper "mix" of control by the conventional three "branches"? To what extent should administration be controlled in *other* ways or be *self*-controlling? Whoever is educating for public administration, wherever the educating takes place, how can such questions be avoided?

Political-Administrative Power—The Outward Dimension. What I turn attention to here are matters suggested by such terms as: service economy, knowledge explosion, postindustrialism, gray area, third sector, transnational corporations. Such matters are of course closely related to the problems just sketched, and "inward dimension" and "outward dimension" may not be the best terms with which to express the relationship. But in any case the questions I am asking are these: What reconstructions and new developments in the theory and technology of public administration are dictated by the emergence of existential conditions significantly different from those of the past? How *should* public administration interact with significantly different conditions—facilitating, restraining, initiating, prohibiting?

To speak to such profound matters in a few setnences canot be done without an air of fatuousness. But no matter, I am of firm opinion that I speak to things that are central to the future of public administration, things so central that they raise questions concerning the future relevance and accuracy of both the adjective "public" and the noun "administration."

Let me put it this way: The nation-state system of "framing" political (and socioeconomic) affairs is, historically speaking, something new. If "nothing abides," then it will be succeeded, and there is much evidence indicating this may take (be taking?) place. From the point of view of Europeans, the United States is in the position of a "preindustrial industrial state entering the postindustrial world"—as one of them put it to me recently. That is, from the Continental perspective the United States has never achieved a "sense of state" and well-developed state institutions, including—*especially* including—those of public administration. To the extent that this is true, it is highly relevant to emergent possibilities and problems, whether advantage or handicap remaining to be seen.

How could public administration not be involved, both acting and acted upon, in profound social change? If it is responsive, how can it be an actor in the drama without as much awareness and intelligence as it can command? If education *for* public administration is responsible, how can it not attend to such matters?

Public Interest/Personal Ethics. Richard Chapman and Frederic Cleaveland, in their above-cited *Meeting the Needs of Tomorrow's Public Service*, take serious note of the problems of inculcating and maintaining the "public-service ethic" in view of forces (such as professionalism and unionism) that would seem to erode such an ethic. Their concern is, I think, properly placed. Indeed, the situation is probably worse than they indicate, if only because their study was pre-Watergate.

One aspect of the situation is that such is the chaos of the area signified by such terms as political theory, religion, philosophy, and ethics that, if one is concerned with building or strengthening a "public-service ethic" he is in a difficult if not downright impossible situation. The idea of a "public interest" may be essential—what else can government "legitimately" be about?—but it seems impossible to sustain by respectable argument (as against the contemporary "Glaucons" and "Adeimantuses") and cannot be discovered by what is nowadays regarded as scientific research.

Another aspect of the situation might be termed "institutional." Our lack of a "sense of state" forbids us to identify the public interest with *state* interest. (If you say, "Thank God!", you demonstrate the point.) Our system of divided powers and separated powers, plus our balance and tension between private rights and majority rule, make it difficult to find an unequivocal position on many matters. Our separation from public law, beginning with the English common law inheritance, proceeding through Political Science's separation from legal studies, and concluding by accepting a definition of Public Administration as concerned with efficiency and not with law (and hence, justice), denies us a way of approaching the problem that "comes natural" in much of the world.

Another aspect of the situation pertains to recent history. The turmoil of the sixties and early seventies revealed new problems or gave a new poignancy to old ones. We have not begun to treat these problems with the seriousness they deserve. The Daniel Ellsberg case, to cite a conspicuous example, raises questions so profound, poses alternatives so threatening, that we are inclined to leave it with those having quick ideological answers. And then Watergate . . . What Watergate has done (whatever else!) is to make it clear that there is not simply a question of identifying and acting on something called the public interest; there are troublesome problems of personal ethics in and about the public service that bear upon the "public interest" in various ways, in complicated ways and even, perhaps, in conflicting ways. That is, there has been (I think) a too ready and too simple assumption that if one acts in "the public interest" he is also acting ethically, morally, as an individual; and vice versa. Of course we "knew better"—any freshman has pondered whether killing in war "in the public interest" is moral or immoral. But it has been no part—at least no important part—of Public Administration to attend to and, possibly, instruct in, such matters.

In the immediate future, I judge, this will not be true, or so nearly true. I so judge because of letters I have received, manuscripts I have seen, and courses in "ethics in public administration" that I am aware of, recently inaugurated or planned. The new interest may prove to be a fad, an episode; and there is serious risk of a spate of pious homilies, sterile formulae, and partisan answers in the guise of science or morality. We shall see.

But in any case the objective *challenge* is there: to respond across a broad area of public-interest/personal-ethics problems. Again, the responsibilities run far beyond Public Administration, just as the problems to be addressed run beyond public administration. And the problems may be insoluble. (One does not necessarily gain a religious faith by studying religions, a personal philosophy by studying philosophies, a political theory by studying political theories, an ethical code by studying ethics.) But if Public Administration simply disregards the problems, will it not then be lacking in a sense of responsibility?

THE PARADIGM PROBLEM

With the publication of Thomas Kuhn's *The Structure of Scientific Revolutions*, "paradigm" became a "vogue word," used so often and in so many senses that perhaps it were best to avoid it. I shall not myself be using it in any strict or careful way. Rather, I use it in the loose sense of "model" or "pattern" to pose some questions and to suggest answers. Or more modestly and realistically, approaches to and considerations relevant to answers. The questions are of this nature: How should Public Administration be conceived? What intellectual structure and valuational set is appropriate to it? What are its proper and optimal disciplinary and professional relationships? And given the answers to these questions, what organizational structure (or set of institutional arrangements) is best for education for the public service?

An appropriate point of departure is the title of a recent book by Vincent Ostrom, *The Intellectual Crisis in American Public Administration.*[28] The crisis is that referred to above as the "identity crisis." Only, one might say, more so: Ostrom finds "the tradition," beginning symbolically and to some degree causally with Woodrow Wilson, to be rooted in error, in what was in fact a "counterrevolution" against the essential American contribution to popular government. We need to do two things, Ostrom believes. One is to repudiate our centralizing, simplifying, unifying approach to the solution of problems: far from curing ills, actions taken in this direction have actually *caused* ills. The other is to move in a "centrifugal" (my word, not his) direction:[29]

> Fashioning the architecture for a system of democratic administration will require different concepts and different solutions from those which can be derived from Wilson, Goodnow, White, and Gulick. Instead, a new theory of democratic administration will have to be fashioned from the works of Hamilton, Madison, Tocqueville, Dewey, Lindblom, Buchanan, Tullock, Olson, Niskanen, and many others. The theory of externalities, common properties, and public goods, the logic of collective action and public enterprise, the concepts of public-service industries, and fiscal federalism will have prominent places in that theory.

Ostrom's book will prove, I think, to be an important one. But this is not the occasion to give it the sustained attention it deserves.[30] For present purposes it serves to indicate the seriousness of the situation: a charge of three generations of almost unrelieved error and mischief. And it serves as a taking-off point for an expression of my own view of the "crisis" and of "paradigm" matters (an early, tentative expression of which, incidentally, was *Ostrom*'s taking-off place).

The Medical Analogy. I believe it is most useful and fruitful at the present time to think of education for public administration as roughly analogous to education for medicine. That is, I think it is sensible and proper to think in *professional* terms. (Engineering or other professions would serve, but medicine strikes me as most apt.)

Some immediate disclaimers and explanations: I do not believe Public Administration—or public administration—is, or is about to become, a profession in any strict sense. I don't even believe that it should, *if* it could, given many contemporary factors pertaining to epistemology, ideology, politics, and what not. I appreciate that the medical (or any other professional) analogy is—as I said— rough; and I am not urging the creation of "doctors of administration" equivalent to doctors of medicine.

I begin with a firm conviction that Public Administration is not and cannot be a "discipline," much less a subdiscipline. If it is so conceived then it is, as some have alleged, dead or dying.[31] Public Administration has as its purpose preparation for careers (occupations, employment, having most of the attributes sociologists attribute to the career concept) in public administration. No single discipline, as these are now constituted and named, provides the knowledge base for preparation for such careers. No single discipline even comes close; instead, many disciplines and foci now contribute and should contribute.

Let me suggest some analogies to medicine both on the "input" and the "output" side. The "softness" of the fields of knowledge on which public administration perforce must rely no doubt will be argued against the analogy. But the "hardness" of medicine can easily be exaggerated or idealized: There is no single, unified theory of illness or health, theories and the technologies based on them constantly change, there are vast unknowns, there is bitter controversy over medical questions of vital importance, the element of "art" remains large and important. "Health" proves, on close scrutiny, to be as undefinable as "good administration." (As a friend who has spent decades studying health care concludes, "Health is a subject, not an object.") While the prominence of the M.D. suggests at first blush a single, uniform, definable product for medical education, this is illusory. By "medicine" *I* mean the medical profession*s*, the many specialties and career lines of the health services. Even "doctor" has a specious unity, since medical doctors vary by title (training) and by specialty.

To think of preparation for public administration as roughly comparable to preparing for careers in health care is liberating and challenging. It frees Public Administration from second-class citizenship in the College of Liberal Arts. It frees us from guilt because we don't have a paradigm in some strict sense. (American medicine has a wide variety of "paradigms," and it appears it will soon be getting another one: acupuncture. We might think, analogously, of adding astrology to our curricula; it is used in some places—successfully, it is claimed—in public planning.) It gives us a license to seek what we need wherever it may be located, whatever the name of the source and whether in or out of academia. It gives us an opportunity (well, subject to various restraints) to experiment with diverse combinations of knowledge, different degrees for different purposes, and varying educational arrangements.

In short, I believe the crisis of identity is properly resolved by recognizing a new kind of identity; and that the paradigm that is most important is an overarching professional paradigm.

On Disciplinary-Professional Restructuring. Public Administration, that is, a self-conscious enterprise under this name is, in the perspective of history, a recent and very "American" thing. That it is addressed to matters of the most vital and grave import—the directions and effectiveness of government—will not need defending to anyone who reads this. But whether it will survive and prosper "as such" is not certain. I conclude with some reflections and observations pertaining to this matter.

The structuring of disciplines and professions in any particular situation is no doubt "necessary" in some sense; but it is also "accidental," in the sense that it is the result of particular circumstances, circumstances different from those that produced a different structuring elsewhere. That American Public Administration came into existence is highly "accidental," the result of confluence of factors that include (but are not limited to) the following:

(1) The separation of the "political" and the "legal" in a particular manner, by way of English history and the common law. This represents a "mutation" from the Roman-derived, Continental, civil-administrative-law approach.

(2) The structuring of the professions in the United States, more in the English mold (largely outside the ambit of state and even universities) than in the Continental mold (within the ambit of state and universities), but differing from both.

(3) The development in the United States of a self-conscious enterprise known as Political Science. This, it must be appreciated, is a new thing under the sun: "—in size, content and method unique in Western intellectual history." (Bernard Crick)

(4) The structuring of the social sciences that occurred together with the rise and growth of the American university. Not only did Political Science gain independence and a particular content, but so did Anthropology, Economics, Sociology, Social Psychology.

(5) The rise of the notion that administration or management is a thing-in-itself, accompanied by the generation of the techniques and ideas that constituted the management "movement."

Public Administration, it might be said, is the result of a process of fractionation—Political Science from Law (more or less also, from Economics, Ethics, History, and Philosophy), Public Administration (via the "politics-administration dichotomy") from Political Science; then the mixture of the derived fraction with elements of scientific management, economics, social psychology, and so forth.

Patently, a product so accidental, so circumstantial, has no claim to universal validity or eternal life. On the other hand, there is no "necessary" reason why the name as well as the enterprise it represents cannot survive and grow in use and acceptance.

With hindsight we shall know what was "desirable" and "possible." If Public Administration should disappear in a restructuring and renaming of the disciplinary-educational-professional universe, the disappearance would be for many a cause of regret. But if this occurs it will be essentially incidental; Public Administration will have served its historical purpose of bridge and matrix and be more or less incorporated into a new pattern or synthesis.

At present there is, obviously, great fluidity and much experimentation—as there should be, I think. At least, one might as well make a virtue of necessity. Let us assess the respective merits and limitations of various educational contexts: schools and programs of Public Administration; schools and programs of Public Affairs; schools of management; centers for policy studies; special attention to preparation for public service in schools of business, law—in the professions generally.[32] Perhaps all these, and other approaches as well, will be found to have a distinctive contribution to make in the complex task of preparing persons to perform better in the public service.

Notes

1. Since so much of my professional work has centered on Public Administration "as such," this will not be easy. Some may wish to refer to two essays that discuss in greater detail some of the matters discussed in this essay: "Public Administration," *Journal of Politics*, 30 (May 1968), pp. 33–8; "Developments in Public Administration," *The Annals*, 404 (Nov. 1972), pp. 217–54. These two essays, in turn, cite other recent essays that treat matters discussed in this one.

2. To emphasize these points it is appropriate to quote from the early pages of *Introduction to the Study of Public Administration* (1926): "The book rests upon at least four assumptions. It assumes that administration is a single process, substantially uniform in its essential characteristics wherever observed.... It assumes that the study of administration should start from the base of management rather than the foundation of law.... It assumes that administration is still primarily an

art but attaches importance to the significant tendency to transform it into a science. It assumes that administration has become, and will continue to be, the heart of the problem of modern government." (Preface, pp. vii–viii.)

"Public administration is the management of men and materials in the accomplishment of the purposes of the state. This definition emphasizes the managerial phase of administration and minimizes its legalistic and formal aspect.... It leaves open the question to what extent the administration itself participates in formulating the purposes of the state, and avoids any controversy as to the precise nature of administrative action.... The objective of public administration is the most efficient utilization of the resources at the disposal of officials and employees." (p. 2).

3. Neutral, that is, with reference to matters other than the basic commitments to science and efficiency.

4. In "Developments in Public Administration," *loc. cit.*

5. With apologies, I again refer to "Developments in Public Administration," *loc. cit.*, where I have discussed what is there called "The Internal Environment of Public Administration."

6. Alvin Toffler *Future Shock* (New York: Random House, 1970). The Toffler book, widely translated, is probably the best known but is not the most "shocking" of its genre.

7. The chief sources of information (apart from personal knowledge) relied upon in this section are the National Association of Public Affairs and Administration's three publications: *Public Affairs and Administration Programs, 1971–72; Graduate School Programs in Public Affairs and Public Administration, 1974;* and *Guidelines and Standards for Professional Masters Degree Programs in Public Affairs/Public Administration* (1974); R. L. Chapman and Frederic N. Cleaveland, *Meetings the Needs of Tomorrow's Public Service; Guidelines for Professional Education in Public Administration* (National Academy of Public Administration, 1973); James A. Medeiros, "The Professional Study of Public Administration," *Public Administration Review,* 34 (May/June 1974), pp. 254–59.

8. In the spring of 1974 the National Association of Schools of Public Affairs and Administration adopted (by unanimous vote) a document titled *Guidelines and Standards for Professional Masters Degree Programs in Public Affairs/Public Administration.* This may prove to be a first step in reversing the trend toward inclusiveness and diversity—we shall see.

9. The growth, while important, and while impressive viewed against recent "cut-backs" in some sectors of academia, must be kept in perspective. Chapman and Cleaveland, *Meeting the Needs...*, estimate that the number of degrees granted by schools of commerce and business is approximately seventy times that from schools of public affairs

and administration. Exact comparisons are difficult because of over-lapping categories and "blended" operations. But in any case, by any constructions, education for "private-sector" employment is over-whelmingly greater than education for "public-sector" employment; and certainly educational effort is not proportionate to present and prospective private and public employment.

10. In the decade 1960–1970 public employment grew from 6 mil-lions to 9.7 millions. Of this, federal employment represented a 19 percent increase, state and local 65 percent. An increase in public employment to 13.5 millions by 1980 has been projected. See: Sterling E. Sonderkind, "The Outlook," *Wall Street Journal*, Nov. 30, 1970.

11. The liberal arts ethos, if one may call it that, is manifested in a number of the Public Administration programs (usually the older ones) in the avowed intent to create "generalists" as against "special-ists." James A. Medeiros, in his "The Professional Study of Public Administration," *op. cit.*, quotes "a typical catalogue statement of such a philosophy": "–the M.P.A. is not a degree in accounting, it is not a degree in budgeting and it is not even a degree on how to find your way through the Washington bureaucracy.... The degree program is first of all an intellectual experience and provides a theoretical as well as an operational understanding of the processes and procedures of governing. It is not a degree in 'how to do it,' for that is perhaps best learned by those officials who serve in governmental roles."

12. If some styles of "reconstruction" were to take place in Political Science, the bond might become stronger rather than weaker. On this, some thoughts below.

13. Until recently, at least, "androgogy" has not been given much attention in the universities. In the federal government the Office of Management and Budget and the Civil Service Commission have taken steps to provide training and education for executive development on an interagency reimbursable basis. The Federal Executive Institute, the regional institutes of the CSC, and the Executive Seminar Centers are maintained through funds on a reimbursable basis. On government in-house continuing-education programs see: Richard C. Collins, "Train-ing and Education: Trends, Differences, and Issues," *Public Adminis-tration Review*, 33 (November/December, 1973), pp. 508–15; Bob L. Wynia, "Executive Development in the Federal Government," *Public Administration Review*, 32 (July/August, 1972), pp. 311–17; Malcolm E. Shaw, "Education Is Not a Place: Connecting Learning and Liv-ing," *Public Administration Review*, 33 (November/December 1973), pp. 516–21; Thomas W. Fletcher, ed., symposium on "Continuing Edu-cation for Public Administration," *Public Administration Review*, 33 (November/December 1973), pp. 487–532.

14. Both newer and older institutions of higher education have re-cently been moving to create new types of advanced education. But

data on these are not at hand and, certainly, I am not well enough informed to comment intelligently on programs and activities. See: Standing Committee on Education for Public Administration, *Education for Public Administration: Action Proposals* (Washington, D.C.: National Academy of Public Administration, Oct. 12, 1973).

15. The following paragraph begins the Summary of Findings in *Guidelines and Standards* (cited above), and pertains to various of the observations made:

"Education and training in public affairs/public administration is presently experiencing a rapid growth and diversification at all academic levels, under graduate, graduate and continuing education. Enrollments at the undergraduate level are more than twice what they were a decade ago, while at the graduate level degree candidates have tripled during the last ten-year period. Recent years have also witnessed the creation of new types of educational and training programs in urban affairs, criminal justice, public health, and other fields as institutions responded to meet the needs for administrative talent in the public service. Of significance is the increased job-oriented outlook of students in programs at both the undergraduate and graduate levels who, in contrast to a few years ago, appear to be seeking training that is occupationally useful. This is especially true for the part-time graduate student who now outnumbers the full-time graduate by more than two to one in public affairs/public administration programs." (pp. 29–30.)

16. See: "Training MBAs for the Public Sector," *Business Week*, June 10, 1972, pp. 82–84. In general, the "public sector" response of schools of business has not involved much engagement of faculty trained in Political Science or Public Administration, but rather has centered on "management science," with outside recruitment mainly from economics, psychology and sociology.

17. NASPAA's *Graduate School Programs in Public Affairs and Public Administration, 1974*, gives (pp. 1–2) the following summary information for the 101 respondents to their late 1973 survey of programs:

Respondents were asked to characterize the type of institution in which the PA/A program is being offered. The five major types and numbers of programs are as follows:

- Separate professional school of PA/A (i.e., reports directly to central university administration in the same or similar manner as a law school) — 25
- Separate department of PA/A in large unit (such as a social science division. college of arts and sciences. etc.) — 23
- Professional school of PA/A combined with another professional school (i.e., business school) — 11

- Department of PA/A combined with another department
  (i.e., business administration)   6
- PA/A program within a political science department   36
                                                        Total   101

Only perusal of the 101 reports that constitute the body of the publication serves to indicate the great diversity in titles, emphases, size, etc.

18. See *The Policy Studies Directory* (1973), published by the Policy Studies Organization in conjunction with the Institute of Government and Public Affairs at the University of Illinois, Urbana. While very informative, this booklet has the limitation indicated by its subtitle: "A Directory of Policy Study Activities in American Political Science Ph.D. Departments as of 1973."

19. Illustrative of diversity, specialization and "hybridization," the creation of institutes designed to provide specialized training for middle-management people engaged in certain functional areas seems to be on the rise. Such institutes may be housed within a school of public administration, draw upon faculty from various departments and from other organizations, and offer a resident course of instruction to the practitioner in the field. At the University of Southern California there are three such institutes: the Delinquency Control Institute, the Environmental Management Institute, and the Institute for Tax Administration.

20. NASPAA's *Graduate School Programs* summary indicates (p. 3) that two-thirds of the respondent programs have more than "five academic fields" represented in their faculties (including part-time faculty). "The fields most commonly represented are, in order of frequency: political science (86 programs), public administration (80), economics (68), business administration (56), sociology (51), statistics-mathematics (40), law (38), planning (37), and psychology (32)." The "course areas," in order of frequency are organization theory and behavior, public policy analysis, urban and intergovernmental administration, public finance and budgetary process, personnel administration, planning, administrative law, comparative bureaucracy. There are obviously other courses, but the summary is not carried beyond this point.

21. This is an appropriate place to note that "administrative regulation" or the "regulatory process"—centering in but not limited to the "independent" agencies—has received decreasing attention during recent years. I say "appropriate" because of the high legal assay of this area.

22. Documentation of these changes is at once easy and, in short compass, impossible. Easy, because thousands of citations could be used to illustrate the changes. Impossible, in short compass, because scores of citations would be necessary to indicate the transformations.

23. Limiting myself to books and to "my" decade, and being illustra-

·tive, not inclusive, I cite: Louis C. Gawthrop, *Administrative Politics and Social Change* (New York: St. Martins, 1971); Harold Seidman, *Politics, Position and Power* (New York: Oxford, 1970); Francis E. Rourke, ed., *Bureaucratic Power in National Politics* (Boston: Little, Brown, 1972); Guy Benveniste, *The Politics of Expertise* (Berkeley, Cal.: Glendessary, 1972); Peter G. Fish, *The Politics of Federal Judicial Administration* (Princeton, N.J.: Princeton University Press, 1972); Lewis C. Mainzer, *The American Public Service Political Bureaucracy* (Glenview, Ill.: Scott, Foresman, 1973); John Rehfuss, *Public Administration as a Political Process* (New York: Scribners, 1973).

24. The following offer an introduction to the policy analysis area (it is not alleged that they are "Public Administration" literature): Thomas R. Dye, *Understanding Public Policy* (Englewood Cliffs, N.J.: Prentice-Hall, 1972); Charles O. Jones, *An Introduction to the Study of Public Policy* (Belmont, Cal.: Wadsworth, 1970); Austin Ranney, ed., *Political Science and Public Policy* (Chicago: Markham, 1968); Charles E. Lindblom, *The Policy Making Process* (Englewood Cliffs, N.J.: Prentice-Hall, 1968); Ira Sharkansky, ed., *Policy Analysis in Political Science* (Chicago: Markham, 1969); Yehezkel Dror, *Public Policy-Making Re-examined* (San Francisco: Chandler, 1968). The newer "policy" journals and the "public choice" literature should, of course, be consulted.

25. Again, documentation for the following paragraphs is at once easy—since examples are so plentiful—and impossible—since documentation of the various matters would run to excessive length. However, a few thoughts: My "Developments in Public Administration," cited in note 1, supplies documentation on some items. The "evaluation" literature illustrates the meeting and mingling of currents. See: Peter H. Rossi and Walter Williams, eds., *Evaluating Social Programs: Theory, Practice, and Politics* (New York: Seminar Press, 1972); Carol H. Weiss, *Evaluation Research: Methods of Assessing Program Effectiveness* (Englewood Cliffs, N.J.): Prentice-Hall, 1972); Orville Poland, symposium on evaluation, *Public Administration Review*, forthcoming. The political-economy/public-choice literature represents the intermingling of various "hard" and some "soft" currents. See Gary Wamsley and Mayer Zald, *The Political Economy of Public Organizations* (Lexington, Mass.: Heath, 1973); Vincent Ostrom and Elinor Ostrom, "Public Choice: A Different Approach to the Study of Public Administration," *Public Administration Review*, 31 (March/April, 1971), pp. 203–16. The "systems" approach often frames an intermingling of currents. See: Ira Sharkansky, *Public Administration: Policy Making in Government Agencies* (Chicago: Markham, 1970). The mingling of politics, economics, sociology, organization behavior, systems concepts and evaluation problems can be observed in a recent textbook, James

W. Davis, Jr., *An Introduction to Public Administration: Politics, Policy, and Bureaucracy* (New York: Free Press, 1974). The meeting and melding of "disparates" is well illustrated in W. B. Eddy, "The Role of Behavioral Science in Public Administration Programs," *Public Administration Review*, 33 (September/October, 1973), pp. 464–68.

26. For the interested, I have discussed these matters in "Political Science," in *Sources of Information in the Social Sciences*, Carl M. White and Associates (Chicago: American Library Association, 2nd ed. 1973), pp. 493–523; and in "Political Science: Tradition, Discipline, Profession, Enterprise," in *Handbook of Political Science*, vol. 1, Fred Greenstein and Nelson Polsby, eds. (Reading, Mass.: Addison-Wesley, forthcoming).

27. I am not by intention either frivolous or insulting when I suggest that the logic of the generic school would, when applied (say) to the field of medicine, dictate that a general school of medicine replace the present division between human medicine and veterinary medicine. An excellent case in logic sustains such a move: there are similar if not identical objectives, the subject matter—animals and their illnesses—has a reasonable unity and coherence, and the problem with a core curriculum would not be to construct one of reasonable size but to keep it of *manageable* size.

28. Vincent Ostrom, *The Intellectual Crisis in American Public Administration* (The University of Alabama Press, 1973; rev. ed. 1974).

29. Ibid., pp. 131–32.

30. My own view, in brief, is that while I believe those upon whom Ostrom relies for guidance have a contribution to make—theories, techniques, and wisdom—they no more than the Wilsons and the Whites have The Answers.

31. *Cf.* Allen Schick, "Coming Apart in Public Administration," *Maxwell Review*, 10 (Winter, 1973/74), pp. 13–24.

32. I do not wish to be understood as arguing against the action of NASPAA in adopting Guidelines and Standards for Professional Masters Degree Programs. These guidelines and standards are far from rigid requirements; they are little likely to halt experimentation and adaptation; official recognition by public hiring authorities will be slow and partial. An attempt to assess and evaluate is the legitimate complement to diversity and experimentation. (The example of the professions generally is relevant. The desirable situation lies between unrestrained charlatanism and unprogressive monopoly.)

6. 1984 and Beyond: Social Engineering or Political Values?

DON K. PRICE

A scientific era breeds its own types of superstition. In our contemporary Orwellian mythology, 1984 is the year of the Apocalypse, when political freedom and humane values are to be destroyed by the dark angels of technology. So you may suppose the title of this essay is to suggest a deadline for doomsday.

Nothing could be further from my mind.

At the end of the first millenium, when much of Christendom expected the world to come to an end by supernatural intervention, sensitive souls were tempted to forget their practical concerns and their moral inhibitions. If you think the world is about to end you can afford to ignore your obligations.

But the fallacy of this approach came to be obvious. Dorothy Parker summed it up:

> Drink and dance and laugh and lie,
> Love, the reeling midnight through,
> For tomorrow we shall die!
> (But, alas, we never do.)

Our contemporary temptation is to look for new scientific equivalents of doomsday. It is obviously possible for civilization to come to an end through nuclear holocaust. It is also possible, I suppose, for overpopulation, environmental pollution, or the exhaustion of our energy resources to bring about various types of spectacular crisis. With such heady possibilities ahead of us, why do we worry about such grubby matters as managerial methods or policy analysis?

The answer, I suppose, is that it is not certain that the world is about to come to an end, and it is even more unlikely that we shall save it by any emotional spasm of moral reform. We are much more likely to have to go on living through various periods of political intoxication and the hangovers that follow them. Year after year the capacity of civilized society to survive will depend on the unglamorous work of public officials. And our job, in schools of public affairs and administration, is to help prepare them intellectually and emotionally to deal not only with the current crisis or the newest crusade, but also with the many that will follow in the normal course of political change.

This is, one may say, an impossible assignment. It calls for the creation of professional skills and a professional attitude—that is to say, a desire for a career that does not depend on the commercial incentive of wealth, or the political incentive of a taste for political power.

On the other hand, public administration cannot be a true profession, in the sense that law or medicine are professions: it cannot be permitted to define the scope of its own responsibilities or control the terms of admission to its ranks. Yet the schools that teach it cannot be content to teach only the systematic thought that is the stuff of the scholarly disciplines, but also must develop in their students a taste for action, a willingness to accept responsibility, and a concern for the accomplishment of humane and public purposes.

As all of us know, it is not easy to do this job within the conventional structure of a university. For that structure is designed to protect the standards of the scholarly disciplines and the traditional professions. But just as the public administrator of the future will have to learn to live permanently with impossible dilemmas—to help mediate all sorts of political conflicts of interest—so in the schools of public administration we must learn to deal with dilemmas of academic organization and curricula, whether we undertake to teach the older types of managerial and staff skills, or the newer techniques of policy analysis and organizational development.

We must be aware, too, of the ways in which the dilemmas that modern government must face affect the educational job that we must do in the university. I think of three that seem especially significant.

The first is the dilemma posed by the apparent conflict between science and values; the second, by the conflict between the generalist and the specialist; and the third, between an elite meritocracy and participatory democracy. Let me take them up in turn.

The first dilemma, that between science and values, is at the root of our old problem of relating administration to policy. Are we concerned only with instrumental skills derived from science and technology, in which the value choices of political decisions are set aside and left to others? Or do we educate administrators for a role in which they are heavily involved in the development of future policies?

A couple of generations ago the intellectual world generally assumed that science and technology were automatically beneficent forces. Today many see them as threats to humane values and challenge our preoccupation with material progress and the intellectual skills on which it is based as the source of the disorder in our civilization.

At the very least, there is much less tendency today to believe that science can save us—that as the social sciences (as well as the natural sciences) become rigorous and effective they will provide the basis for the determination of our political issues, even if they do so only by clarifying alternatives and quantifying their costs and benefits.

There is much less attraction today in the notion of a scientific system of politics than there was in the nineteenth century. This loss of faith in scientific materialism as a basis for politics is in part the result, I suppose, of the layman's observation of how scientific materialists really behave. Marxists may profess a belief in the inevitability of revolution, just as capitalists used to profess a belief in the inevitability of progress, but both were likely to resort to vigorous political action to cooperate with the inevitable.

This has nothing to do with the utility of the sciences, and especially the social sciences, as guides to policy decisions or administrative action. The main limitation on using the sciences to make policy decisions is not that any science is useless but that for any practical purpose there are too many of them that are essential. In dealing with any concrete problem, the administrator is likely to find that he must combine the intellectual skills drawn from a great variety of sciences. At any given moment he may indeed find that a single science provides the solution to the crucial issue—but if he does he is likely to find a year later that the nature of the problem has changed and the earlier scientific answer is less relevant.

In the actual conduct of affairs, the administrator's role in the formulation of policy must be something more than that of a scientific analyst. For the analysis and development of policy and the execution of policy decisions are inseparable functions. No person can separate completely the processes of thinking and acting. In any institution, how old policy is carried out will determine the new options and pose the issues for the responsible political authority that must make the major decisions. In this continuum, all branches of knowledge have their contribution to make. The dynamic of modern science has broken down the boundaries between the application of the several disciplines and the several scientific professions, and has also made it plain that the manager or administrator must be concerned as much with the formulation or development of policy as with its execution.

This has nothing to do with the question of his involvement in partisan politics or his subordination to the politician who is responsible for policy decisions. But it is a duty that flows inevitably from the fact that the options for the policy maker are determined by the previous decisions and by the current state of both technology and the nature and capability of the administrative organization. Those reactionary politicians who undertook to keep public management weak and corrupt so as to discourage liberal programs and policies had a perverse but accurate logic. An English scientist once remarked that invention is the mother of necessity.

One might add that effective administration is equally the mother of policy decisions, because if we learn how to manage effectively programs that people like, the demand for the programs will increase. Administrative reorganization and managerial reform have often disappointed those who have promoted them for the purpose of cutting taxes; even when they are successful in effecting true economy, the characteristic response of political leadership has been to use the saving to increase services rather than to reduce taxes.

The lesson for our academic curricula is a plain one. We do not accept the dilemma between policy and administration—between the substantive purpose of what we undertake to do in government, and the efficiency of our method of carrying it out. We must continue to be concerned with problems of formal organization and systematic management. At the same time we must take advantage of all the most modern intellectual skills for the comprehension and analysis of substantive policy issues. It makes no sense to be frightened of the ways in which, in recent years, the useful skills of PPBS or systems analysis have been abused or made into fads from time to time. If properly developed and used they offer administrators useful tools for opening options that their political superiors may exploit.

At the same time, if we drill only these skills into the heads of our future administrators we may produce a distortion—a kind of institutional reductionism—that would seriously cripple our political process. While we teach sophisticated systematic theories of a highly scientific nature, we need to balance them with an equally sophisticated understanding of our problems of fundamental values and social injustice.

Our reaction against science and technology too often takes the form of a flabby appeal to vague emotional attitudes. It is worth recalling that in the prescientific age philosophers and theologians recognized that value choices—problems of love and justice—were not questions to be decided merely by an appeal to emotion but required rigorous analysis. The moral and ethical problems that lie ahead for the public administrator will not be solved by purely scientific modes of thought. These are problems that relate both to the inner ethics of his own profession—the relations within administrative organization and between it and political authority—and also to the ethical dilemmas posed for government by advances in modern technology. To mention the conflict between environmental protection and the need for energy, or the dilemma between the advancement of medical care and problems of overpopulation or the care of the dying, will suggest the nature of these issues.

Our second dilemma is an equally ancient subject of debate within our trade. It is the dilemma between the education of generalists or specialists.

As a part of my first dilemma, I noted the problems that arise in the relation between the specialized knowledge of administrators and the general value system of political authority. But now I am talking about another dimension of the problem—not the vertical dimension of tension between the level of management or administration and what ought to be the superior level of political decision, but the horizontal dimension of conflicts between functional programs in different departments and agencies.

I have been one of those who in the past have been disposed to argue that our main need is to educate generalists, whatever they are, but it is clear that we do not develop a curriculum or create a discipline simply by noting a problem. The main problem of American government, as well as the source of many of its strengths, has been its pluralism—a pluralism sometimes approaching anarchy. The administrative aspect of this pluralism is the predominance in the upper reaches of the career service of officers educated and experienced in various specialized professions rather than in the liberal arts or in general administration.

And yet an administrative system must correspond to and support the constitutional system that it is designed to serve. Our Congress is a pluralistic system and so is our society, and the executive and the administration are forced to organize themselves along similar lines. The limited degree of unity that has been established in the Presidency has turned out to be a weaker and more corruptible force that many of us would have hoped.

But the weakness of the generalist formula has not come merely from the pluralism of American politics. Even in the classic home of the generalist administrator, modern society and technology have made the amateur generalist incapable of dealing effectively with the problems of modern government. As evidence of this I recommend the report of the Fulton Commission in the United Kingdom, which pointed out the shortcomings of the Administrative Class that was for so long taken as the model by American civil-service reformers.

It is plain, as the Fulton Commission understood, that the upper reaches of the civil service must include not only mere generalists but also generalists who have first mastered some specialized form of knowledge in sufficient depth to cope with the complex problems of modern society. If this is true in an administrative corps that has the traditional authority and the weight of experience of the British civil service, it is clear that what we have thought of as a weakness in the American civil service might actually be converted into an advantage.

Yet it would not do to be complacent on this matter. The effectiveness of specialized techniques may be a virtue if they are asked to solve the right problems, but they can be a menace if they capture policy for particular specialized ends. Pluralism is not enough. The big issues arise not within particular specialized professions or individual functional programs but in the interrelations among them.

It is all too easy to find illustrations. The headlines of the hour, dealing with the newest crisis or with the latest formula for social salvation, will provide ample evidence. Our current obsession is an energy crisis, which lets us forget the environmental crisis, which in turn grabbed the headlines from the urban crisis. But the effort to solve any one of these within the terms by which some one professional specialty defines it is bound to be self-defeating— bound to create another crisis in turn. When we were "solving" the environmental crisis, it would have been prudent to think about the effect of our actions on the future supply of energy, or on the shape and structure of our metropolitan areas and the social problems that we were building into them. As we deal with the energy crisis we may find that we have to worry about the effect of payments for foreign oil on our international balance of trade, on our system of foreign aid, on our diplomacy with the Third World, on our military posture, and indeed on the domestic policies that we have followed for many years of dealing with our urban problems by creating a suburban sprawl of housing indirectly subsidized by highway grants and housing credit and dependent on cheap gasoline for commuters.

What lesson should we draw from this dilemma with respect to our governmental institutions? Perhaps the main lesson is one of Constitutional and political adjustment, which is beyond the scope of our present discussion. But however the executive may be organized in relation to legislative leadership—at any level of government—it is clear that political leaders cannot deal with the complexity of the modern world unless they have an underpinning of career administrators and policy advisers with much more intellectual flexibility, and much more understanding of the interrelationship of policies and programs, than those we have been accustomed to produce.

Many administrators in both local and national government and many educators have been aware of this need for at least a half century. The first valiant efforts to meet this need were made by those who experienced it in municipal government. The work of bureaus of municipal research and the early experience under the council-manager plan contributed to the thinking of those leaders in personnel administration who shifted their emphasis from fighting patronage to developing a career basis for effective general administration.

Leonard White's interest in city managers prepared him for his efforts as a member of the U. S. Civil Service Commission to recruit management interns not for specialized immediate tasks on the basis of specialized knowledge, but for long-term careers in general management on the basis of their general ability. Those efforts were the lineal ancestor of the present Federal Executive Service proposal. Although I do not like some aspects of that proposal—the increase in partisan patronage in the federal service in recent years makes me suspicious—I believe that its general direction is one that the federal service must follow in the future. And if the Intergovernmental Personnel Act is ever funded on the scale it deserves and is then administered with an eye to the big opportunity it may help the nation develop administrative leaders who will move, in the course of their careers, from one level to another within the federal system, as well as from one functional program to another. The cause of local self-government cannot be furthered by the old idea of Home Rule in this era of grants-in-aid, federalism-by-contract, and quasi-governmental community-action programs. That cause will depend instead on the creation of satisfying careers for men and women interested in working at all levels of government to build a more humane and civilized society. And to many students today, the most appealing opportunities are in local and state government.

But to develop such careers, we must not rely entirely on a corps of people educated solely in general management—which all too often means not a capacity for generalization but only a collection of management specialties. We have to help accomplish something more difficult: to take people who have started—both in their university education and in their governmental careers—as professional specialists, and add to their specialized knowledge the capacity for comprehending its relationship with broader interests and a dedication to the general purposes of government and society rather than to narrow professional ends.

This calls for a flexible system of personnel management in the higher civil service, and for a pattern of career development that puts a high premium on one's going beyond one's particular program or specialty to a concern for the comprehensive policies of the government as a whole.

It is not easy to say just what should be done within a university curriculum to contribute to this ambitious end. I would hope for a very great variety in university experiments for this purpose. But within such variety I would look for two general themes.

The first is to recognize the greater need for those intellectual skills that enable an official to deal with the complex interrelations of policies and programs, by comparison with competence in any one specialty. As Brooks Adams put it, more than a half century ago, "Administration is the capacity of coordinating many, and often conflicting, social energies in a single organism. . . . probably no very highly specialized class can be strong in this intellectual quality. . . . yet administration or generalization is not only a faculty upon which social stability rests, but is, possibly, the highest faculty of the human mind."[1]

But it is one thing to echo Brooks Adams' eulogy of administration and a very different thing to look at what we have taught and practiced as public administration. Both in its older form of managerial processes and in its newer fashions of policy analysis, it is all too easy for it to put emphasis on specific, rather narrow skills and to neglect the more difficult but less definable, perhaps less teachable, skills that constitute the application to unmanageable problems of wisdom as well as techniques.

The second point is to recognize the difficulties of the problem and not to try to solve them within our type of school alone. To concentrate on any specific skill is to risk retreating into a new kind of narrow specialism. But within a university the variety of approaches and interests that are built into the several professional schools, with their concern for the attainment of social purposes as well as for the teaching of academic disciplines, offers some hope for the development of a continuously open and varied approach to our impossibly difficult problems. For at least a decade we have talked a great deal in these circles about the obvious fact that in American government the specialized professional, scientific, and technical fields in practice offer the most regular route to high administrative positions. Many professional schools now recognize that their graduates are not destined solely for the private practice of their professions. Some are eager to see a limited number of their best students acquire those skills outside their professional curricula that will help them direct the processes by which policies are developed and decisions administered.

If schools of public affairs and administration can ally themselves with the schools that educate students for the older and more traditional professions, they may find that the future administrator who is interested in the substance of some functional program will be just as able to learn to deal with a wide variety of complex problems as he would be if he had been trained solely in the abstractions of administrative and analytic techniques. There is much to be gained, I think, by seeing that students concern themselves in depth with the substantive content of some field of policy at the same time that they study the skills of the generalist.

The problems of modern government are so complex and so obviously require a blending of the skills of the specialized professions with those of general policy analysis and management that no single school or faculty can pretend to cope with the problem of educating for public service. That job can be confronted only by drawing on the reserves of a university as a whole, including the resources of the entire range of professional schools as well as the most pertinent academic disciplines.

Our third dilemma, as we usually think of it, is between elite meritocracy and participatory democracy. The problem is: how can we make government competent and authoritative without destroying the values of democratic participation and responsibility? This is really a mixture of two quite different problems. One has to do with the composition or representative character of the career service. The other has to do with its degree of authority and continuity.

As our federal civil service developed more than a century ago, it became not only pluralist in its basic pattern, but representative. By contrast, the British civil service, as it was modernized, followed the ideas of the utilitarian reformers. They were prepared to accept the idea of sovereignty so long as it could be controlled by an elected assembly, and the idea of a bureaucracy so long as it could be recruited and administered on a competitive-merit basis. The two ideas were combined in the concept of Her Majesty's Civil Service, a politically neutral agent of the parliamentary majority. And the formation of that majority would cancel out local and corporate vested interests and ensure by political trade-offs the greatest good of the greatest number.

Americans, in the Jacksonian era, rejected not only the idea of sovereignty but the corollary idea of a unified and politically neutral bureaucracy, as well. The Jacksonians thought that the civil and military services should be representative of the electorate: party patronage, control of Presidential appointments by Senatorial courtesy, and nomination of entrance to West Point and Annapolis by members of Congress were all designed to ensure that representative quality.

Even when the worst patronage abuses were restricted by a merit system, the representative idea persisted. In the higher civil service, patronage was eliminated less by a move toward an elite class of generalists than by the insistence of the professional and scientific societies that those who represented their functions in government should meet their standards rather than pass the test by party loyalty. And in the lower ranks, the civil service was still required to be representative: state quotas ensured the representation of geographic regions. Even veterans' preference and loyalty oaths demonstrated that civil servants were not expected to be morally and politically neutral: on fundamental issues their political function was recognized.

Now, as the moral sentiment of the country becomes more egalitarian, the pressure for making the civil service representative of the population as a whole is expressed not on a geographic basis but in terms of demands for opportunity—and perhaps proportional quotas—for all sorts of underrepresented groups in the population.

It is, of course, all too possible that our concern for maximum feasible participation may become something like a new form of patronage with benefits distributed—at the expense of the general public—to minority groups rather than to wardheelers. But now that even the most naïve student of public administration has lost his faith in the complete separation of policy and administration that we formerly considered the main argument for a merit system, we need to think through more clearly how far we are willing to push our notions of meritocracy as against the demands for equal participation by groups that are underrepresented.

I am not uncritically optimistic about our chances for striking a good balance on this issue. But I am not nearly so worried about it as I am about the second aspect of this dilemma. That is the problem of reconciling the need for authority and continuity in the career service with democratic responsiveness. On the former aspect—the question of representativeness versus competitive merit —we at least have plenty of debate, which gives rise to some appreciation of the costs and benefits of the two horns of the dilemma. But on the latter part of the dilemma, our national neurosis is the belief that it simply ought not to exist.

The most damaging criticism of the federal civil service during the past several administrations has not come from patronage politicians. They have pretty well given up on this issue. It has come instead from scholarly idealists and from zealous White House staff members who are dissatisfied whenever the career service is not instantly responsive to the new policies of a new administration.

But we cannot have it both ways—not, at least, without striking a lot of clumsy compromises. We cannot give scientific specialties influence over segments of policy, by means of our personnel promotion and classification systems, without slowing down the responsiveness of their bureaus to changes in the direction of Presidential policy. We cannot give disadvantaged groups control of community action programs, by contracting their administration out to private corporations, without restricting the freedom of a new administration to abolish the Office of Economic Opportunity. And we cannot desocialize, by contracting them out, a postal service or an Amtrak without putting some checks on the flexibility of control by higher political authority.

Many of the idealists, of course, are less sure now than they were a decade or more ago that instant responsiveness to top authority is an absolute good. If you distrust the President or the President's staff, you begin to talk more about the moral virtue of "whistle blowing"—the practice of speaking out in public against the offenses of one's superior officer—than about the virtue of responsiveness. Our current crisis certainly suggests that, for the higher civil service, democratic responsibility is not defined simply as instant responsiveness to the executive chain of command: the civil servant's duty is to uphold the Constitution and the laws, and the processes by which he works must be accountable to the courts and the Congress as well as to the Presidency.

If we applaud a civil servant in Internal Revenue who refuses to take orders to punish the President's political enemies, or a lawyer in the Justice Department who subpoenas the President's tapes or papers, we should ask ourselves what administrative system and what legal principles make it possible for a subordinate to act on such distinctions between official duty on the one hand and hierarchical orders on the other. Some degree of security of tenure, and even more important, some sense of responsibility to professional standards as well as legal procedure, are necessary to buttress the individual's devotion to ethical standards when the political heat is on.

Such corporate or professional spirit can make democratic responsibility difficult to enforce in any system in which the bureaucracy cannot be checked by legislative committees that are politically independent of the executive, and by courts that are independent of the legislature. But in the United States, the Constitutional checks not only greatly reduce the danger that the career service will become an irresponsible bureaucracy, but they make it an ally of the courts and the Congress in restraining arbitrary executive power. Especially if we equip the Congress, as well as the President, with the kind of staff that it needs.

But, once a reasonable degree of confidence in the Presidency is restored, it should be clear that the main case for strengthening the higher civil service rests not on its negative function but on its positive role of making the government more representative and more responsive.

It is clear that the civil service will have to be representative, in the sense that it will include minority groups of various kinds and specialists in the several professions and sciences that dominate many of the specialized programs of government. It is not so clear that the general public interest will be adequately represented. The typical political scientist assumes that the public interest cannot be defined, even though he may believe that it is something more than a mix of competing private interests. But it is not easy to define private interests either; those who try to speak for them often lose their followers, when it comes to the test of an election, to a general party leader. Can we provide the career staffs that are needed by those political authorities—legislative as well as executive—who are responsible for representing the public interest in its most general form?

In the structure of our civil service, we are willing to give permanent status to, and permit the development of a strong sense of corporate identity by, officials who control specialized programs, and still we worry about giving the same privileges to generalist administrators. Yet it is the specialized operating official, whose zeal is focused by his education and career incentives on the promotion of a narrow program, who poses the greatest problem with respect to political responsibility, and whose independent initiatives pose the greatest dangers in modern technological society. Irreversible damage can be done to our environment, for example, if technological programs are pushed ahead by zealous specialists without adequate regard for other interests. The widespread use of nuclear power will create situations that will require regulation and control by some agency with high general ability and permanent dedication to duty. Nothing less than the kind of loyalty and competence that we hope for in our military services can possibly do the job.[2]

But here we are inhibited by our curious double standard between military and civilian administration. We fear in the civil service what we insist on in the military service: a strong corps of general officers. For practical politicians realize that in military affairs they have no freedom of choice unless they have the support of a dedicated set of career subordinates. Without effective military services, we would have no options in the conduct of power relations with other states.

There is no doubt—as our experience with the military proves—that a strong career service is not always properly responsive to democratic control. On the other hand, the voters and their representatives can find their options closed off equally effectively by the lack of a career civil service with sufficient continuity, competence, and loyalty to democratic principles to help identify issues and present them early enough—regardless of partisan consequences—for rational consideration by Constitutional procedures.

Such a suggestion will have hard going at a time when political sentiments are strongly egalitarian. But the most noted philosophical advocate of equality concedes that a measure of inequality is justified if it adds to the welfare of all, and especially if it gives its greatest benefits to the least advantaged.[3]

It is intriguing to consider how far this principle would extend to permit a strong career service in government. Clearly the rest of us are better off if we pay something extra—whether in taxes or fees—to make possible, for example, the existence of a medical profession commanding higher than average talents and higher than average remuneration. But how far do we extend this principle? It seems clear to me that the new risks that have been imposed on all of us throughout the world by the nature of our technology and of the modern economy require such a high degree of competence to avoid disaster—to say nothing of attaining potential benefits—that a measure of special status within government is justified for those who commit themselves on a long-term basis to loyalty to the public welfare.

This is not to say that this status needs to be translated into rewards of income anything like those now permitted to great industrialists or professional entertainers. But it is to suggest that neither politicians nor scholars should scorn the maintenance of the competence, the integrity, and the incentive system that establish continuity within our major governmental institutions, especially at those levels which must cope with the crucial interrelationships of public policies.

If we appreciate the implications of our third dilemma, what lessons do we draw for the development of our schools of public affairs?

The most obvious one has to do with the composition of our student bodies. If the government service is to be adequately representative of groups that are now underprivileged, it should have a chance to employ those who have had the highest-quality education of which they are capable. Our own efforts at recruitment and admission should go well beyond the formal duties imposed on us by affirmative-action programs.

As for the content of our curriculum, we have long since learned the importance of the behavioral sciences and the lessons that they have to teach us for management. On the whole, they have led us in the direction of an appreciation of the need for democratic participation within administration. This of itself is a value that is important and useful, but it is no more to be given absolute and overriding weight than an emphasis—than the contrary emphasis—on economy and efficiency.

To rise above the dilemma between cost effectiveness and free participation requires some closer study of the basic theory of politics and of the relation of moral and political values to technical means. The basic theory of the relation of the career administrative service to the legislative and executive powers in modern Constitutional government needs to be rescued from legalistic abstraction and studied and taught in relation to the policy imperatives of a modern technological society.

At a more mundane level, it seems to me that the field of personnel administration needs to be rescued as a subject of study from the technical preoccupations that have dominated it in the past. Our whole study of budgeting as a set of routine techniques has given way, under the impulse of economists, to the study of the ways in which resources are allocated within modern government and society. Similarly it seems to me that personnel administration should be seen today as no longer the improvement in the management of the more routine aspects of appointment, recruitment, classification, and labor relations.

Personnel administration has bigger questions to worry about, for government by its actions now has a dominant influence on the distribution of talent to various roles and functions in society. By its support of teaching and research and by the wide range of its regulatory and operational decisions, it affects the distribution of talent to the several professions and the major social interests, without stopping to consider how it does so. What functions should be discharged by those in the federal career service and how much through grants in aid—controlled to what degree and on what conditions—to states and local governments? How much should be kept within the formal framework of government, and how much contracted out to private institutions and to corporations? To what extent should the development of the higher administrative and professional careers within government be pursued on a specialized basis within particular departments, and to what extent should it be changed to a broader system of promotion?

We have not yet faced the policy implications of such questions regarding the civilian personnel system as effectively as the Army did in 1921, when it changed to a unified promotion list and away from promotion lists dominated by specialized arms and services, or when it developed its own system of staff colleges and of relationships with civilian universities.

And above all, what should be the Constitutional and political status of the higher administrative service? Does a career status require that its members refrain not only from participation in political campaigns but from public discussion or advocacy of their programs or policies? The ethical and indeed constitutional implications of our personnel systems are subjects essential for study—just as in practice they set the limits as to what it is feasible for politicians to accomplish by their formal enactments.

If we are to try to cope with these dilemmas, it is important to recognize both the strengths of the universities and their limitations.

As for the latter, it seems to me that universities, in the main, cannot do the job of conducting the more immediately practical types of training as well as the government agencies can. Universities may indeed be of service by demonstrating, in special cases, what useful training projects are possible, and how they may be managed. But their essential contribution, it seems to me, should be to make the best use of their institutional skills and habits, which commit them to a more fundamental and indeed theoretical approach, at both the preentry and midcareer levels of education for public service.

For the student who has not yet embarked on his governmental career, the university should not only teach him the fundamental intellectual skills but should also seek to instill the professional commitment that public service requires.

As for the public official in midcareer, the universities' primary opportunity is to give him the chance to broaden his competence by adding to his earlier professional or specialized education and experience an appreciation of the broader context within which his agency must work, and a knowledge of the essential skills that can help him become a more effective policy analyst or manager at higher levels of responsibility.

But these are pallid platitudes that will be of limited use to anyone who seeks to lift education for public service to an effective status in our universities.

What such an effort requires is, first of all, shrewdness of judgment about the strengths and opportunities that are peculiar to each university, and enough patience to develop them in spite of the delays and frustrations that are normal in academic administration.

At our university (Harvard), I am now deeply hopeful that we are developing a program in which we can make better use of the resources around us than we have ever done before. It adds to our old midcareer program, which had always enlisted limited cooperation from other faculties, a new curriculum in policy analysis and administration, the Public Policy Program. That program will provide preservice education more specifically professional in purpose and managerial in nature than our older offerings. And this new curriculum—with appropriate research behind it—is beginning to provide teaching materials that serve not only its own degree candidates but also our midcareer students and a great many students in other professional schools, as well. We are building a small core of faculty fully committed to the professional purpose of the school, and we profit from the collaboration of professors drawn from seven other faculties of the university.

But for all my enthusiasm about our new program, I do not think of it—or any other university's program—as being suitable for slavish imitation elsewhere. For much of what we have done has been to take advantage of whatever opportunities we found at hand. And I am painfully aware of strengths and virtues in programs at other schools that it would be useless for us to try to copy.

But if there is no single pedagogical theory to pilot us, we can steer by a common vision—the vision of a society that is rejecting material abundance as its primary goal and unconstrained technological advancement as its measure of progress, and that is searching for ways to further material welfare as only one value among others—such others as freedom, social justice, respect for the natural environment, and democratic responsibility. If men and women are to be educated who share this vision, and who understand that it can be made real only through the disciplined effort of responsible public administration, our universities must seek to discover the most effective ways in which they may individually organize their best efforts.

It is high time we got under way, for we will not only be guided by the gleam ahead, but will be propelled by a push from behind. The student generation that will be following us is impatient, and with good reason. There are a great many young men and women who no longer worship power or material success, and are looking for ways to be of humane service to society. There are even a good many of them who realize that such service requires something more than revolutionary ardor or commitment to simple slogans, and who are willing to tolerate the dilemmas of public life and accept the discipline of intellectual effort. It will be hard for us to stay a jump ahead of them.

NOTES

1. Brooks Adams, *The Theory of Social Revolutions* (New York: The Macmillan Company, 1913), pp. 207–08.

2. I do not mean to say that any conceivable administrative arrangement could take care of this situation safely. See the argument on this point by Allen V. Kneese, "The Faustian Bargain," in *Resources*, number 44 (September, 1973), (Resources for the Future, Inc., Washington, D.C.)
For a somewhat less alarmist view see Harvey Brooks, "Technology and Values: New Ethical Issues Raised by Technological Progress," in *Zygon, Journal of Religion and Science*, vol. 8, no. 1 (March, 1973).

3. John Rawls, *A Theory of Justice* (Cambridge, Mass.: Harvard University Press, 1971), p. 302.

7. George Maxwell had a Dream

A HISTORICAL NOTE WITH A COMMENT ON THE FUTURE

LUTHER GULICK

George Maxwell was not only an imaginative and purposeful man, but a stubborn man, as well. He was a hard-working patent attorney and inventor, a successful business organizer and promoter, and a true believer in religion, morality, democracy, education, and the American Way as it was defined in New England in 1900. He lived and worked in Boston, and knew at first hand the degradation of American city politics at the time Lincoln Steffens immortalized it in *The Shame of the Cities*.

World War I disturbed him even more seriously than Boston politics did. As he observed some years later, it demonstrated to him "the general ignorance among the masses of our history, the principles of our government, its aims and safeguards." "The blind patriotism of our young people," he continued, "was pathetic. Almost every strenuous agitator found a large following. This was simply because the crowd did not have the mooring or background of actual knowledge of what we are, have been and should stand for."[1]

Out of his disgust over American politics and his despair over the ignorance and lack of character of the masses and of the rising generation, Maxwell was impelled to action. The result was his dream.

The idea did not come to him all at once in a single flash. He worked it out gradually over a period of years.

From the first he knew that the problem was both educational and moral, if not religious. He therefore turned first to the Theological School of Boston University in 1916 with a gift of $60,000 to establish a chair of "Practicalities and Homely Virtues." This soon troubled his own "practicalities," however, so he transferred the endowment two years later to a chair of "United States Citizenship" in the Arts College. Dr. Frederick A. Cleveland, one of the organizers of the New York Bureau of Municipal Research and also of what is now the Brookings Institution, was appointed to the professorship.

Not satisfied with the results thus achieved, Maxwell proposed in 1919 a series of lectures on American citizenship at his alma mater, Syracuse University, of which he was then a trustee, to be given by a New York State senator, Dr. Frederick M. Davenport, a former Methodist minister with a doctorate in sociology, who was then a college professor of political science, whom Maxwell had met and come to admire.

Before these lectures could be arranged, however, Maxwell followed up his proposal in discussions with Chancellor Charles W. Flint of Syracuse University and finally offered to donate a fund of $500,000 to establish a "School of American Citizenship." He suggested Davenport as the man to organize the program.

Maxwell's letters at the time indicated that his chief purpose was "to make a signal contribution to the growth of stalwart Americanism among our people . . . and to produce a constant outpouring of enthusiastic young specialists who will make it more or less their life work to promote intelligent patriotism. . . ."[2] And to this end he suggested that the school should be geared primarily to the undergraduate level. Maxwell wrote that he was not interested in "politics" or "political science" or "philosophy." He wanted his school to concentrate on facts rather than on theory and, in his words, "utopian idealism."

The chancellor, though somewhat baffled by Maxwell's dream, was understandably enthusiastic, as the university was in need of funds, and wrote to Maxwell, "I think I can grasp your idea and

ideal and am inclined to think it can be worked out education-
ally."[3] In search of an answer to this problem, he wrote immediately to Dr. Davenport, who had become a New York state senator, putting Maxwell's proposals before him, and offering him the
directorship of the proposed new school. In keeping with Maxwell's desire to remain anonymous, partly because of modesty and
partly to avoid the charge that a man of means was trying to
"warp" the minds of youth, Davenport was not shown the Maxwell correspondence or told who was back of the idea.

At that time I was working night and day to finish the annual
report to the legislature of the Committee on Taxation and Retrenchment, of which Davenport was the moving spirit and I was
staff director. It was this report that proposed the then revolutionary principle of equalization by formula of state aid for local
schools inversely weighted by wealth, and a massive increase of
the state-aid program. This proposed move necessitated a substantial increase in state taxes, and we were hunting high and low for
politically acceptable tax proposals.

In the midst of a serious and painful discussion of what I had
drafted on school needs and state taxes, Davenport asked, out of a
clear sky: "What would you say, Luther, if you were asked by
the head of an unnamed up-state university to draw up plans for
an ideal school of American citizenship to be generously financed
by an anonymous donor?" To say the least, this question struck
me not only as rather iffy, but also as irrelevant to the business at
hand. So I tried to brush Davenport off, and get him to concentrate on our tax problem. But he continued to press, and at lunch
disclosed confidentially that the donor had offered the then impressive endowment of $500,000 for the program. I did a quick
take, noting that such a fund would produce about $25,000 annu-
ally, a sum that was only half of the current budget needs of the
Training School for Public Service of my Institute of Public Administration, and replied, "Five hundred thousand dollars? You
had better tell your donor that that is only half enough to start
the project."

So we went back to taxes, and I forgot the anonymous donor.
But the following week, when the senator came back to New

York to see how I was coming with the final text of the committee report and with the reach for $3 million of new taxes, he
greeted me with: "Luther, I got the million!" It took me a little
while to realize that he was talking about the mysterious donor for
the School of American Citizenship, not about my state tax problems. However, it was then that we did take time to talk about
the practical, philosophical, curricular, staff, and administrative
problems of creating an ideal School of American Citizenship
on a university campus.

When I agreed to put some ideas down on paper, I did not
know Maxwell or what he really wanted, nor do I think Davenport had too clear an idea, either. So I naturally took off on the
basis of the program of the New York Training School for Public Service, which we at the Institute of Public Administration
were then running. I had been supervising that school until Dr.
Charles A. Beard resigned as director of the New York Bureau
of Municipal Research in 1920, when I became director of the
bureau, and persuaded Dr. William E. Mosher of our staff to head
the training school.

It was at that point that the bureau itself was reorganized and
refinanced as the National Institute of Public Administration, with
the help of Raymond B. Fosdick, the Rockefeller, Carnegie, and
Rosenwald foundations, and a number of our New York supporters, especially Mr. R. Fulton Cutting, Mr. Richard S. Childs, Mr.
Carl H. Pforzheimer, and Mrs. E. H. Harriman.[4]

I refer to Mrs. Harriman especially because she, single-handed,
had established the Training School for Public Service and placed
it under the Bureau of Municipal Research in 1911. Her action
was an essential step in the prehistory of the Maxwell School.

In the exciting days of railroad finance and development, the
Harrimans were a notable power in New York. Mrs. Harriman
had an important place in the social life of the city, and her salon
was brilliant and significant.

During one of her many trips to Europe, she was impressed by
the able and ambitious young men who sought careers in English
public life and by the preparation for these careers that they received through the universities.

Reflecting on these observations, and comparing British public life with that in America at the time, Mary Averell Harriman had a dream. She wanted to find a method of drawing young men of ability and character into our public life. Like George Maxwell a decade later, Mrs. Harriman decided that educators and universities had to get involved. At a number of her brilliant dinners, she tried out the idea on several noted university presidents. First was Charles W. Eliot of Harvard, then Arthur T. Hadley of Yale, then Nicholas Murray Butler of Columbia. She asked each of them why young Americans of outstanding backgrounds and promise avoided politics, and why the universities didn't aim or prepare men for public life, but sent them straight into business, finance, and law. Each of the presidents in turn, she told me, were polite but amused. They assured her that in America politics was no career for a gentleman, and that a responsible college could not send its graduates into a blind alley.

This did not stop Mary Harriman. She soon found support in the New York Bureau of Municipal Research, which her husband was helping to support, and in Professor Charles A. Beard, then at Columbia. Working through these men, she took her idea, and the quarter of a million dollars she had raised and given all by herself for a Training School for Public Service, and in 1911 turned the idea and the money over to the Bureau of Municipal Research to develop and manage.

This was the school that existed a dozen years later when Davenport asked me his question. It was a school with a small student body, a nonacademic but practical program, several hundred enthusiastic alumni busily at work in government and government research, and dire financial needs. We thought that we had the formula, that it was working, and that all it needed was a university campus and adequate funds. Thus it was that Mrs. Harriman through us, helped Syracuse to set up what became the Maxwell School, when we transferred to the Syracuse campus not only the training-school program but also the registered students and the director of the program, Dr. William E. Mosher, who became dean of the new school.

Five major original streams of thought and effort were, in due

course, merged to form what is now the Maxwell School. None
of the founders got precisely what he or she initially wanted, but
I think that each one would be pleased to see what has now
emerged.[5]

Reviewing these initiatives in point of time, the first was that
of Mary Averell Harriman. She wanted a university program that
would draw young men of promise and character into the higher
levels of political leadership, including those who were free to
serve because they had acquired or inherited adequate economic
security. When no university was prepared to help her in this
effort, she made a start nonetheless with the Training School for
Public Service in New York, and its programs for city managers,
civic workers, researchers, budget officers, personnel directors,
health and welfare executives, and various other professional public administrators and public-administration teachers. Many of
these "graduates" did in fact win their way to the top of the civil
service, federal, state and local, as able public servants, dedicated
missionaries for good government, and pioneer teachers of administration.

Next came George Maxwell. He was a classical liberal-conserva-
tive who wanted, by traditional educational methods, to develop,
primarily at the undergraduate level, morally sound and ethically
committed Americans who would make it their concern to promote intelligent patriotism both directly and through the reform
of teaching programs of American schools and colleges, thus advancing the cause of good government.

Though somewhat thwarted in his initial aims, he accepted a
less frontal approach to the task of inculcating morality and patriotism and permitted his funds to be used also to expand social
science and graduate work in public administration and practical
politics, as proposed by Davenport and Gulick. He regarded this
as a somewhat indirect approach, but one that he hoped would
lead eventually to his true goals.

The third initiator was Frederick Davenport, a Bull Moose Progressive, who wanted a school that would turn out men who were
morally committed to progress, social welfare, and reform within
the framework of the American Constitutional system, men with a

good practical knowledge of American politics and expert competence in government administration. On this last point, he thought the New York Training School program was a sound beginning.

Fourth, Chancellor Flint and his faculty were concerned and interested not only in having the university serve as the instrument of George Maxwell and his good citizenship endowment, but also in fitting the new program into the needs of the university, especially by supporting the social studies and political science program, without upsetting existing arrangements. There were those who urged, no doubt with some reason, that all education contributes to "good citizenship" and that what Maxwell sought is the subtle by-product of a broad and fundamental education.

Finally, the Training School for Public Service program that Davenport, Gulick, and Mosher transported to the Syracuse campus was at the start, perhaps, "the most important influence on the development of the Maxwell School," to quote from Peter Johnson's excellent history of Maxwell in the recent winter number of the *Maxwell Review*.[6] This was an eclectic, nonacademic, interdisciplinary professional program dealing with the then current structures, interrelations, and administrative procedures and problems of state and local government and politics, based largely on field work, research, seminars, case studies, and apprenticeship in civic work, politics and management, under the supervision of senior officers and faculty members.

At the time of the transfer to Syracuse, the training school was looking for a hospitable university campus and for more financial support, it having become evident that the students required a much broader array of disciplines and skills than could be furnished by any institute or bureau (though such institutions were, of course, useful for laboratories and internships). Also desirable were scholarships, dormitories, libraries, and recruitment and placement services. But of prime consideration, in addition to academic freedom, was the interdisciplinary broadening of the scope of the work and research to include what we now call the "policy sciences." It is not without significance that the first faculty addition for the Maxwell School program, after Dean Mosher, was a social psychologist.

The interdisciplinary nature and scope of the "citizenship" course initiated at Maxwell in 1924 merits special notice. It began as an introduction to civics and civic responsibility, but it soon came to deal more generally with "man in society," drawing also on history, anthropology, economics, sociology, and education. The collection of readings for this course, which appeared in print in 1941 under the title *Introduction to Responsible Citizenship*[7] was used in a number of other colleges as well.

It is from these diverse yet complementary trends that the deans of the Maxwell School, with their colleagues over the past fifty years, have fashioned what is still a unique educational experiment, an experiment that is increasingly, as the years pass, fulfilling the dreams of the founders.

MOTIVATION AND COMMITMENT

One aspect of this experiment in education deserves special emphasis in view of the other papers in this volume. It concerns itself with motivation and commitment. Both of the major financial donors, George Maxwell and Mrs. Harriman, were concerned with something more than knowledge and skills; they were searching for moral and ethical standards, and for commitment to the public service. They were looking for dedication.

What actually came about incorporated several intertwined elements:

1. As to skills, the program has developed, and is keeping up-to-date, various "systems" and tools that range all the way from accounting to zoning, from budgeting and personnel classification to semicybernetic decision techniques and proliferating methods of input, output and end-up indicators, measurements, and analysis.

2. As to increasing the chances for broadly valid decisions, the program has found methods for expanding the field of operational acquaintance with relevant disciplines and technologies.

3. As to general competence and "wisdom" in administration, the program has proceeded on the theory that an art is mastered especially during the early years, not through book knowledge,

but by working with mature and dedicated artists, by actual participation in real work situations, and by continuous criticism of work experience by the workers with the help, where possible, of a master.

4. As to motivation, admissions were screened with care, novices were associated with dedicated and highly motivated teachers and operators, and early work experience was designed to be distinctly rewarding from a public-service standpoint. To this end, carefully selected internships were arranged under the continuing supervision of dedicated teachers.

5. Throughout the entire training process the arts of communication were emphasized, both in sensing and being guided by the inputs of democracy and in developing the educational component of administrative action, verbally and through reports and "public relations."

6. Professional associations of practitioners in general and specialized fields were established and encouraged to develop a constructive, vital and cohesive influence.

In this brief summary you will note that the part of education for the public service that is intellectual we treat as the universities do history, literature, or science, but with more attention to the case method (which we adopted in 1911, a decade before this was done at the Harvard School of Business); the part of our education that is skill, we treat as a trade, with procedural handbooks, practical work, and apprenticeships with master technicians; the part that is an art, we handle by working at the art with established artists (or as Dwight Waldo might say, as an intern with a master surgeon); and finally, the part that is value laden and motivational, we handle by blending the cognitive with the emotional in a framework of direct association with men who are themselves deeply committed.[8]

PROBLEMS FOR THE FUTURE

In the field of government and its operation, nothing stays put. This is inevitable because government is a major instrument by which man adapts his social system to the changing environmental challenges, most of which he now creates for himself.

In this process, the spinning off of new and deeper areas of theory and of experimental practice is not, as I see it, a mark of decadence and decay but rather a proof of vitality and growth. When a constituent phase or unit of a broad field of interest, knowledge, technology, or study is significantly redefined and elaborated, even to the point of questioning or modifying prior paradigms, and when this is accepted by those most concerned, the process is an enrichment, not an impoverishment. In such cases, there is no problem of something "coming apart", there is, on the contrary, a demonstration of expansion and growth. Medicine, with its many specializations, and physics, with its extraordinary proliferations, are cases in point. Are they demolished by their new fractions and branches?

So long as government exists, so long as men work together in formal or informal frameworks of power dedicated to the purpose of human welfare and justice, men will be concerned with public administration and public management. The more we have specialized fields of operation, analysis, theory, and purposeful manipulation, the greater will be mankind's need for those arts and that body of knowledge about government management that we call "public administration," and for men and women educated to function effectively and responsibly in these fields and with these tools. If you wish, you may call this knowledge and this education something else, but until all government "withers away," until power and specialization cease to play a role in human society, public administration will endure as an existential fact. If the philosophers overlook this, the oversight will discredit their philosophy; it will not change the realities of the world.

Even so, looking into the future, schools of public administration and public affairs do face important challenges arising from (1) ongoing changes in the environment and (2) significant advances in knowledge and theory.

These have been noted and commented on by the deans of the Maxwell School in their annual reports of recent years. Both faculty and students have been drawn into international public-administration problems, working not only for the United Nations, the World Health Organization, and the Agency for International Development, but also for foreign governments and universities in vastly different and contrasing social, political, and economic environments. It has enriched and sobered American scholarship to come into contact with less materialistic and more idealistic cultures that have perdured successfully for thousands of years longer than our own. The extension of Maxwell's theater of operations from New York State to the whole world has significantly changed the program of the school. It must be obvious to all, however, that the full significance of this extension of American interest abroad, and consequently of the scope of "citizenship" in the modern world, has barely been appreciated thus far, and is destined to call for further and much more fundamental adjustments in the decades that lie ahead, especially as we consider the new problems for policy and administration that are already emerging in such pronouncements as those recently made by C. P. Snow and UN Secretary General Kurt Waldheim on world population, poverty, and food.

While the American adjustment to this new world outlook lies urgently in the future, we must note also an important change that has been going on here at home. When we began to train people for the public service in New York City in 1911 we started with a trade school for local government researchers and local civic and management reformers. Charles Beard expanded this program considerably in 1915 when he broadened the curriculum to include history, economics, sociology, and politics, and later he, William E. Mosher, and I developed specific work for city managers and budget and personnel officers. But even when the program was shifted to the Syracuse campus in 1924 it continued to concentrate on preparing people for state and local governmental research, and civic work. It was not until the New Deal days in Washington that we began to look also at the federal services and at the broader problems of policy.

This step up from primarily local and civic reform to the full range of federal, state, and local administration has played an important role in reformulating the content of public administration thinking and training.

Even more significant, however, was the shift that was taking place in the American concept of government itself. When we started work, both in New York and in Syracuse, we were dealing with a laissez-faire government that was seeking to maintain the status quo, to preserve the "market mechanism," to make democracy effective, and to keep the masses reasonably comfortable and satisfied. There were some departures from these negative ideas in practice, but none in theory. We did have tariffs and taxes and banking laws, which served to protect certain economic interests, but it was only with Theodore Roosevelt and Woodrow Wilson that we began seriously to restrain the most predatory corporations and monopolies. It was only after the turn of the century that we began to extend the already established free education for the masses and to make "public" our largely voluntary system of helping the poor and the weak. But the accepted general doctrine was still "the less government the better" and "the devil take the hindmost," under which formula public administration was, I suspect, helping the devil!

With the New Deal, this began to change in fundamental ways. As a nation we found we had to use our government as a positive force: (a) to change the rules of the game, not simply maintain the status quo; (b) to render important services that the market could not supply, nationally, locally and by states; (c) to ameliorate the status and enrich the opportunities of underprivileged and weak groups of the population; (d) to bring about a shift in the distribution of the GNP, so as to increase the share going to the lower third of the population, to labor and agriculture, and to the southern and western parts of the continent; and (e) to undertake and to encourage developmental research, ideas and experimentation.

Public administration as a branch of knowledge and study, and even more as an educational field, has been slow indeed to adjust to the significance of this revolutionary shift in American history. Nor have the other social sciences done any better. Much recent criticism of public-administration education and theory is due to this adjustment lag. It is a valid criticism, but the reasons for the slow and limited adjustments are not far to seek.

In the first place, the nation and its various power blocs do not see what has happened even now, nor do they welcome illumination on this point. While the publicists and the political "leaders" still bask in the "free enterprise" and "free market" lingo, we are forced to operate *in fact* not only with irresponsibly managed prices and commodity options, but with brainwashed consumerism, shrinking freedoms and standards of living for the middle classes as well as for the masses, and government-induced unemployment and precipitous inflations, all apparently tolerated intentionally by a government without a helmsman, and all having the effect of diminishing the status of the weak and allowing the well-placed and well-organized to escape the inflationary trap by their economic and legal power to "pass it along."

The intellectuals and idea leaders are not much help, either. Unconsciously they split into "conservative" and "radical" wings in every substantive field, all the way from economics and social work to ethics and theology. They all know where we have been; some of them know where we now are and how we got that way; but few even try to predict honestly what will happen next (just look at the President's economic advisors and their consistent string of booboos); and still fewer agree on what can and should be done next. They are not in posts of authority, nor are they as gifted, say, as Adlai Stevenson or Harriet Beecher Stowe, who could exercise power with their pens.

In the second place, educators in public administration have been confronted with a most confusing and explosive array of new ideas, theories, and "laws" in all the social sciences. The MAN with which we deal in politics and administration today is not the same man who was in the mind of Plato, Aristotle, Saints Paul and Augustine, el Ghazzali, Malthus, Burke, Paine, Madison, Jefferson, Hegel, Hobbes, Comte, Mill, Darwin, Marx and Lenin, Spencer, Kierkegaard and Sartre, Pareto, Weber, Freud, Goodnow, Wilson, James and Dewey, Beard, Taylor, Keynes, Bentley, Fayol, and Follett, or even Gandhi and Mao. Our MAN is a new creature, and even he is being reconstructed, step by step and gene by gene, by modern biology, anthropology, ethnology, ecology, sociology, genetics, psychology, psychoanalysis, and political science. You have to turn around and look over your shoulder to see even the shadow of "the child of God," the "noble savage," the "original sinner," the "economic man," the "rational man," the "average man," the "dominant id," the "foreigner,' the "Pavlovian man," and, of course, the "organization man."

The more we discover about man, the more we find that he is tied to his evolutionary, biological, and cultural past and that most human traits are distributed among men, as are variations in the dimensions of the leaves of a tree, so that they fall in a bell-shaped frequency distribution. As a result, most studies of human capacities, behavior, and institutions fit only that small part of the curve that we are able, or choose, to analyze. Not a few of our most cherished Western "values" and "ideals" may well turn out to be such partial "truths"—even such concepts as freedom, democracy, justice, honesty, and the devoutly-to-be-desired supersession of hierarchy, which may, in fact, have roots in the genes of men.

Most of the stereotypes and shadows of "man" have receded into the past during the short half century that we are talking about. Is it any wonder that public-administration education has faced, and still faces, problems of adaptation?

The NEW MAN (and WOMAN) who is emerging is more complex, more unpredictable, more worthwhile, more creative, more willful, more motivated by group loyalty and love, more exciting, lovable, and *real* than any of the older shadows. We in public administration must deal with this man/woman/child in our thinking and in our work because he is the producer and the consumer, the manager, the civil servant and the client, the foreigner and the native, the ruler and the ruled.

Herein lies the challenge of the future.

NOTES

1. Letter to Frederick M. Davenport, Sept. 10, 1926. Davenport Papers, Box 7, Syracuse University Archives.
2. Letter to Flint, Oct. 11, 1923. Flint Papers, Syracuse University Archives.
3. Letter from Flint to Maxwell, Oct. 24, 1923. Galpin Papers, Syracuse University Archives.
4. "National" was dropped from the Institute title in 1921.

5. Students of administration will note that the managers influenced the structure and realization of the program even more than did the donors.

6. *Maxwell Review*, Vol. 10, No. 2 (Winter, 1973–74), p. 8.

7. William E. Mosher (Ed.) and Associates (New York: Henry Holt & Company, 1941).

8. This is "confluent education" as defined in the University of California studies (Santa Barbara), (Unpublished), 1974.

Appendix: Case Histories of Early Professional Education Programs

ALICE B. STONE AND DONALD C. STONE

Each major effort to create a school of public administration or its equivalent is an interesting story in itself. In the aggregate, they provide a means of assessing and comparing causes of success and failure. In this Appendix we have selected for special analysis ten institutions that appear to have made the most significant contribution by 1933. The case histories have been based on university reports, accumulated files, personal correspondence, and the works of several authors, principally George A. Graham in *Education for Public Administration* (1941) and Leonard D. White in *Trends in Public Administration* (1933). We beg indulgence for any oversights or inaccuracies that may have occurred in our efforts to reconstruct a poorly recorded past.

The Training School for Public Service. Because it was the apparent founder of professional, multidisciplinary education in public administration and had penetrating influence on later university initiatives, we give the New York Training School first place in the history. It was founded in 1911 and formally consolidated with the New York Bureau of Municipal Research in 1922 to form the National Institute of Public Administration. (The word "National" was dropped soon thereafter.)

We are indebted to George A. Graham for a vivid and detailed account of the training methods employed in the school's different stages.[1] Referring to the first stage, 1911–1915, he says in substance: its plan of training—new, stimulating, and almost startling at the time—in retrospect seems to have been a natural development of the era, a reflection of the conditions or convictions that influenced Frederick Taylor's scientific management, John Watson's behaviorism, and Theodore Roosevelt's progressivism. The idea was to learn through doing, but not through doing alone, rather through doing plus observing freshly, critically, and optimistically. Men were set to work immediately on the current projects of the Bureau of Municipal Research. Some specialized early and intensively. The younger men were more apt to have a variety of assignments. The plan of supervision was threefold: general supervision by officers of the bureau (later by a director of field work), immediate supervision by a senior staff member, and close association with a public official. There were formal written assignments, frequent reports, time sheets, staff and luncheon conferences. Precision of statement and development of facility in speaking were encouraged. Officials spoke informally at staff sessions. There were visits to municipal institutions and to state and federal departments. All worked on the New York City budget, handled office correspondence, got out the bulletin, criticized published reports, prepared publicity for papers and magazines.

When Charles Beard became head of the training school in 1915, he introduced formal lectures and seminars as the core feature of a two-year program. The "announcement of courses" for 1916/17 listed the following subjects:[2]

First semester: law and municipal government taught by Howard Lee McBain; legislative drafting and administration, by Thomas H. Parkinson; municipal highway engineering, by Arthur H. Blanchard; government of the City of New York, by Ernest P. Goodrich; politics and administration, by Charles A. Beard and E. Berl Shultz; and elements of municipal accounting, by E. M. Freeland.

Second semester: principles of management taught by Frederick A. Cleveland; engineering administration, by Goodrich; charities, school and health administration, by Samuel McCune Lindsay, Russell H. Allen, and Carl E. McCombs; police and fire administration, by C. J. Driscoll and Raymond B. Fosdick; budget-making, accounting, and reporting, by Frederick Cleveland.

Students enrolled in these courses were expected to devote the second year to supervised field assignments. Experienced and well-grounded persons with suitable backgrounds could undertake such assignments immediately. Some students could combine both. Special courses were also offered special groups.

In 1922/23, after the bureau and training school were incorporated to form the (National) Institute of Public Administration, a third training format was developed. It provided for full-time enrollment in a selected-course program from September to May. Courses were conducted on a workshop or clinical basis, and students were viewed as apprentices or junior employees. Graham reports the following subjects: charter and municipal corporations, budgets and budget making, public accounting and financial reporting, civil service and personnel administration, purchasing and supplies, taxation and revenues, public debt administration, engineering administration, police and fire administration, public health and welfare administration, and educational administration. Minor subjects were statistics and graphic methods, committee management, publicity, and special problems of city management.

Students elected courses to fit their interests. By February, each student selected a subject for intensive study. In May, each was put on a full-time assignment from three to six months with an institute staff member. A formal report was required.

After 1924 the institute dropped this kind of program (which the Maxwell School instituted) and accepted advanced graduate students as apprentices, while continuing to offer special courses for special groups.[3]

The authors recall a visit with the Beards in their Connecticut home in 1928. Young William Beard was enrolled in one of the institute courses and accompanied them. He had a problem, and wanted his father's advice on how to index his report. After the perusal, his father looked up and said, "Why, Billy, you can't index a fog."

Between 1911 and 1930, 1,544 men and women enrolled in the school's announced program. The following distribution by five year periods is taken from White's *Trends in Public Administration:*[4]

Period	Full Time	Part Time
1911–15	94	90
1916–20	32	244
1921–25	34	848
1926–30	36	166
	196	1,348

Excluded from the above figures is a large number of persons for whom special courses were arranged at the New York School of Social Work and City College, and lectures provided by the staff at numerous other colleges and universities.

Luther Gulick, who served for many years as director of the New York Bureau and Institute of Public Administration, reports that roughly 80 percent of the full time graduates entered government or unofficial public service work. In 1928, twenty-five bureaus of municipal research gained directors and forty-eight staff members in this way; twenty-six universities appointed professors from this source; twenty-two went into city management.

Gulick describes subsequent developments as follows: "The new and comprehensive character of the training course was formally recognized by Columbia, New York, Chicago, and other universities which made arrangements for the interchange of students and for the granting of credit toward advanced degrees on account of work in the Training School. . . . The development of definite graduate degrees in public administration, as at Michigan and Syracuse universities, and the expansion of university courses in public administration as at Columbia, New York, Harvard, Johns Hopkins, Northwestern, Chicago, Illinois, Wisconsin, Iowa, Minnesota, Oklahoma, California, Stanford, and Washington, during the decade which followed the establishment of the Training School, gradually altered the situation. It became no longer necessary for the Training School and Institute in their training work to deal directly with the problem of elementary graduate instruction in public administration."[5]

The development of correspondence courses in 1922 was another innovation of the Training School for Public Service. They were transferred to Syracuse in 1925 and later taken over by the International City Managers' Association (ICMA) when Clarence E. Ridley became its executive director.

The Institute of Public Administration was affiliated with Columbia University from 1931 until 1942, when the relationship was terminated. In a personal letter (May 16, 1974) Luther Gulick writes: "Our difficulties with Columbia arose largely from lack of funds which created personality problems. The University was a reluctant partner, and those who developed the relationship died or got involved elsewhere, and things fell apart. My absences in Washington from 1939 to 1945 for the war were a factor. The split on campus over the New Deal in Washington was also a factor, a split that started when FDR was governor, 1928–31."

Michigan. The first distinctly graduate, professional program in public administration was a one-year masters course in municipal administration, established at the University of Michigan in 1914. Three months of field work were also required.

Jesse S. Reeves, chairman of the political-science department from 1910 to 1937, was largely responsible for conceiving the program. About the same time a Bureau of Reference and Research in Government fostered research and assisted public officials. Robert T. Crane, with a background in the consular service, was brought to head both the bureau and the municipal program. The bureau (soon called Bureau of Government) provided both library facilities and work space for public-administration students. It developed a splendid collection of state and municipal materials.

By the 1920s the enterprising Michigan Municipal League and the Detroit Bureau of Governmental Research were partners in the municipal administration program. Lent D. Upson and C. L. Rightor, respectively director and assistant director of the Bureau, offered courses at Ann Arbor and provided supervised internships in Detroit. In 1922 Thomas H. Reed was appointed director of the Bureau of Government, instructor in municipal administration, and supervisor of the master's students.[6] Arthur Bromage joined in 1928 as a municipal specialist, and continued association with the public administration programs through their fiftieth anniversary in 1964.

About 1930, several public-service training interests at the university—municipal administration, public health, sociology, economics, etc.—were combined under a joint committee of the departments represented, with Reed as curriculum director. Enlistment of talented students was aided by a three year allocation of $10,000 for senior and graduate fellowships.

In a July, 1932, report on Training Public Administrators, Mssrs. Leet, Nolting, and Paige stated: "Twenty-four of the graduates of the Michigan municipal administration course are now engaged in public work as follows: four city managers, one assistant city manager, eight in some county or city position, five with public and private agencies, five with chambers of commerce or community funds, and one secretary of a state municipal league."[7] The latter was Harold D. Smith who later became budget director of Michigan and in 1939 director of the U.S. Bureau of the Budget. By 1935 sixty degrees had been granted.

The Depression took its toll. In 1933 this program was at first curtailed and later abandoned. After a gap of four years a new curriculum in public administration was organized as part of an Institute of Public and Social Administration, to become the Institute of Public Administration in 1946.

A joint degree program with civil engineering leading to a master's degree in public-works administration dated back to 1914. A master's in natural-resources administration, a pioneer in the field, was first offered in 1936 in cooperation with the School of Natural Resources. The public-administration program, under several plans and names, never gained full control over its curriculum and budget until 1950.

Significant in the Michigan efforts were the strong support to the instructional program provided by the independent Bureau of Government, involvement of a number of university departments, effective relationships with the Municipal League and Detroit

Bureau of Governmental Research, and the progressive character of Michigan municipal government, made possible by the home rule provisions of the 1908 constitution.

While the institute had enough freedom to develop a good program, it was always dependent either upon the ephemeral support of persons whose primary loyalties were to other purposes, or on the limited attention the dean of the graduate school could give. But for the dedication of the successive directors of the public-administration curriculum, the institute would not have survived. The history written for the fiftieth anniversary emphasized that the orientation of the institute was "one of continuity rather than change." A rather optimistic view of things! The institute was subsequently changed to the Institute of Public Policy Analysis.

University of California, Berkeley. This institution established the Bureau of Public Administration in 1920, first within and later outside the political-science department. Under Samuel T. May the bureau became a very substantial reference, research, and service center covering municipal, state, and federal affairs. It developed what is without doubt the most extensive collection of documents in these fields of any university. (The bureau ultimately became the present day Institute of Governmental Studies.)

The bureau became a catalyst in stimulating the political science department to offer course work in public administration and enlisting interest in other parts of the university. It provided a work center for students as well as research experience. In 1922 the first cluster of courses was offered to upper division students. In 1924 graduate seminars in federal, state, and municipal administration were introduced. Personnel administration, police, and criminal justice were featured for the first time in 1931. In 1931/32 the public-administration program enrolled about fifty graduate students, including fifteen public employees each semester.

Under the dynamic and largely individual efforts of Sam May, who developed a wide number of contacts both within and especially outside the university, California provided many of the inputs of a professional school of public administrators. For years, May with one toe in the political science department, seven toes in the Bureau, and two in outside agencies—gave some institutional vitality to public administration. Only after Frederick C. Mosher and Victor Jones arrived on the scene did it become possible, with the support of Joseph Harris and Dwight Waldo, to create a MAPA program within the political-science department—and ultimately a separate School of Public Affairs (with a name change, even before it was organized as planned, to that of Graduate School of Public Policy).

California is a story of substantial contribution to public service conducted without an enduring legal/political mandate. Until the 1960s the program was fragmented and fragile, sustained largely by the enthusiasm of Sam May. It is a story of what might have been if university leadership had had enough vision in early years to create an autonomous school.

Stanford University. Few persons today think of Stanford University as a pioneer in public-administration education. Thanks to the wisdom and resourcefulness of Professor Edwin A. Cottrell, head of the department of political science, it was a leading institution in this field for some years.

The program was started in 1921 as a three-year course, with two years of college preparation required for admission. According to the editors of the July, 1932, issue of *Public Administrators' News Letter*, courses were offered in administrative law, municipal corporations, public-utility law, public management, school finance, school administration, governmental research, sanitary engineering, and general administrative subjects. In some of the courses, field work was required. For thesis purposes, graduates were placed in city, county, and state governments and in bureaus of municipal research.

Sponsored by the chairman of political science with support and cooperation from other departments, the program flourished for as long as Edwin Cottrell was its mentor. This ad hoc arrangement was in the Stanford tradition. Without enduring structure, the program atrophied after Cottrell's departure from the scene. While some students continued to have an interest in public administration, faculty leadership gradually disappeared. The final result has been the emergence of a well-financed school of business management dedicated to the proposition that since government needs business management, it is equipped to provide the administrative talent for government.

Syracuse University. The origin of the Maxwell School of Citizenship and Public Affairs is in striking contrast to that of other institutions. There were few early university inputs and no delays in gestation. It happened all at once.

A Boston industrialist, inventor, and attorney by the name of George A. Maxwell started things off by offering an endowment of $500,000 (with roughly $25,000 in annual earnings) to his alma mater for the purpose of establishing a program for the education of better citizens. The president of the university enlisted another alumnus, state senator (later congressman) Frederick Davenport, formerly professor of political science at Hamilton College, as counsel to work out plans. While serving as chairman of the New York State Special Joint Committee on Taxation and Retrenchment, Davenport had come to know Luther Gulick, director of the National Institute of Public Administration, which had provided staff for Davenport's committee. Davenport reported Maxwell's offer and proposal for a school of citizenship to Gulick, who advised Davenport that establishing the program would cost $50,000 a year, Maxwell immediately doubled the endowment and the new school was on the way to delivery.

Davenport's keen interest in better-trained state and local administrators, buttressed by Gulick's advice, led to the decision to make a graduate program in public administration a principal feature of the new school. Dr. William E. Mosher, who was then in charge of the training programs of the New York Institute of Public Administration, was persuaded to become dean of the new school. Since the institute's full-time course of instruction was being phased out anyway, Dr. Mosher was literally able to transfer it intact to Syracuse.

At its inception, the Maxwell School of Citizenship and Public Affairs had three purposes: (1) providing citizenship courses for all students, (2) establishing social-science leadership, and (3) organizing a program leading to a Master of Science degree in Public Administration. From the beginning then, the school combined education and research in the social sciences and professional education for public service. It is almost unique among the early programs in that public administration was not incubated in the department of political science.

The entering class in 1924 consisted of six persons, all of whom were recipients of fellowships. The curriculum featured city management. Subjects were taken up sequentially so that students could give their undivided attention to one field at a time, whether for three days or three weeks. This arrangement made it possible to import about half of the instructors. The overall aim was excellence, both in format and quality of instruction.

An introduction to American government and politics, municipal government, and administrative law was followed by units in civil service and personnel, public finance, accounting, purchasing, community organization, municipal engineering, public health, school management, problems of city management, and a sprinkle of city planning. In early February the class moved to New York for seven or eight weeks of instruction at the National Institute of Public Administration where professors Gulick, Buck, Cornick, Studensky, McCombs, Bartlett, and Smith served as tutors in their respective fields: administrative research, budgeting, tax administration and assessing, debt management, health and welfare, public works, and police and fire administration.

A distinctive and most valued feature of the entire program was the focus on substantive policies and operations—on application of administrative concepts to public-service fields. Visits to waterworks, sewage-disposal plants, police headquarters, health departments, and other public offices were arranged. In later years this kind of field work was carried out partly through the Rochester Bureau of Governmental Research.

The Maxwell program was designed for the students and was not simply a collection of courses that faculty members liked to teach. Clarence R. Ridley, a product of the New York Bureau of Municipal Research and a former city manager, while completing his doctorate at Syracuse, was the general supervisor, almost the vicar. For the students of the first years, he tied it all together.

A good working library was established at the outset, enriched by duplicates of surveys, proceedings of associations, and public reports that had been assembled over the years at the institute's library in New York. There were few available textbooks in the public administration field, and the group literally watched the librarian open new packages to see what they contained. Two students were in the office of Dean Mosher when he unwrapped a package out of which popped Leonard White's *Introduction to the Study of Public Administration*. Glancing at the table of contents, the good dean looked up and said, "He beat me to it." The moral is that academics who are successful in establishing schools seldom have the time to write books, and those who spend their time writing are seldom able to organize schools.

The thesis was viewed as a means of applying what had been learned. Students worked on practical problems faced by municipal administrators in real situations. An oral exam covering both course work and thesis capped the program.

For inexperienced students, internship was an integral part of the program. Placement possibilities were naturally on the minds of students. The market in this era of fumbling government was pretty thin. The two most likely possibilities were assignment to a city manager or to a governmental-research agency. Such internships often led to permanent posts.

With rare exceptions, the graduates of Maxwell embarked on careers in public or quasi-public agencies. They had become imbued with the importance of public service and professional dedication. Among them we find city managers, research agency directors, budget and personnel officers, agency administrators, college presidents, community leaders, governor's assistants, directors of finance, deans and directors of public administration centers, etc.

The early Maxwell history continues to provide guidance for today: a purposeful and well-managed program strongly supported by the dean and university administrators, a professional and operational orientation, focus on management in relation to functional or substantive fields, effective promotion, readily available fellowships, competent instructors, field work, and good student/instructor interaction.

Lacking, however, were effective relationships with other professional schools within the university. We refer again to Graham's report of 1940.[8] "It was the university center for social science training, but it was hardly a university center for public administration training." The single-track ride for public-administration students did not permit extra passengers. No courses were offered to accomodate students of other schools or part-time students until much later. Moreover, there seemed to be no interest in offering short-term courses. Linkages between the school and governments in the area were very limited, partly due to unprogressive city and county governments. Fruitful connections with Albany came only later.

The public-administration student saw himself as a part of an exciting and unique program in a protected unit of a complex school. Many of the regular faculty were primarily interested in other fields of teaching and research. Public administration lacked a multidisciplinary faculty of its own. The arrangement was excellent in many ways, broadening the scope of the social sciences and increasing their concern with application, but not in creating a professional school or department of public affairs/administration. Unlike most institutions reviewed in this account, the Maxwell school has held steady to its course, with continuous growth and outreach.

University of Cincinnati. The public-service training program began at the University of Cincinnati in 1927 under the leadership of S. Gale Lowrie, chairman of the political-science department. Three major factors contributed to its initiation: (1) the advent of council-manager government (1924) in the city and reform in the county, (2) the feasibility of the cooperative plan of education (work-study) in which the College of Engineering had pioneered since 1906, and (3) a grant from the Rockefeller Foundation.

At the start, the program consisted of a curriculum in public administration in which a graduate student could specialize, and a program in municipal engineering in which an undergraduate engineering student could pursue a certificate option in public administration. The engineering program was subsequently moved to the graduate level. A program in welfare administration was added.

The entire program was based on a mix of formal courses and work experience as employees of public agencies. At first, master's degree students engaged in alternate months of work and study for a period of twenty-one months. The format was soon changed to one in which first-year graduate students attended classes in the morning and/or evening, and in the afternoon worked in city hall, the county building, or at some other location. The following summer and the first semester of the second year were spent in full-time work, usually outside of Cincinnati to give broader experience. The second semester required full-time study and completion of a thesis.

During the early years, the following courses were offered: public administration (as though a course covered the total field), local government, public finance, public utilities, taxation, governmental accounting, administrative law, municipal corporations, city planning, personnel administration, purchasing, public-welfare administration, police administration, economics of labor, labor problems, engineering problems, and administrative problems.

Not all courses were taught every year. Instructors were drawn about equally from the political-science department, other units of the university, and city hall. The latter contributed such well known professionals as C. A. Dykstra, John B. Blandford, Jr., and Fred K. Hoehler.

The courses attracted a few part-time students. For example, while working in Cincinnati, the authors of this appendix enrolled in public finance, administrative law, international law, and international organization. The time was probably premature to include international affairs in the program. Students in the master's program were drawn from all parts of the country. George Graham reports that by 1938/39, 136 persons had been enrolled in some phase of the program. Only 57 had completed the course in public administration, an average of less than 5 per year.[9]

The Cincinnati program had a favorable university, community, and geographical location, and enjoyed attractive features. But it never gained a critical mass of faculty and students. It was never given a suitable status as a department, school, or institute. Structurally it was a floating element of one department with some loose collaborative relationships with engineering, economics, and law. The program had paternal guidance but little management. It suffered from insufficient promotion, negotiation, supervision, and follow-up. No real effort was made to involve public employees in part-time study. After Lowrie's retirement, the program deteriorated. In later years it was partially revived as a professional master's program.

University of Southern California. USC, like Syracuse, moved quickly to establish a genuine school headed by a dean, but that is where the similarity ended. An appeal by public officials in the Los Angeles region to organize courses for public employees begat what ultimately became the School of Public Administration. In August, 1928, the first annual short-course institute was staged. "Four hundred officials and employees from more than fifty governments declared it to be a most effective instrument for the improvement of the organization, administration, and management of government."[10] These participants were the nucleus of what became thousands of supporters for the school.

The academic response was simple and direct. An inventory of all university resources applicable to public service was made, together with an analysis of problems and objectives. With the enthusiastic support of the president and the dean of the graduate school, a decision was made to establish a new professional school of public service. In February, 1929, the University Board of Trustees authorized what was first known as the School of Citizenship and Public Administration,[11] with Emery E. Olson as dean, reporting directly to the president. USC is thus second in sequence to Maxwell as a school headed by a dean, and the first school fully devoted to professional education in public administration.

USC's was no narrow, trade-school approach. It was unique in its involvement of public officials from many fields in a focussed effort to develop a professional spirit backed by the necessary pre-service and in-service education. Said Olson: "We believed that the science and art of public administration demanded imagination and flexibility in all of human knowledge. . . . We accepted both policy *and* administration, academic research *and* field survey, organization structure *and* motivation, line *and* staff, techniques of administrative procedures *and* the behavioral sciences as equally important bases for investigation and study."[12]

The announcement of courses for 1929 shows that from the beginning USC offered both a bachelor's and master's degree in public administration, and a joint degree with the school of law. At its downtown Civic Center, the school catered to public officials of the region who wished to pursue either a degree or certificate program, while at the same time providing well-developed, professionally focussed public-administration curricula at its University Park campus. John Pfiffner taught three courses the first year and by 1930 had developed a textbook. Gordon Whitnall, the city planner who started teaching part time at USC in 1921, also taught in the new program and continued until 1971.

The curriculum reflected a broad sweep of interest. No other school approached USC's success in utilizing and integrating university-wide resources with new course work. Cross listing of courses and cooperative programs were characteristic from the start. Even the first year, joint degree and joint certificates with degrees were scheduled in several engineering fields and in social work. The program in police administration was also launched at that time.

Client-centered programming, negotiation of agreement, and promotion produced exceptional support, both within and without the university. Plans and proposals were formally presented to the League of California Cities, professional and civic organizations, city councils, county and state groups, and other institutions. A "Civic Air Tour" in 1928 captured the imagination of press and public. A three-motored Ford plane carried a group of county supervisors, city councilmen, city manager, college deans, and the

USC president to other cities. The newspapers became strong allies. Later, radio was used to report on civic progress, special courses, educational exhibits, equipment demonstrations, and the results of surveys and research. These "youthful and uninhibited efforts," as Olson called them, paid off in academic and short-course enrollments, requests for advisory services, and support from many quarters.

With rapidly increasing enrollments—about 60 full-time and 250 part-time within four years—a variety of programs and courses became possible. The school's announcements listed what were considered relevant courses in architecture, commerce, economics, engineering, geography, political science, psychology, social work, sociology, etc. Joint seminars abounded.

Dean Olson points out that while appropriate attention was given to staff and analytical subjects, the main thrust was on line management—on the functions of city managers, police chiefs, public-works engineers, public-health directors at the local level, on the heads of state-government departments, and departmental administrators and bureau chiefs in the federal government.

The encompassing interfaces uniquely developed by USC were sustained both by Dean Olson's catholic interests and the mechanism of an advisory committee that he chaired, consisting of the heads of some ten other schools and departments. Instructors were also drawn from these units and from government and community agencies, and business firms.

The school had a great impact in both region and state. Assisted by a network of committees of public officials, it carried out short courses of great diversity. The annual institute of government of a week's duration enrolled 1,000 participants in the early 1930s. Later, as a visiting lecturer, we faced groups of 300 and 800, with additional discussion groups of 100 and 200. More than 3,000 officials participated. In retrospect, the high quality of government in southern California can be attributed to a large extent to the professionalization and administrative orientation of public service fostered by the University of Southern California. Each graduate student placed and each official upgraded was a potential proponent of USC's education and research efforts.

USC offers several lessons worthy of emulation: an autonomous professional school well supported by the president; appointment of a dean with administrative competence; development of cooperative relationships with many other schools and departments on a mutual benefit basis; recognition that most administrators/ managers are engaged in functional or specialized fields and the consequent need of relating administration to the problems and technologies of those fields; involvement of public agencies of all kinds in the school's programs; and resourceful promotional and publicity measures. Almost uniquely, USC applied to itself the requisites of public administration and consultative management that it espoused in its curriculum.

We should take note that these accomplishments were achieved with meager university and external financing. Almost all programs were self-supporting. On the other hand, the school benefitted greatly from rapidly developing, high-quality local and state government. The solid institutional base and other supportive factors enabled the school to gain in both capability and prestige. By 1933 its resourceful grasp of opportunity could foretell that it would ultimately have the largest enrollment and the most varied program of any comprehensive school. It had a mandate and it went about fulfilling that mandate with vigor, never mind the funding.

University of Minnesota. Although the public-administration center at the University of Minnesota was not fully operative until 1935, the initial steps were taken in 1869 when its first president, William Fowell, in his inaugural address, advocated teaching in government. Fifteen years later, in "stepping up" to a professorship in political science, Fowell advocated the training of administrators to fulfill the Pendleton Act of 1883.

In 1913 the university established a Municipal Reference Bureau as part of the Extension Division, and related it to the League of Minnesota Municipalities. Course work in government and municipal administration was soon started. In 1916 William Anderson appeared on the scene as professor and later chairman of political science. By 1919 he had succeeded in getting the university to establish—on a shoe string, so far as financing was concerned—a Bureau of Research in Government on the New York Bureau of Municipal Research model, except that it was interested in research that would lead to a longer range program of improvements.

In 1922 Morris Lambie was recruited to serve as teacher of public administration, director of the Municipal Reference Bureau, and secretary of the League of Municipalities. Two years later John Gaus arrived to strengthen the team in public administration.

Two programs were publicized: one for state and federal administration at the higher levels, and one for city management. The latter had inputs from and the support of the Department of Civil Engineering. Even though funds were lacking to promote and extend the program as announced in the bulletin, students were received and taught. Financial support at this stage could have produced a full-blown school.

In 1929, with President Coffman's support and with national participation, Anderson and Lambie organized a conference on training for public administration.[13] This was the precursor of the Commission of Inquiry sponsored by the Social Science Research Council's Committee on Public Administration, chaired by President Coffman.

Then the economic depression hit. Nevertheless, President Coffman responded to an Anderson/Lambie proposal to appoint an all-university committee on training for public service. The committee proposed a center for graduate education of both generalists and specialists. The plan adopted featured the development of public-administration courses for students enrolled in a substantive field such as agriculture, forestry, engineering, health, welfare, etc. With a Rockefeller Foundation grant for fellowships and Lloyd Short on deck as director, the Public Administration Center soon became a leading one.[14] With Anderson as chairman, the all-university committee continued as a supervisory group. The center reported directly to the president.

The reasons for the center's ultimate success were: sound ideas emphasizing an interdisciplinary approach, good leadership (including presidential support), involvement of other parts of the university, a distinct organization, good promotion, and, last but crucial, fellowship funds. These qualities led eventually to the center's becoming the School of Public Affairs. In retrospect, one wonders why a great university could not find enough funds during twenty or more years of fragmented effort to develop a solid school.

Columbia University. This university could have easily become the mecca for professional education in public administration. Beginning with its first public-administration courses in 1888, Columbia became a germinal center and wellspring for scholarship and academic study. In other fields it spawned renowned schools: law, medicine, teacher education, library science, journalism, business administration, international affairs, and architecture (with curricula in housing and planning.) But in public administration it drifted, without plan or organization.

There were a number of things going for public administration at Columbia during the first third of the century: first rate professors (Schuyler Wallace in international affairs, Raymond Moley in criminal justice, the Legislative Drafting Fund under Joseph Chamberlain, Seligman and Haig in public finance, Joseph McGoldrick, and the inspiring teacher Arthur Macmahon in public administration and politics); the university extension program; a publicly oriented law faculty; and relevant programs in other professional schools.

Beginning in 1915, many Columbia students took some of their course work and engaged in field studies under the tutelage of the New York Bureau/Training School/Institute of Public Administration. Students had much freedom during the 1920s to work out their programs. Guidance depended upon enlisting a professor's interest. Traditionally, the professors went their separate ways, making effective cooperation or mechanisms to produce operationally viable programs between departments difficult.

When the institute became a part of Columbia University in 1931, its director, Luther Gulick, was appointed to the chair of Eaton Professor of Municipal Science and Administration in the Department of Government and Public Law. Institute staff also taught courses in the department, thus establishing Columbia for a season as a strong center for professional studies in public administration. Lack of support by the chairman and some others of the department, coupled with declining interest of the institute staff in academic effort, severed this marriage in 1942.

George Graham's concluding statement about Columbia in his survey is a classic understatement: "The absence of any all-university organization for public service training purposes was probably a handicap to that function."[15]

The University of Chicago. Like Columbia, the University of Chicago played an important role in education for public administration. Charles E. Merriam, in his early writings on politics and government, foreshadowed many of the requisites of administrative management, and he helped put some of them in practice as a member of the Chicago City Council in the 1920s and the President's Committee on Administrative Management in the late 1930s.[16]

In the twenties, Merriam and Leonard D. White spearheaded the study of public administration, Merriam as chairman of political science, and White as teacher and researcher. In 1926 White produced the first general textbook, *Introduction to the Study of Public Administration*. Merriam's interest in administration was so keen that he early espoused a consolidated school of business and public administration at the university. The proposal was short-lived owing to the business faculty's lack of understanding of, and regard for, the field of public administration.

Beginning in 1929 the International City Managers' Association (ICMA) and other governmental associations (which became known as the "1313" East 60th Street Public Administration Center), began to locate on the University of Chicago campus and contributed instructional resources. The Public Administration Clearing House (PACH), headed by Louis Brownlow, provided general liaison with the university. Aided by substantial research grants, the university and PACH sponsored a wide variety of significant studies.

In 1932 we find an announcement of the following faculty:

Charles E. Merriam (politics and administration), Leonard D. White (public administration), Simeon E. Leland (public finance), Clarence E. Ridley (city management), Ernst Freund (administrative law), Jerome Kerwin (municipal government), Louis Brownlow (municipal government), Harold F. Gosnell (political parties), Henry W. Toll (legislation), Harold D. Lasswell (public opinion), Fred Telford (public personnel), A. H. Kent (constitutional law), and Edith Abbott and Sophenisba Breckenridge (public-welfare administration). In reality, this was not a program; it was merely the listing of isolated and uncoordinated, albeit excellent, courses. Students developed their own programs, worked part time on "1313" projects, and a few found posts there.

In 1932 a university-"1313" ad hoc committee explored the feasibility of a formally organized training center to be jointly sponsored by the university and the "1313" organizations. The members—Glen Leet, Marietta Stevenson, Leonard White, and Donald C. Stone—developed a comprehensive plan.[17]

There was support for the proposals on both sides of the Midway. However, President Robert Hutchins did not believe that administration could be taught, and the melon died on the vine.

Since the successors to Merriam and White did not share their interests, and no one else grasped the torch, the inevitable end of public administration at Chicago was a shallow grave. Group luncheons at the Quadrangle Club and friendly encounters on the squash courts were not enough to hold the pieces together.

Brookings Institution. No story would be reasonably complete without mentioning the education/training vicissitudes of the Institute of Government Research (1916), the Institute of Economics (1922), and the Robert Brookings Graduate School of Economics and Government (1924), three Washington-based organizations, sponsored by Robert Brookings of St. Louis, that were merged to form the Brookings Institution in 1927.

Following some cooperative arrangements in 1923 between the Institute of Government Research and Washington University (St. Louis), of which Robert Brookings was also chairman, the

Robert Brookings Graduate School of Economics and Government was incorporated in the District of Columbia in 1924. "The purpose of the school," said Brookings, is "to teach the art of handling problems rather than to impart accumulated knowledge; and its end is to turn out craftsmen who can make contributions to an intelligent direction of social change."

A year later, when steps were taken to merge the school with the Institute of Government Research and the Institute of Economics, Walton Hamilton, dean of the school, objected. He viewed the school as an experiment in graduate social-science, education, whereas Brookings and others viewed the role of the school as one of training for public service, i.e. professional education. Brookings saw that the school's emphasis on educating doctors of philosophy had diverted interests from government to university service. When the merger occurred in 1927, Dean Hamilton resigned, students protested, and the newspapers had some lively stories. Charles Beard, ever ready to side with the oppressed, got into the act, but after studying the matter, supported Brookings' view. He stressed the necessity of "relating the teaching of higher graduate students more vitally to the realism of the research work. . . ."

The last class of Ph.D.s was graduated in 1930. Seventy-four degrees had been awarded. From 1928, predoctoral and postdoctoral fellows, recruited annually, participated in seminars, worked with the research staffs on projects, but took their degrees, if any, at their home institutions. Many of these entered public service, thus fulfilling Robert Brookings' aspirations.

The depression, with its declining funds and its controversies between Brookings Institution and the New Deal administration, prevented development of Brookings' training efforts. As a result, the institution was unable to expand or to establish a continuous program of courses in public administration, or to establish collaborative programs with universities. The Brookings case is unique in that its public-administration education was primarily the outgrowth of economic concerns and action by economists.

NOTES

1. George A. Graham, *Education for Public Administration* (Chicago: Published for the Committee on Public Administration of the Social Science Research Council by the Public Administration Service, 1941), pp. 135–45.

2. Ibid., p. 139.

3. In a personal letter Gulick states: "That which we transferred to Maxwell was the formalized courses for city managers, government reserachers, budget officers, and personnel and planning administrators. What we continued after the 1924 shift included only post-graduate work for special students."

4. Leonard D. White, *Trends in Public Administration* (New York and London: McGraw-Hill Book Company, Inc., 1933), p. 260.

5. Luther Gulick, *The National Institute of Public Administration*, NIPA, 1928.

6. Graham, *Education*, p. 151.

7. *Public Administrator's News Letters*, vol. II, no. 5, issued by the Public Administration Clearing House in Chicago.

8. Graham, *Education*, p. 173.

9. Ibid., p. 181.

10. Emery Olson, "Twenty-five Years of Building Better Government," in *Proceedings of the Twenty-fifth Anniversary Celebration*, School of Public Administration (USC Press, 1955), p. 10.

11. Renamed School of Government in 1933, and later School of Public Administration.

12. Olson, "Building Better Government," p. 14.

13. See "University Training for the National Service," *Proceedings* of a conference held at the University of Minnesota, July 14 to July 17, 1931, (Minneapolis: The University of Minnesota Press, 1932).

14. Some of this history is drawn from a recorded talk by William Anderson in 1960 reporting on the development of public-administration education at Minnesota; other parts derive from a personal letter from Lloyd Short to the authors.

15. Graham, *Education*, p. 315.

16. Charles E. Merriam, *American Political Ideas, 1865-1917* (New York: The Macmillan Company, 1920). See especially Chapters 4, 8, and 13.

17. Donald C. Stone, "Proposals for Training in Public Administration by the Public Administration Group and University of Chicago," Feb. 7, 1933.

Index

[Notes to the essays in this volume have not been indexed]